Your Divine Goodly Heritage

JOSEPH 'SOLA ADEDOYIN

Your Divine Goodly Heritage

Don't Surrender It To Demonic Hosts!

Readability Statistics
Flesch Reading Ease: 66%
Flesch-Kincaid Grade: 8

Cover designed by Joseph 'Sola Adedoyin

The work of this book is a non-fiction. Names, characters, places, and incidents are real, based on revelations by the Holy Spirit, personal careful study and experiences of the author's over 30 years as a servant of God. In case otherwise stated as fictitious, any resemblance to actual persons, living or dead, events, or locales is entirely coincidental.

Joseph 'Sola Adedoyin
Visit my website at www.josephadedoyin.com

First Edition: October 2020
Joseph 'Sola Adedoyin

ISBN- 9798699413607

All scripture quotations from the Holy Bible are so noted. The emphasis of italics has been added to all portions of quoted scripture.

Scriptures marked "KJV" are taken from the KING JAMES VERSION (KJV): KING JAMES VERSION, public domain.

Scriptures marked "ASV" are taken from the AMERICAN STANDARD VERSION (ASV): AMERICAN STANDARD VERSION, public domain.

Scriptures marked NKJV are taken from the NEW KING JAMES VERSION (NKJV): Scripture taken from the NEW KING JAMES VERSION®. Copyright© 1982 by Thomas Nelson, Inc. Used by permission. All rights reserved.

Scriptures marked "NIV" are taken from the NEW INTERNATIONAL VERSION ("NIV"): Scripture taken from The Holy Bible, NEW INTERNATIONAL VERSION ®. Copyright ©1973, 1978, 1984, 2011, by Biblica, Inc.™. Used by permission of Zondervan.

Scriptures marked "MKJV" are taken from the MODERN KING JAMES VERSION ("MKJV"): Scripture taken from the Holy Bible, MODERN KING JAMES VERSION copyright ©1962-1998 by Jay P. Green, Sr. Used by permission of the copyright holder.

Scriptures marked "AMPC" are taken from the AMPLIFIED BIBLE, CLASSIC EDITION ("AMPC"): Scripture taken from the AMPLIFIED® BIBLE, Copyright ©1954, 1958, 1962, 1964, 1965, 1987, by the Lockman Foundation. Used by Permission. (www.Lockman.org)

Scriptures marked NAS are taken from the NEW AMERICAN STANDARD (NAS): Scripture taken from the NEW AMERICAN STANDARD BIBLE®, copyright© 1960, 1962, 1963, 1968, 1971, 1972, 1973, 1975, 1977, 1995 by The Lockman Foundation. Used by permission.

Scriptures marked ESV are taken from the HOLY BIBLE, ENGLISH STANDARD VERSION (ESV): Scriptures taken from THE HOLY BIBLE, ENGLISH STANDARD

Publisher:

Published by JOSEPH 'SOLA ADEDOYIN
London
United Kingdom

E-MAIL: josephadedoyin.rhemaaflamepublishers@outlook.com

adedoyin.rhemaaflamepublishers@gmail.com

Worldwide Distribution:

This book is only available at Amazon.com for worldwide distribution

Dedication

I humbly dedicate this book, *'Your Divine Goodly Heritage'* to every Christian in the Body of Christ across the globe, particularly those that are earnestly contending for the Christian Faith—*Jude 1:3*. May they be always maximally equipped with all the might of God; always having the confidence of assured victory in the face of any battle of life, until they keep all satanic hosts totally under their feet now and perpetually, in Jesus' Name. Amen.

Acknowledgements

I am so grateful to the Lord God Almighty, in the Person of the Holy Spirit, for the inspiration, strength, and encouragement He granted me to write this book. He has been there with me on every stage of this book as I prepared the manuscript. Indeed, He is my Parakletos; my Father; my greatest Friend; my best Companion, and most excellent Teacher. Hallelujah!

Contents

Introduction

Surely the world is a battlefield for myriad souls. As souls make progress on their courses, they are faced with many challenging issues. Some are easily tackled, and others are compounded by mysterious forces that make life so unbearable.

Oftentimes, these battles manifest on different stages of life's events now and then. However, victories are attained in phases, irrespective of the fierceness of the battles. As efforts are made to resolve them, some battles become walkovers and others, because of their mysteriousness, rage on and on. Nevertheless, no matter how mysterious the battles may be, victories can be achieved every time, through God.

Unknowingly to many, a life's battle does not just rage on and on without a mysterious opposing force working behind the scenes. And except the opposing force is detected and tackled on time, the battle can be prolonged unnecessarily and weigh down a soul.

Indeed, there are two main mysterious forces at work in the world of man, as they both contend with each other for mastery over a soul, to direct their affairs. Regardless, whichever one a soul succumbs to, controls its affairs; either to compound life's issues by bondage to aggravated afflictions, or to bring deliverance and victory and make things better now, and for all eternity.

Satanic hosts are one of the mysterious forces. They have an organized kingdom and always, they are the masters of deceit as they use weapon of deception   omplish their evil intentions. Everyone under their spell alwₐyₛ ₁ᴄels in ignorance and confusion. Unless you know their power structures, see through their arsenals, and understand their game plans, you may be beaten now and then. Now their operational hierarchies are laid out in depth in this book for their objectives to be entirely grasped.

Notwithstanding, God's kingdom is greater, and God is the greatest Strategian of all times, and victories over the satanic forces are always realized through Christ. While you realized your victories, you can assert your dominion and decisively utilized to rule over your world, protect your territory and preserve *'Your Divine Goodly Heritage'*--marriage, children, finances, social life, community, entire nation, etc. for posterity in Christ.

Hitherto, dominion is yours because you have triumphed in Christ Jesus. Hence, as the Lord Jesus Christ triumphed where Adam failed, you too can triumph through God, by the mighty weapons available to you. At your command, all satanic hosts can now be rooted out from all facets of your world. Afterwards, you can plant and build up God's righteous intentions wherever you are, to preserve *'Divine Goodly Heritage'* for posterity.

Unquestionably, you are God's ambassador wherever you are on earth; you are appointed to govern according to the blueprints of heaven. So, comprehend your eminent role and claim your territory for God. As you govern to fulfill the purpose of your divine appointment and exhibit the essence of the heavenly kingdom by your dominion, the difference will be clearer to the people of the world, as your light will shine forth. By your positive impact, hopeless souls will accept Jesus Christ as their Lord and Saviour.

All the same, you are already an overcomer in Christ because you have been born of God, and an overcomer is a winner, whenever: *"for everything that has been born of God overcomes the world. And this is the victory that overcomes the world, our faith. 1John 5:4 MKJV.*
If you continue to keep the faith in Christ and fully equipped with God's might, you can never lose on the battlefield of life. However, the place of communion and intercessions is where you can acquire more power to exert your authority and prevail. Certainly, you will be many steps ahead of all satanic hosts and beat them in their guile.

Ultimately, *'Your Divine Goodly Heritage'* will be preserved for generations to come, and God will be glorified now and forever. Hallelujah!

Joseph 'Sola Adedoyin

Chapter 1

Two Hands Behind The Scenes Of Life

Until I came to know Jesus Christ as my Lord and Saviour, I was unaware that there are two powerful forces at work behind life's scenes in the world of man; and they have very different objectives.

Born and raised in a Muslim home, I obeyed the tenets of Islamic religion. Always, I prayed five times a day and was well acquainted with the names of Allah and Mohammed, whom, in the day of trouble I called for help continuously, and the help never came. Religiously, I recite verse after verse from the Koran and observed the Muslim's Ramadan with a 30-day fast for many years. These were essentially all I knew about the spirituality of the religion and the unseen spiritual forces.

In days of ignorance and despairs, I did not know that there were two hands operating behind the scenes of my life. One was drawing me deeper into torment, confusion, horror, and growing thoughts of suicide while the other, a gentle, loving voice was calling me to the Master: Jesus Christ, the Son of God.

In 1975, because of cruel demeanour of my Islamic Religion Knowledge ('IRK') secondary school teacher towards me and other classmates, I decided to change from IRK to Christian Religion Knowledge ('CRK') without informing my parents.

One day, during my CRK class, my teacher told a beautiful story of Jesus Christ and God's redemption plan for man. She narrated the man's sinful nature and the eternal consequences of sin. The story left an indelible remorseful impact on my heart that day.

As soon as I returned home after the school hours, I secretly went into a secluded area and invited Jesus Christ into my heart. However, due to the fear of my parents and the consequences of my embracing Christianity, I continued to practice Islam. Nevertheless, my life was dramatically transformed by God's love in 1987 when for the second time, I received Jesus Christ now publicly as my Lord and Saviour and became a citizen of the kingdom of God.

As my spiritual eyes were opened, I began to see beyond the natural realm and understand that there are many mysteries surrounding the world of man, especially concerning the conflicts that have engaged mankind for so many generations. These conflicts are still raging and have successfully withstood the material forces that humans have garnered to extinguish them.

Generally, people in various fields of endeavour have tried many times to find lasting solutions to too many problems confronting humanity to no success. Regardless, now is the right time for all mankind to know that answers cannot be found from the material realm; they are in the spiritual realm.

Natural-minded people cannot resolve the issues because they are well rooted in the spiritual realm than what mankind can fathom with their minds. Only men that are filled with the Spirit of God can determine the resolutions.

Universally, God has never been more gracious to any generation than all mankind in this present generation as the Church of Jesus Christ anticipates the day of rapture. The reason is because He is now unfolding the mysteries of His plan that have been kept for ages before our very eyes. If we care to search, we will discover that today, Bible prophecies are being fulfilled than before, and presently many events in the world are confirming their exactitude.

The Only Best Alternative

Furthermore, a great cognizance is needed to understand that, man lives in a world where everything that occurs does not just happen, but they have their origins from the unseen world.

There are always two hands behind the scenes of life, and each strives to control everything that happens in the terrestrial world. Both belong to very distinctive camps.

There is a hand that works for man's wellbeing, and there is another that influences miseries and places mankind in perplexed hopeless conditions. One is the Hand that gives relief and peace during life's turmoil, and the other is torturous, and it aggravates pains and eventually brings eternal death.

While one hand tends to preserve life and gives hope for all eternity, the other delivers the means to destruction on indiscernible souls. Albeit one is extended in love to convey man to a glorious, expected end, and the other is feigning stretched to lure people into hellish terminal. One is ultimately mighty in strength and acts valiantly to save, and the other is weaker and cowardly in deeds, and cannot save everlastingly.

The mysteries of both hands must be resolved, or else, due to ignorance, mankind's miseries will never diminish, and life's anguish will not dissipate. Nonetheless, the Creator of all things, the Lord God has never left a man without a way of escape from whatever their life's turmoil may be. Now, everyone has an obligation to quest and discover the exit 'Door' that God has provided for their eternal peace.

In sundry times, God has heralded the good news that reveals the 'Door' to all mankind, yet, only a few have accepted the good news as an authentic divine message. The remainders of mankind grope in ignorance and unable to have decisive victories in the battles of life. Therefore, their situations are hardly changed while their problems persist.

The Lord God knows the origin of man's fiery attacks and their insurmountable challenges and how they could be terminated. Thus, He has given the only *'Best and Perfect Alternative Means'* for all mankind to triumph in the battles of life. This only *'Best and Perfect Alternative Means'* is the only 'Door' that leads to real rest during turmoil and adversities of this world.

While many have refused to seek the Maker for His only 'Best and Perfect Alternative Means', they deluded themselves with fruitless hopes as they lean on creatures. Hence, they have never grasped what God's good eternal plans are for them. However, a few that are truly chasing after God are discovering the Way.

A True Life Story

As a former Muslim, before I became a born-again Christian, I was engaged in so much life's battles. Day and night, I cried out to Allah and Mohammed for help to no avail. Regardless the oftentimes I called on Allah and Mohammed for help, answers never came from anywhere to really alleviate my despair.

When no answers came, I pursued a higher means by reciting many verses from the Koran to resolve the mysteries and miseries surrounding my life. Yet, I only found myself in desolated deafening silence as I sought for answers; and enduring help never came.

My parents, being staunch Muslims engaged the help of many Islamic clerics on my behalf in hopes that they would be able to find solutions to the challenging issues of my life. Notwithstanding, none could offer any breakthrough and deliverance.

The more verses they gave me to recite from the Koran, the more the battles raged on and on, becoming fiercer on daily basis. At times, they gave me some prepared peculiar water to drink to offer solutions, because a renowned Islamic cleric had recited some verses of the Koran into the water. All exercise ended in great disappointments.

On many occasions, the Islamic mediums would write some verses of the Koran on a small wooden board with some specially prepared ink. They washed the ink on the wooden board with water into a basin and gave it to me to drink or wash myself. Regardless, nothing brought relief. No solution came from all these mundane practices.

Despite all steps employed by my parents in their best ignorant efforts to resolve the problems, they compounded the miseries and never unfolded the mysteries. These resulted in repeated attacks. In retrospect, it was like going through the valley of the shadow of death and no one could deliver me from my despair.

For example, one a day, then I was still a Muslim, I felt fagged out and was trying to catch some sleep during the day. All entrance doors in the flat were securely locked and bolted from the inside.

Suddenly, in my sleep, I heard that one of the doors was being opened, and I jumped up quickly out of my sleep to check which door it was. After a quick check and I confirmed that all the doors were still locked, and I was sure that there was no intruder in the house, I returned to bed to continue my sleep.

As soon as I lay down, I started hearing some footsteps coming towards the door of my bedroom. Again, I got up to see what was going on. and I looked around to understand the mystery, yet I saw no one.

I was rattled by this experience and did not know what to do. After a while, I went to lie down on my bed again, filled with the unexplainable thoughts of the fearful experience.

While I lay down, I drifted off to sleep. Not long after this, "an invisible force," which I later discerned to be a demonic spirit of witchcraft came upon me, wanting to strangle and suffocate me. I struggled with him a little and woke up; now I was struggling for every breath to stay alive. It was indeed a great horrible experience.

I wept profusely as the spirits of fear took hold of me; I became so agitated while my legs were shaking and could not hold me in an upright position. Without hesitation, I got in touch with my parents and narrated my ordeal to them. The only thing they could do was to give me some verses from the Koran to recite whenever I wanted to sleep and drink the special prepared water.

In addition, I was given some special incense to burn on the advice that it would drive away demons. All these endeavours could not overpower the demonic attacks that were coming after my life. The problem persisted for about five years until I openly gave my life to Jesus Christ in 1987 and committed everything to Him.

It happened after my two years as a born-again Christian, I had a similar experience. This time it occurred at night. Having heard the footsteps from my sleep, this horrible demon came again. I struggled for a while and shouted the Name of Jesus out in my sleep; then I felt the spirit left. I woke up panting and full of fear. "What is going on. Now I am a born-again Christian, why am I still having all these attacks again?" I asked myself"

I was desperate for answers; hence, as a child of God, I decided to table everything before Him in prayers. I asked Holy Spirit to unfold the mysteries surrounding these demonic attacks to me. He told me specifically about a neighbour that was the demonic human agent, possessed with the spirit of witchcraft. He was filled with envy and unforgiveness and was hell-bent to terminate me.

God told me the way to overcome is through consistence spiritual warfare by declaring judgment by His Word and unleashing terror on the devil and his agent in the Name of Jesus Christ. He said I have the greater power to prevail over the host of darkness.

In earnest, the warfare started. I took authority over those demonic forces that had possessed the satanic human agent. I declared *'IT IS WRITTEN'* and the judgment by the Word of God, in the Name of Jesus Christ.

A few days after this, the man behind the satanic attacks mysteriously took ill and was taken to the hospital. The doctor could not precisely diagnose the mysteries of the sickness because it was spiritual, and he was discharged to die at home. While I observed his suffering, I cried to the Lord to have mercy on him; God heard my prayers and healed him.

To cut a long story short, that was the last time I had such a terrible attack. Since that day, if the man sees me coming from any direction he would speedily turn into another direction and did not dare to directly look at my face or gaze at me eyeball to eyeball.

Through this experience I came to realize that the real enemy behind the mystery and barrage of attacks was Satan and his demons. Immediately I exercised my authority in the Name of Jesus Christ, and the judgment was issued by the Word of God, the demons left, and the satanic human agent lost his power totally.

My parents could not save me or rescue me from all these problems. Recitations from the verses of Koran and Islamic mediums efforts brought no relief; they could not unfold the mysteries behind my troubles. Deliverance, freedom, and victory came only from God by the power in the Name of Jesus Christ.

Another True Life Story

In my early years in primary school, learning was very easy for me. As I got to secondary school, everything was reversed; I did not have intellectual acuity as before. I could no longer grasp whatever I was being taught rapidly as previously.

My parents and close relatives were concerned. They knew of nothing they could do concerning the problem other than to give me some verses of the Koran to recite at the beginning of each lesson. Believe me, nothing changed.

I had to take my West African Certificate Examination (WAEC — an equivalent of GCSE) four times and General Certificate Examination (GCSE) twice before I could have enough requirements to enter a tertiary institution to become a graduate. Astonishingly, the problem only manifested in connection with anything related to my academics.

One day, during my first semester examination, as I was writing one of my papers, a man came from the institution's admin office and served me an 'advice to withdrawal' letter. I tried to imagine what I had done wrong to deserve the letter, and I could not arrive at any reasonable conclusion.

As I was thinking about this, a voice that I later recognized to be the voice of Holy Spirit spoke loudly in my heart in such a way that I could hear it audibly. It said: "Ensure you finish all your papers. No one would set their hands on you before you finish your examinations."

I heeded the voice, even though it was a strange one, and I completed all my papers. Day by day, moment by moment I became very troubled; I always thought that one day the institution's authority would come and chuck me out and that would be the end of my academic pursuits.

In Nigeria, particularly within the family that I was born into, getting education to the minimal of first degree or its equivalent is a must achievement. If you are not educated to at least first-degree level, you could be classed as inferior to others that are graduates. Due to this family criterion, I could not return home after I had finished my examinations to discuss the issue with my parents.

Out of despair, a few days after I had completed my examinations, I planned to commit suicide on a certain day. On the night before the dawn of the day, I had an encounter with the Lord in the dead of the night.

On the fateful night, I was alone in my hostel room on the institution's main campus, even though I shared the room with two other students. The remaining roommates had gone out all night to prepare for their next examinations. Between 12 midnight and 1.30 am, while I slept, I felt a hand gently touching me as if someone were trying to wake me up. I looked round and could not see anyone, so I drifted into sleep again.

At about thirty minute's intervals, I felt the strange hand came on me the second time with its gentle taping. Once again, I looked around and could not see anyone. This time around, I was a bit concerned, but I thought it was just my imagination, or a dream, or a sort of nightmare, and I drifted into sleep again.

Again, at about thirty minute's intervals, the hand came on me the third time and shook me out of sleep. Now I was entirely awakened. I looked around; and no one was in the room with me, and I was afraid exceedingly.

Suddenly, I heard the same voice that spoke to me while I was taking my examination, on the day I got the 'letter of advice to withdraw' speaking audibly. I heard it clearly while it said, "Why do you want to kill yourself? You have Christians as friends. Go with them to church and pray and the problem will be over."

The voice was very gentle and so comforting and more assuring. It sounded if it were nearer and at the same time coming from afar-off. After the encounter, I could barely sleep; regardless, I noticed that all thoughts of suicide had disappeared.

When the day finally dawned, early in the morning, one of my roommates, a born-again Christian, an architectural student just returned from his all-night preparation for his next examination. After we exchanged pleasantries, without knowing what I had already encountered the previous he offered me an invitation to attend a Varsity Christian Fellowship (VCF) Crusade on the campus.

Surprisingly to me, he suggested we should go to the crusade together and pray, even though he knew that I was a Muslim. Thus, I wondered how he was able to speak along the line of the instructions given to me by the invisible being that visited me in my hostel room a few hours ago at night, since I was alone in the room.

Instead of accepting his invitation at once, pride raise its ugly head within me, and I courteously rejected his kind gesture. However, not quite a while after, I had a rethink and collected the necessary information about the event. I told him that I might consider attending the event. Later that day, I attended the crusade, just to observe.

The guest minister, Greg Alabi from Faith Clinic Ministries, Ibadan, Nigeria was preaching as if he had a movie in front of him, as he narrated the story of my life briefly. He gave the assurance by Scriptures as he emphasized repeatedly that I was not attending the event by accident; it was divinely put together for me to be saved. I concluded that my experience within the last almost twenty hours could not be an accident. At the end of his message, he made an altar call. I went forward and before everyone, for the second time, I publicly gave my life to Jesus Christ, the only begotten Son of the Living God.

The exceptional event occurred on the very day I wanted to execute a suicide agenda. The very day Satan was inducing me to end my life and go to hell became the very day God gave me a new lease of life. Instantly His life earnestly began in me, and I started basking in its glory. Since, I have realized that no matter what, life is worth the living to fulfill God's purposes.

A few weeks after I became a born-again Christian, a course mate, by name David Adetiloye who also became a born-again Christian the same night, offered me an invitation to attend a healing and deliverance meeting at Faith Clinic Ministry at University College Hospital (UCH), Ibadan. He advised me that God could unfold certain mysteries concerning my life and set me free from mysterious demonic bondage. I gladly accepted his invitation, and I attended the event.

By God's arrangement again, it was Greg Alabi that came to preach the night I publicly gave my life to Jesus Christ that ministered to me on one-to-one. As he continued to minister to me, I felt something like a chain was cracking as it was being cut off around my head, and immediately I regained my brilliancy and soundness of mind. I experienced total recovery within moment.

My family members were amazed at what had happened to me after I graduated. They asked how I was able to recover and finish my academics with one of the best grades in my department. Before then, some of them had said, "academically, nothing good could ever come out me"; because all hope for my recovery had gone. Surely, amazing excellent things that rewrote their prediction of a bleak future about me manifested in me through Christ Jesus, my Lord. Jesus Christ turned my captivities around and gave me total freedom and astonishing testimonies.

Since that day, many glorious things have been manifesting in me and through me. To God Almighty belongs all glory in the Name of Jesus. Amen.

Although,

"The thief does not come except to steal and to kill and to destroy. I (Jesus Christ) have come so that they might have life, and that they might have it more abundantly."

John 10:10 MKJV

Dear reader, I believe you have gained something from my true-life stories? There were indeed two hands that were controlling my life before the night I gave my life to Jesus Christ. One was the hand that was pushing me towards destruction; the other was a Hand that was guiding me to God's only 'Best and Perfect Alternative Way' to eternal life, and it eventually brings me into abundant life.

To apprehend the solutions that God has provided for you to overcome any problems you may face at any time, you must have sound knowledge of their origins by the Holy Spirit. He will unravel their mysteries to you.

While you know the origins of those issues, you will recognise the real enemy that is working behind their scenes. As you know the real enemy, then you take all the necessary steps to overcome him in any battles of life.

Life is full of battles; and the battles are in phases. Nevertheless, you can only overcome when you acknowledge the living God, through His Son Jesus Christ. And by Holy Ghost, you will know His master plans for ages, in relation to you. God did not create you to be His enemy but for an everlasting, divine relationship, thereby manifesting His sovereign glory and governance on earth by you.

Subsequently, if God is not your enemy, who is it? And how did things go out of God's original intentions for your life? Now is the time to unmask the real enemy behind the battles of life.

Chapter 2

Dissecting And Unmasking The Adversary

In chapter one, I narrated some personal testimonies to buttress that life is full of battles, and the battles are in stages; in many cases, they are mysterious and intensified by miseries. In addition, it was established that the Almighty God is not your enemy, but a Friend, closer than your blood families, and by His Hand He wants to guide you into His good everlasting plans. So, who is the 'enemy'?

Your first perception on the *'enemy'* is that he is a spirit being, tirelessly working behind the scenes of your life unobserved.

Let me dissect and unmask the mysteries surrounding him to you. You will be amazed to discover the mysteries of his creature and attributes. Please note that I will be using more of the original Hebrew and Greek words from which some scriptures were translated. It will enable you know his nature and mode of operations better.

In *Genesis 1:1-2*, the scripture says:

"In the beginning God created the heavens and the earth. And the earth was without form and empty. And darkness was on the face of the deep. And the Spirit of God moved on the face of the waters."

Genesis 1:1-2 MKJV

As stated in the above scripture, follow me to look at other translations of the words, *'beginning'* and *'created'* to have a full understanding of what happened at the beginning.

The word translated *'beginning'* is the Hebrew word *'Raysheeth.'* Other translations are first (in time, place, order etc.), best and chief.

Likewise, the word *'created'* was rendered from the Hebrew word 'Bara.' It has other interpretations as, to create, shape and form.

From the numerous interpretations derived from the Hebrew words *'Raysheeth'* and 'Bara', we can conclude that, God, Who has no beginning, at the beginning of time, a time not known to any creature, began the procedure of creation; that is, He created and shaped the heavens and the earth.

The beginning at the time of creation referred to in Genesis 1:1 did not start with the present world of man, which is just about 6,000 years. It can be said to be some billions of years or more before Adam was created. It is a transfinite period.

Many discoveries by men through science and technologies--in space, on earth, including archeological breakthroughs and the other uncovering in the world of man, which scientists estimated to have existed for some billions of years--were the confirmations that the previous world indeed existed for a period. The then previous world was angelic world. Likewise, they prove the existence of the Creator called God.

"...the thing which may be known of God is clearly revealed within them, for God revealed it to them. For the unseen things of Him from the creation of the world are clearly seen, being realized by

the things that are made, even His eternal power and Godhead, for them to be without excuse...."

Romans 1:18-22. MKJV

Classes of Angels Created By God

Angels are some foremost creations of God; they were created ever before Adam and Eve were created. Therefore, no man knew when they were created. They are divided into five categories, even though some school of thought claim they are more than five categories. However, we will only examine the angels in these five classes.

> ➢ Seraphims
> ➢ Cherubims
> ➢ The Four Living Creature Of The Book Of Revelation
> ➢ Arch Angels
> ➢ Man-Like Angels

Now let us examine them briefly on their individual categories.

Seraphims

Seraphs are the highest-ranking angels of God. They are majestic six-winged angelic beings that are always before the presence of God. With two wings, they cover their faces; with two wings they cover their feet; with two wings they fly around before the throne of God. They have human hands, and like man they have voices. Day and night, they proclaim God's holiness and glory, and whenever they cry holy, holy, holy, God's presence is always revealed as smoke of fire. They have never left God's presence.

"...I saw also the Lord sitting upon a throne, high and lifted up, and his train filled the temple. Above it stood the seraphims: each one had six wings; with twain he covered his face, and with twain he covered his feet, and with twain he did fly. And one cried unto another, and said, Holy, holy, holy, is the LORD of hosts: the

whole earth is full of his glory. And the posts of the door moved at the voice of him that cried, and the house was filled with smoke..."

Isaiah 6:1-5 KJV

To better understand their nature, let us look at the Hebrew word that was rendered Seraphim in the above scripture. It is called *'Saraph.'* The word *'Saraph'* is rendered Seraph, burning, serpent, fiery serpent, and poisonous serpent.

With the above interpretations, they are fiery as serpent in their nature; they burn with great passion to show they're for God.

Moreover, they are God's spiritual agents of purification.

"...Then said I, Woe is me! for I am undone; because I am a man of unclean lips, and I dwell in the midst of a people of unclean lips: for mine eyes have seen the King, the LORD of hosts. Then flew one of the seraphims unto me, having a live coal in his hand, which he had taken with the tongs from off the altar: And he laid it upon my mouth, and said, Lo, this hath touched thy lips; and thine iniquity is taken away, and thy sin purged."

Isaiah 6:5-7 KJV

Cherubims

Cherubims are the four-winged angelic beings that dwell in God's presence. Two of their wings are stretched upwards and the other two downwards to cover their bodies. Also, they have two man-like hands.

Each of the Cherubims has four faces of man, an ox, an eagle, and a lion. They bear the likeness of man and have straight feet with soles like a calf's that sparkled like burnished copper. Moreover, they look like burning coals. Whenever God speaks, their wings make reactive sounds. They are always where God's glory is present.

"Also out of its midst came the likeness of four living creatures. And this was how they looked; they had the likeness of a man. And

four faces were to each, and four wings to each. And their feet were straight feet; and the sole of their feet was like the sole of a calf's foot. And they sparkled like the color of burnished copper. And the hands of a man extended from under their wings on their four sides; and the four of them had their faces and their wings...And the likeness of their faces: the face of a man, and the face of a lion, on the right side to the four of them; and the face of an ox on the left side to the four of them; and the face of an eagle to the four of them. So their faces were. And their wings were stretched upward; to each, the two wings of each one were joined; and two wings covered their bodies...And the likeness of the living creatures: they looked like burning coals of fire; like the appearance of torches..."

Ezekiel 1:6-13 MKJV

"And four faces were to each one. The first face was the face of a cherub, and the second face was the face of a man, and the third the face of a lion, and the fourth the face of an eagle."

Ezekiel 10:14 MKJV

Additionally, they are known as angels of glory. God's throne is situated above them, and they are toters and movers of God's throne in heaven. They have whirling wheels that are always moved with them by their spirits. They look like burning coals.

Moreover, they are also angels of judgment, and they safeguard the Most Holy place of God; they were symbolically positioned as covering Cherubims over the Mercy Seat as seen in the tabernacle and temple that Moses and Solomon built for God.

They protect the glory and most holy place and things of God. After Adam and Eve were driven out of the Garden of Eden, Cherubims were positioned to protect the garden.

However, if comparisons are made, Cherubims are different from the 'Four Living Creatures' the John the Beloved saw as recorded in the Book of Revelation.

The Four Living Creatures Of The Book Of Revelation

The Four Living Creatures John the Beloved saw in heaven and recorded in the Book of Revelation are different from the living creatures that Ezekiel saw. The Four Living Creatures of the Book of Revelation have six wings full of eyes within.

One of the four 'Living Creatures' has the face of man, another the face of a lion, another the face of a calf and another the face of a flying eagle. They have eyes at the front and behind.

Day and night, they worship and proclaim God's holiness and give glory and honour to Him. As they proclaim God's holiness, the twenty-four elders in heaven fall before God and cast down their crown and worship Him.

"...And in the midst of the throne, and around the throne, were four living creatures, full of eyes in front and behind. And the first living creature was like a lion, and the second living creature like a calf, and the third living creature had the face of a man, and the fourth living creature like a flying eagle. And each one of the four living creatures had six wings about him, and within being full of eyes. And they had no rest day and night, saying, Holy, holy, holy, Lord God, the Almighty, who was and is and is to come. And whenever the living creatures gave glory and honor and thanks to Him who sat on the throne, who lives forever and ever, the twenty-four elders fell down before the One sitting on the throne. And they worshiped Him who lives for ever and ever, and threw their crowns before the throne"

Revelation 4:6-10 MKJV

Archangels

The word *'Archangel'* was stemmed from the Greek word *'Archaggelos.'* It was also translated as 'Chief of the Angels.' The word 'Archaggelos' was also derived from two Greek words: *'Archo'* and *'Aggelos.'* The word *'Archo'* was reded as chief, to lead and to rule. 'Aggelos' was interpreted as a messenger, envoy, one who is sent, an angel and a messenger from God.

Unlike Seraphims and the Living Creatures that are heavenly based and are always serving God before His throne, Cherubims and other angels, including archangels serve God beyond heaven. Archangels are always God's special messengers to His people on earth or sent to execute some specific assignments elsewhere on earth.

Even though mostly, Cherubims are heavenly based before the throne of God, there was an exception in the case of Lucifer, who later became Satan after his rebellion. He was an 'Anointed Cherub that covers.' He was formerly based in the Garden of Eden. More things about him will be elaborated later in this chapter.

Specifically, only three archangels are named in the Bible. They are Michael, Gabriel, and Lucifer even though there are more. Thus, I will limit their names to these three. While Michael is mainly regarded as a warring angel, Gabriel is principally regarded as special messengers of God to His people. However, both Michael and Gabriel also function on any of the two assignments.

"And while I was speaking, and praying, and confessing my sin, and the sin of my people Israel, and presenting my cry before Jehovah my God for the holy mountain of my God; yes, while I was speaking in prayer, even the man Gabriel, whom I had seen in the vision at the beginning, touched me in my severe exhaustion, about the time of the evening sacrifice. And he enlightened me, and talked with me, and said, O Daniel, I have now come out to give you skill and understanding. At the beginning of your prayers the commandment came out, and I have come to explain. For you are greatly beloved; therefore understand the matter, and attend to the vision:"

Daniel 9:20-23 MKJV

"But the ruler of the kingdom of Persia withstood me twenty-one days. But lo, Michael, one of the chief rulers, came to help me; and I remained there with the kings of Persia."

Daniel 10:13 MKJV

"Then he said, Do you know why I come to you? And now I will return to fight with the ruler of Persia. And when I have gone out, lo, the ruler of Greece shall come. But I will show you that which is written in the Scripture of Truth. And there is none who holds strongly with me in these things, but Michael your ruler."

Daniel 10:20-21 MKJV

"And answering, the angel said to him, I am Gabriel, who stands before God. And I am sent to speak to you and to show you these glad tidings."

Luke 1:19 MKJV

"And in the sixth month the angel Gabriel was sent from God into a city of Galilee, named Nazareth, to a virgin betrothed to a man whose name was Joseph, of the house of David. And the virgin's name was Mary."

Luke 1:26-27 MKJV

"And there was war in Heaven. Michael and his angels warring against the dragon. And the dragon and his angels warred, but did not prevail. Nor was place found for them in Heaven any more."

Revelation 12:7-8 MKJV

Moreover, apart from Satan, archangels are always the dominant angelic rulers over the main kingdoms and governments of the nations of the world.

Also, an archangel as God's special messenger will blow the last trumpet on the day that the Church will be raptured from the earth to heaven.

"For the Lord Himself shall descend from Heaven with a shout, with the voice of the archangel and with the trumpet of God. And the dead in Christ shall rise first."

1Thessalonians.4:16 MKJV

Man-Like Angels

High ranking angels have wings, however, there are myriads of low-ranking angels that do not have wings; they have the likeness of a man in their appearance. Occasionally, they have appeared to some people in the Old and New Testaments eras. Regardless, many Christians have claimed to have encounters with some angels of God during this Church dispensation.

Manoah and his wife had encounters with an angel of God in Judges 13.

"And there was a certain man of Zorah, of the family of the Danites, whose name was Manoah. And his wife...And the Angel of Jehovah appeared to the woman and said to her...And the woman came and told her husband, saying, <u>A man of God came to me, and His face was like the face of an Angel of God, very terrifying.</u> But I did not ask Him where He came from, neither did He tell me His name."

Judges 13:2-6 MKJV

Lot, Abraham's nephew had an encounter with two angels that appeared like men to him in Genesis 19.

"And <u>there came two angels to Sodom at evening.</u> And Lot sat in the gate of Sodom. And Lot rose up to meet them when he saw them. And he bowed himself with his face toward the ground, and said, Behold now, my lords, please turn into your servant's house and stay all night, and wash your feet, and you shall rise up early and go your way. And they said, No, but we will stay in the street...And they called to Lot, and said to him, <u>Where are the men which came in to you this night?</u> Bring them out to us, that we may know them...But the men put out their hands and brought Lot into the house to them, and shut the door. And they smote the men that were at the door of the house with blindness, both small and great, so that they wearied themselves to find the door...And when the dawn rose up, then the angels hurried Lot, saying, Rise up! Take your wife and your two daughters who are here, lest you be consumed in the iniquity of the city.

Genesis 19:1-15 MKJV

A man-like angel also appeared to Mary Magdalene and Mary the mother of James and Salome at the tomb of the Lord Jesus Christ on the day of His resurrection in Mark 16.

"And very early in the morning, the first day of the week, they came upon the tomb, the sun having risen. And they said among themselves, Who will roll away the stone from the door of the tomb for us? And looking up, they saw that the stone had been rolled back, for it was very great. And entering into the tomb, they saw a young man sitting on the right, clothed in a long white garment. And they were frightened. And he said to them, Do not be frightened. You seek Jesus of Nazareth, who was crucified. He is risen, He is not here. Behold the place where they laid Him."

Mark.16:2-6 MKJV

Therefore, Paul admonished Christians to entertain strangers, because they could be angels.

"Do not be forgetful of hospitality, for by this some have entertained angels without knowing it."

Hebrews 13:2 MKJV

The Beginning Of Lucifer's (Satan) Abode On Earth

Before Adam and Eve were created by God, some angels were custodians of the earth, and they dwelt on earth as permitted by God. Among these angels was Lucifer (Satan); he was their earthly leader.

"...So says the Lord Jehovah: You seal the measure, full of wisdom and perfect in beauty. You have been in Eden the garden of God; every precious stone was your covering, the ruby, topaz, and the diamond, the beryl, the onyx, and the jasper, the sapphire, the turquoise, and the emerald, and gold. The workmanship of your tambourines and of your flutes was prepared in you in the day that you were created. You were the anointed cherub that covers, and I had put you in the holy height of God where you were; you have walked up and down in the midst of the stones of fire. You were perfect in your ways from the day that you were created, until iniquity was found in you. By the multitude of your goods they have filled your midst with violence, and you have sinned. So I cast you profaned from the height of God, and I destroy you, O covering

cherub, from among the stones of fire. Your heart was lifted up because of your beauty; you have spoiled your wisdom because of your brightness. I will cast you to the ground; I will put you before kings, that they may behold you. By the host of your iniquities, by the iniquity of your trade, you have profaned your holy places; so I brought a fire from your midst; it shall devour you, and I will give you for ashes on the earth, before the eyes of all who see you."

Ezekiel. 28:12-18 MKJV

Who is Satan?

Now, let me unfold some mysteries relating to Satan to you through the Word of God. The word *'Satan'* was rendered from the Hebrew word *'Satan'* in Job 1:6. It has other renditions like an opponent, the arch enemy of good, adversary and withstand.

In other words, as deducted from the above translations, Satan is the arch enemy or an adversary that always opposes or withstands whatever that is divinely and purely good. Not only what is good that is invented by man but also anything good that God has created or given for the benefits of mankind.

Many examples are seen today from the fields of science and technology; some things invented by man for a good cause, oftentimes, have been perverted by the demonic spirits controlling the heart of the people of the world, and they are used for evil cause.

Many times, what man calls natural wisdom has procured foolishness and destruction for them, because it has been corrupted by the satanic hosts and seized to achieve initial godly and good intentions. Therefore, natural wisdom does not take mankind to God's purposeful end. However, God's wisdom is pure, and it is one of the best gifts of life that anyone can possess to accomplish excellence in all endeavours.

"For it is written, 'I will destroy the wisdom of the wise, and I will set aside the understanding of the perceiving ones.' Where is the

wise? Where is the scribe? Where is the lawyer of this world? Has not God made foolish the wisdom of this world?"

1 Corinthians 1:19-20 MKJV

Creation of Satan

The Lord God Almighty, the Creator of heavens and earth is eternal, and He inhabits eternity, a indefinite period before the beginning of time.

"Before the mountains were brought forth, or ever You had formed the earth and the world, even from everlasting to everlasting You are God."

Psalm. 90:2 MKJV

"For so says the high and lofty One who inhabits eternity; whose name is Holy..."

Isaiah 57:15 MKJV

"But Jehovah is the true God, He is the living God, and the everlasting King."

Jeremiah. 10:10 MKJV

God created all things. As stated earlier, some of His numerous creations before man were angels. The angels have been in existence before God renewed the earth for Adam and his generations to live in. Angels are spirit beings and very powerful in nature.

"And Jehovah answered Job out of the tempest, and said, Who is this that darkens counsel by words without knowledge? Now gird up your loins like a man; for I will ask of you, and you teach Me. Where were you when I laid the foundations of the earth? Tell if you have understanding! Who has set its measurements, for you know? Or who has stretched the line on it? On what are its bases sunk, or who cast its cornerstone, <u>when the morning stars sang together and all the sons of God shouted for joy?"</u>

Job 38:1-7 MKJV

From the above scripture, God was denoting a time before Adam was ever made. The sentences *'the morning stars'* and *'all the sons of God'* are referring to angels.

"Now there was a day when the sons of God came to present themselves before the LORD, and Satan came also among them."
Job 1:6 KJV

So, if God says when He laid the foundations of the earth the *'sons of God'* shouted for joy in Job 38:4-7, this signifies that the angels were the sons of God then and were created before man. It also indicates that they have been in existence before God created the earth. They indeed saw the finished works of the earth and shouted for joy.

The words *'shouted for joy'* are derived from a primitive Hebrew word *'Rooah.'* Other words rendered from it are to shout, raise a sound, cry out and give a blast. The angels saw something they had never seen before and were amazed and cried out for joy for what God did.

If Satan is an angel, where was he then in Job 38:4-7? He was among the angels that shouted for joy. At that moment he was on God's side; his loyalty to God was undivided. In fact, he should be the one that led other angels in joyful praise to God.

Light-Bearer's (Lucifer or Satan) Bodily Formation

Bible really gives some clues on Lucifer (Satan's) creation. Ezekiel 28:13 says:

"...Every precious stone was your covering, the ruby, topaz, and the diamond, the beryl, the onyx, and the jasper, the sapphire, the turquoise, and the emerald, and gold. The workmanship of your tambourines and of your flutes was prepared in you in the day that you were created."
Ezekiel. 28:13 MKJV

25

When God created Satan, he was a full spiritual being, having mind faculties, and he was covered with every precious stone as a body.

Let us look at the word *'created'* from Ezekiel 28:13. It came from a primitive Hebrew word *'Bara.'* It has other renditions as, to create, shape and form as of transformation.

In other words, while God was creating the angel that is now known as Satan, He (God) selected every precious stone and caused them to go through a process of transformation to create a body for Lucifer (Satan). The word *'Bara'* (created) was also used in *Genesis 1:27* for the creation of man.

God through the process made Lucifer (Satan) have a spirit and mind covered with shaped body of precious stones instead of flesh. The implication is that, as man is a spiritual being having faculties of mind and covered with the body of flesh made from dust, and living on earth, Lucifer (Satan) is a spiritual being having faculties of mind covered with a body of precious stones and lives in the spiritual world.

God was totally satisfied with His completed work on Lucifer (Satan). He did not see any flaw in him, but perfection. We will see more of this as we continue.

Satan's First Name

I want you to grasp this: everything God creates He gives a name. When God finished His work of creation on Satan, He gave him the name, *'Morning Star'*, which was translated from the Hebrew word *'Haylale.'* It was further rendered as *'Shining Star'*, *'Day Star'*, *'son of morning'* and *'Lucifer.'* *'Haylale'* was his first name and not Satan as it is generally known in the world today. I will buttress on the implications of these names later in this chapter.

Satan Is Not A Creator; He's A Creature

From the above information on Satan's creation, it can be concluded that Satan is not God or Creator of creations as he often portrays himself to many that believe and worship him in the world today. He is one of the creations of God. He did not just exist from nowhere; he was *'made'* from some materials. Devil has a beginning, and his end is at hand.

I chose to use the word *'made'* in the last sentence above to further shed light on the process of Satan's creation, which was similar to the process of Adam's creation.

In the Bible, the word *'made'* was derived from a Hebrew word *'Asah.'* Other interpretations from it are to do, fashion, accomplish and make. David used a similar word when he described God's process of man's creation in *Psalm 139:15*. Also Moses recorded the same Hebrew word in *Genesis 1:25*.

In earnest, God created Satan and finished the work of his creation and called him 'Haylale' *('Morning Star', 'Shining Star', 'Day Star', 'son of morning' and 'Lucifer.')* as stated in *Isaiah 14:12*: *"How art thou fallen from heaven, O Lucifer, son of the morning! how art thou cut down to the ground, which didst weaken the nations!"*

If Satan is not a Creator, then how did he get power to impact the world of man with miseries, sorrows, destruction and death? The answer is this: everything God creates, He gives strength to their nature and empowers them to function according to His intentions.

When God made Satan, He gave strength to his being and empowered him to fulfill His godly purpose as one of the Cherubims. It is the reason he is called 'anointed cherub.' One of the things anointing does is spiritual empowerment to fulfill God's given purpose, particularly in righteousness. Ezekiel says this about him:

"You were the anointed cherub that covers, and I had put you in the holy height of God where you were; you have walked up and down in the midst of the stones of fire."

Ezekiel 28:15 MKJV

As stated earlier, when God created Satan, he was flawlessly made. Also, he was empowered with pure wisdom; he was perfect in beauty.

"...You seal the measure, full of wisdom and perfect in beauty."
Ezekiel 28:12 MKJV

One more time, let us look at words that were translated *'full'*, *'wisdom'*, *'perfect'* and *'beauty'* in the above scripture for more revelations.

The word *'full'* was derived from the Hebrew word *'Male.'* It has other renditions like full, fullness and that which fills.

The word *'wisdom'* interpreted from the Hebrew word *'Chokmah.'* Other interpretations are wisdom, shrewdness, wit, and skill.

'Kaliyl' is the Hebrew word reded *'perfect.'.* This has other interpretations like entire, all, and perfect.

Lastly, the word *'beauty'* was construed from the Hebrew word *'Yophiy.'*

From the above interpretations, it could be said that Satan was a paragon of beauty among God's creations. God perfected him with beauty, skill, and wisdom more than any of His creations.

God's Original Purpose For Satan

"You have been in Eden the garden of God...The workmanship of your tambourines and of your flutes was prepared in you in the day that you were created. You were <u>the anointed cherub that covers,</u> and I had put you in the holy height of God where you were; you have walked up and down in the midst of the stones of fire."
Ezekiel 28:13-14 MKJV

Analytically, the conclusion from the above scripture is that Satan is in the category of the Cherubim angels--*'the anointed cherub that covers'*; he was created and assigned to the garden of God, Eden, to spread over or cover.

The word *'covers'* was rendered from a primitive Hebrew word *'Sakak'*. Other interpretations from it were to entwine, fence in, cover over, protect, defend, hedge in, shut in, etc. In other words, God appointed and empowered him to cover over, protect and defend His purpose on earth from Eden, and not his.

Please note, God will not leave you destitute regarding His purposes for you. Whatever He has called you to do; He will empower and give you the free will to fulfill it, in righteousness.

Furthermore, the scripture *"the <u>workmanship</u> of your tambourines and of your flutes was prepared in you in the day that you were created"*, in *Ezekiel 28:13* tells us of another purpose for which Lucifer was created. The word *'workmanship'* was interpreted from the Hebrew word *'Melakah.'* It was also rendered as deputyship (ministry), employment, work, occupation, service and business.

Tambourines and flutes are musical instruments. In other words, Satan's ministry service to God and primary occupation and business on earth, apart from the ones stated earlier were to praise and worship God with music. He was also to lead other creatures in praise and worship of God.

While Satan was within God's purposes, any steps he made disseminated perfect rhythm of sound and music acceptable to God. Subsequently, he served as a priest that offered sacrifices of praise to the LORD from the holy mountain of God on earth.

Inclusively, he was anointed a ruler to rule from the holy heights of God, a lofty kingly position.

"...and I had put you in the holy height of God where you were..."
Ezekiel 28:14 MKJV

Indeed, he was exalted until his fall; and he falls forever.

Christian, I advise you to discover God's purposes for you and remain within them. They are your service and ministry to Him. Let them be your primary occupation on earth. God who has called you would not leave nor forsake you. The beginning may be very small and the road, somehow very rough, however, your later end shall be exceedingly great and glorious.

Never step out of your divine call to be something else; limit yourself to the boundaries of grace while you obey its blueprints. Trying to be like something else could take you out of God's plan entirely and the consequences could grievous.

Jesus Christ, the Son of the Living God, is our perfect example. He lived by exemplary obedience and fulfilled God's purposes. Our aim in life should be to imitate Him, as we grow into the fullness of His stature.

"Be imitators of me, even as I also am of Christ."
1Corinthians 11:1 MKJV

"Faithful is He who called you, who also will do it."
1 Thessalonians 5:24 MKJV

Satan Falls Forever

"How you are fallen from the heavens, O shining star, son of the morning! How you are cut down to the ground, you who weakened the nations! For you have said in your heart, I will go up to the heavens, I will exalt my throne above the stars of God; I will also sit on the mount of the congregation, in the sides of the north. I will go up above the heights of the clouds; I will be like the Most High. Yet you shall be brought down to hell, to the sides of the Pit."
Isaiah 14:12-15 MKJV

"You were perfect in your ways from the day that you were created, until iniquity was found in you. By the multitude of your goods they have filled your midst with violence, and you have sinned. So I cast you profaned from the height of God, and I destroy you, O covering cherub, from among the stones of fire.

Your heart was lifted up because of your beauty; you have spoiled your wisdom because of your brightness. I will cast you to the ground; I will put you before kings, that they may behold you. By the host of your iniquities, by the iniquity of your trade, you have profaned your holy places; so I brought a fire from your midst; it shall devour you, and I will give you for ashes on the earth, before the eyes of all who see you."

Ezekiel 28:15-18 MKJV

Earlier, it was revealed that when God created Satan, he was flawless; perfect in all his ways and in everything.

The words translated to *'perfect'* and *'ways'* in Ezekiel 28:15 were rendered from the Hebrew words *'Tamiym'* and *'Derek'* respectively.

The interpretations show that Satan was entire, without spot and upright. He exhibited innocence in all his custom and conversations as he went about God's purposes. He manifested godliness *'until'* he conceived iniquity in his heart; as a result, God's judgment came on him.

God is a perfect God. His ways are perfect and all His creations including man, in their initial states were perfect without any flaws. Satan was without sin while he remained within the boundaries of the purposes of his creation.

Satan Has No Eternal Connections With God

Satan was created an arch angel in the same rank with arch angels Michael and Gabriel. By the names of angels Michael and Gabriel, they have connections with God. Michael means *'Who is like God'* and Gabriel means *'Man of God'* or *'Warrior of God'*. Endlessly, there shall be no one like God, and God will everlastingly be a Warrior.

Names in the Bible are like prophesies that reveals what a person is and would be. For example, for Abraham to precisely align with

God's purpose for him and become the father of many nations, God changed his name from Abram to Abraham -- *Genesis 17:5*.

Likewise, the name Joseph means *'Jehovah Has Added.'* Therefore, anywhere he was, he brought great increase, stamping indelible marks of flourishment upon the sands of time.

David means *'Beloved',* and he became a man who loved God and was called a man after His heart -- *Acts 13:22*.

Also, Elijah also speaks on the same note. It means *'My God is Jehovah'*, and he was used to revealing God as the God of Israel. He brought revival and demonstrated God's power to prove His existence. As a result, the children of Israel acknowledged God as authentic. Indeed, *'Jehovah Is God'* -- *1 Kings 18:21-40*.

Another reference is Jabez. He was an Israelite under the Abrahamic covenant and supposed to be honourable. Regardless, his life endeavours always ended in sorrow. Then, a day came when he realised that his name gave him no connection to God. He knew that under the Abrahamic covenant he was supposed to be blessed and the blessings of God make rich and add no sorrow; but "sorrow" was always the testimony of his efforts.

Therefore, he called on God for an intervention, and He heard him, changed the destiny his name had brought on his life. He 'Magnanimously Blessed and Increased' him; He shielded him by His mighty hand and evil came on him no more. His story changed, and he had a new testimony -- *1 Chronicles 4:9-10*.

While Satan, by his names has no connection with God, and he opposes everything godly, however, by their names and positions, both angels Michael and Gabriel are always on God's side and stand against everything that exalts itself against His will.

So, God knew ahead of time what would be the end of Satan. God knew that, at a point in time, by pride he would abuse the purpose of his creation and fall from the exalted glorious position into everlasting damnation.

Christian, names have some spiritual forces working through them. You may have names that do not connect you directly to God, however, today, you have a new Name that everlastingly connects you to God at your spiritual birth. It is the Name, 'Jesus', the Son of the Living God. The meaning of 'Jesus' is *'Jehovah Is Salvation.'* So, do not exchange it for any reason for any other.

Satan Is the Originator of Sins And Death

Sin never existed in any creation of God until Satan invented sin and sinned. His sin can be summarized in two words -- pride and lust. Lust transmuted him to want to be what God did not create him to be, and pride made him to lust after God's sovereign position.

By lust and pride, he took steps he should not have taken, and sin metamorphosed out of his actions. Now, he is a doomed creature forever.

After God created Lucifer (Satan), He ordained him a king and priest. He ruled the world of angels on earth from Eden as king and offered sacrifices of praise to God on the holy mountain of God as a priest.

However, pride manifested in him and his heart was haughty. Satan thought he was all in all among the angels he had rule over. Possibly, because of his beauty and wisdom and the influence he had over other angels, he lusted after God's eternal sovereign position; he wanted to be like the Most High.

"I will go up to the heavens, I will exalt my throne above the stars of God; I will also sit on the mount of the congregation, in the sides of the north. I will go up above the heights of the clouds; I will be like the Most High"

Isaiah 14:13-14 MKJV

He abandoned his original position and the purpose of his creation and exalted himself above everything that is of God. Ezekiel said:

"By the iniquity of your trade, you have profaned your holy places." Ezekiel 28:18.

The word translated 'trade' is a Hebrew word *'Rekullah.'* It has other translations like peddling, merchandise and traffic.'

In other words, after sin originated from Satan, he moved from place to place between heaven and earth peddling corruption. His merchandise was perverted, as he abused the authority of his office. By violence, he became unrighteous in his dealings.

"And a day came when the sons of God came to present themselves before Jehovah. And Satan also came among them."

Job 1:6 MKJV

Furthermore, by the beauty of his nature, he corrupted his wisdom.

"You have spoiled your wisdom because of your brightness."

Ezekiel 28:17 MKJV

From the above scripture, the word translated *'spoiled'* was a primitive Hebrew word *'Shachath.'* Other rendition from it were 'to decay, destroy, corrupt and ruin'.

By choice and through pride, he destroyed the pure wisdom he had to execute holy assignments. Therefore, all his dealings in the holy assignment were corrupt and ruined. He fell from glory to shame, never to rise again, forever.

Pride and lust did not originate from God, and Satan did not acquire them from Him. He became haughty, and his haughtiness gave way to lust, and lust procured his downfall and everlasting judgment. He would never be pardoned.

"For if God did not spare sinning angels, but thrust them down into Tartarus, and delivered them into chains of darkness, being reserved to judgment."

2 Peter 2:4 MKJV

"And those angels not having kept their first place, but having deserted their dwelling-place, He has kept in everlasting chains under darkness for the judgment of a great Day."

Jude 1:6 MKJV

Satan's actions were the genesis of sin among the creations of God. He is the originator of sin, man is not.

"He who practices sin is of the Devil, for the Devil sins from the beginning..."

1 John 3:8 MKJV

While he sinned, he underestimated the heights of God's power to checkmate him. He thought he could override God, and then become God. However, God dealt with him decisively.

From *1John 3:8* above, the word translated *'beginning'* was from the Greek word *'ache.'* It has other interpretations like commencement, chief, origin.

Sin was already in existence before Adam was created. John, in *1John 3:8* was not referring to the beginning of man but to the first world that existed before Adam was created, when Satan was then Lucifer.

Lucifer first conceived sin in his heart and then sold the idea to one-third of angels by deception; afterwards to Eve, and by Eve's influence, Adam fell for Satan's wiles.

Satan Is Cast Out Of Heaven Forever

From the revelations in *Isaiah 14:15-17* and *Ezekiel 28:16-19,* God announced Satan's crimes and judged him; likewise, the angels that took side with him; and the then angelic world was destroyed. Now, Satan is eternally judged and doomed.

God cast him out of the holy convocation of the righteous creations and would be atemporally destroyed—' *"So I cast you profaned from the height of God, and I destroy you, O covering cherub, from among the stones of fire."* -- Ezekiel 28:16 MKJV

The word *'profaned'* in the above scripture was translated from the Hebrew word *'Chalal.'* Its other renditions were wound, dissolve, defile, pollute, desecrate, prostitute, stain, sorrow, etc.

Hence, before God, Satan and his host have brought stains and pollution on their nature, and they are counted as defiled, desecrated and prostitutes. They have been wounded and are now sorrow personified.

Moreover, God also cast him out of His presence to the ground as profaned -- 'I will cast you to the ground...' and God has -- 'brought a fire from your midst; it shall devour you, and I will give you for ashes on the earth, before the eyes of all who see you.' - *Ezekiel 28:18 MKJV*

Along the notes of God's judgment, Jesus Christ declares:

"Concerning judgment, because the ruler of this world is judged."
John 16:11 MKJV

'...I beheld Satan as lightning fall from heaven.'
Luke 10:18 KJV

"Now is the judgment of this world. Now shall the prince of this world be cast out."
John 12:31 MKJV

Nonetheless, you must know that Satan is never remorseful of his evilness towards God and man. Consequently, after rapture, he and his spiritual hosts will attempt to invade heaven to accuse the saints in heaven; a war will breakout, and they will be judged and cast out of heaven forever. John the Beloved amplifies God's judgment on them in the Book of Revelation:

"And there was war in heaven: Michael and his angels fought against the dragon; and the dragon fought and his angels, And prevailed not; neither was their place found any more in heaven.

And the great dragon was cast out, that old serpent, called the
Devil, and Satan, which deceiveth the whole world: he was cast
out into the earth, and his angels were cast out with him."
Revelation. 12:7-9 KJV

Beloved child of God take note, Satan and his hosts have been
banished from God's heaven and will again be expelled forever.
You have gained heaven forever with God's saints. Do not let him
rob you of it.

Satan Was Sentenced To Utter Darkness

As a result of Satan's insurrection as stated in *Ezekiel 28* and *Isaiah
14* his operational headquarter, the then Garden of Eden was
wholly destroyed with the earth - *Ezekiel 28:13a; 17b; Isaiah
14:12; Job 1:7*. So, as God's judgment came, its impact was
apparently revealed in *Genesis 1:2a*.

*"...The earth was without form, and void; and darkness was upon
the face of the deep..."*
Genesis 1:2a KJV

In accordance with the pattern of this book, let us further consider
some words from the above scripture. They are 'without form',
'void', and 'darkness.'

The words *'without form'* were translated from the Hebrew word
'Tohu.' It has other interpretations as to lay waste, worthless,
formless, confusion, desolation, and emptiness.

The word *'void'* was rendered from the Hebrew word *'Bohu.'* Other
words reded from it were to be empty, ruin and waste.'

'Darkness' was construed from the Hebrew word *'Khoshek.'* Other
interpretations from it were dark or darkness, misery, destruction,
death, ignorance, sorrow, wickedness.'

The deduction from these translations is that, since the fall of Satan
and his hosts, the previous earth became worthless and laid waste.

It became empty with no creation in it. Lucifer (Satan) and his hosts now have a new nature that exhibits curses of darkness, confusion, misery, destruction, death, ignorance, sorrow, wickedness, waste, and desolation from that day of judgment.

Thus, if there are any traits of spiritual darkness, confusion, misery, destruction, ignorance, sorrow, wickedness, waste, untimely death and desolation manifesting in anyone or at any place, they are signs of divine judgment and satanic attacks.

Some people from certain religious movements believe in death, waste, and destruction of lives while they claim they are serving the living God. They should know that they have been deceived by satanic hosts; they are not serving the Living God.

The God of Christians is Love, and His love is everlasting. Satanic hosts are the forces of the spiritual darkness, misery, confusion, destruction, death, ignorance, sorrow, wickedness, waste, and desolation of this world.

Another aftermath of God's judgment on Satan and his angels includes their separation from God, evermore. Although they are still very much active, however, they have been separated from the life of God; they are dead awaiting their final extinctions.

In addition, satanic angels still possess their angelic nature-powers like the true angels of God and use them for unrighteous purposes after their new nature. Even though Satan still possesses his angelic prowess, nevertheless, he lacks the rights to reign over any creatures of God.

God revealed that Satan does not have any right to rule over any mankind, especially Christians as in the case of Job in the book of Job ' *Job 1:6-12*. Job was righteous, and he was under the rule of God and not Satan's. Thus, before he could attack Job, he had to take permission from God.

Another reference is Peter, in *Luke 22:31-32*. Satan demanded from God to sift Peter, but God did not grant his desire because

Jesus Christ had prayed for Peter. Therefore, he could do nothing to him.

Child of God be confident that no satanic hosts can touch you except God allows them. Surely, God will not permit any evil on you.

While God's judgment lasts on Satan, he lost his angelic dominion to rule over the earth. Hence, God manifested another master plan; He created man in His image and after His likeness. I will expatiate on this along the lines of this book.

Nevertheless, assuredly, greater punishment awaits Satan and his hosts; it is for all eternity. They are damned everlastingly, and they will not escape their doom.

Chapter 3

Satan Will Not Escape His Eternal Doom

All truths devoid of hypocrisy will duplicate legitimacy. Hence, as things are spiritually, often, they are materially in the world of man. After a trial in the court of law and a person is guilty of a crime, a specific day is set aside for his conviction. Likewise, Satan and his host of darkness, while they have been found guilty in the court of God, God has chosen a day for their final sentence.

There is no doubt, the day that Satan and his hosts would earn their final sentencing to eternal doom is sooner than anyone can imagine. They will be bound and cast into hell fire and God will rain brimstone upon them. The book of Revelation shows us this.

"And the devil that deceived them was cast into the lake of fire and brimstone, where the beast and the false prophet are, and shall be tormented day and night forever and ever"

Revelation 20:10 KJV

You should remember that after trial, God declared a sentence on Satan and his fallen angels because of their sins. They were cast out of Eden as profaned, and since then, they never have a permanent base on earth. They go from place to place, moving up and down as wanderers.

The second judgment came on the hosts of darkness as God cast Satan out of Eden and destroyed the earth and world they once occupied. These two judgments were explained earlier in chapter two.

Third Judgment Was Declared On Satan

After Satan was found guilty of deceiving Eve to sin, and Adam was influenced by Eve to sin, and he stole Adam's dominion, the third judgment was pronounced on him and serpent. So, God said:

"And Jehovah God said to the serpent, <u>because you have done this you are cursed more than all cattle, and more than every animal of the field. You shall go upon your belly, and you shall eat dust all the days of your life. And I will put enmity between you and the woman, and between your seed and her Seed; He will bruise your head, and you shall bruise His heel.</u>"

Genesis 3:14-15 MKJV

It is very crucial we know the meaning of the word *'this'* from the scripture above. From the English dictionary, it is an interjection, a function word. It means, 'to indicate the speaker's strong approval or agreement with the previous material.' Also, it could be used to mention something that the speaker thinks are not previously known to a listener.'

Taking a clue from these meanings, what God was saying was that He concurred with what Eve said—she did not lie against Satan (masking as Serpent). Therefore, God said, "Satan, because you have done what Eve accused you of, you are guilty."

During the cause of trial, if Satan (masking as Serpent) had a defense, he would have objected what Eve said and presented his defense. But he kept quiet to give his consent to what Eve accused him of.

Jesus Christ Is The Seed Of The Woman

In earnest, Satan (masking as Serpent) was found guilty of crimes of deception, lies and theft of dominion. God judged him and sentences were read out.

God said: *"you are cursed more than all cattle, and more than every animal of the field. You shall go upon your belly, and you shall eat dust all the days of your life. <u>And I will put enmity between you and the woman, and between your seed and her Seed</u>; He will bruise your head, and you shall bruise His heel."*

God used the *'Seed of the woman'* allegorically in *Genesis 3:14-15* above to point to the Lord Jesus Christ. Although, God pronounced the judgment of destruction on Satan, but it is the Seed of the woman, the Lord Jesus Christ that would execute the judgment at an appointed time. So, the execution of this sentence was deferred to the time Jesus Christ would manifest on earth as the *'Seed of the woman.'*

In a court of law for example, when an accused person is found guilty of a murder offense and possibly sentenced to death, the execution of the judgment may not be instant. It could be deferred to a certain date.

Some people hold the view that the personality referred to in *Genesis 3:15* was serpent and not Satan. No! Do not be deceived; it is Satan; he is the culprit. God was not speaking to the material body, but to the 'spiritual being' that worked out the crime by Serpent's material body at the time of the incident.

To buttress that God was speaking to a 'spiritual being' that used the body of Serpent, Jesus Christ demonstrated a similar scenario in *Matthew 16:21-23*. Jesus Christ was telling His disciple that He would suffer in the hands of elders in Jerusalem. He would be killed and on the third day He would rise from the dead.

While Jesus Christ was laying bare before His disciples what would happen to Him at Jerusalem, Peter began to rebuke Him.

However, Jesus Christ knew that it was not Peter that was speaking but Satan. Instantly, Jesus Christ rebuked Satan and not Peter.

Although God judged Serpent for allowing Satan to use his body in Genesis 3:14, as He said, *"Because you have done this you are cursed more than all cattle, and more than every animal of the field. You shall go upon your belly, and you shall eat dust all the days of your life"*, however, in *Genesis 13:15,* God was speaking to the *'spiritual person'* that used the body of serpent to deceive Eve, and that was Satan.

Therefore, *'the seed'* that would bruise the heel of the Seed of the woman was Satan and *'the Seed'* of the woman that would bruise the head of Serpent' was Jesus Christ. At this point in time, Serpent had become Satan personified; he had become the *'head of Serpent'* because Serpent had submitted to his authority and influence. Jesus Christ, the Seed of the woman would execute God's judgment on Satan that was allegorically the head of Serpent to destroy him.

Jesus Christ has crushed Satan and destroyed his works of sin and power of death for all mankind on the cross. Sin and second death shall not have dominion over you and me. Hallelujah!

By Ignorance Satan Miscalculated God's Purpose

Satan influenced the religious leaders of the days of Jesus Christ to crucify Him purposely to stop God's plans for man's redemption; he miscalculated as he became clueless of God's strategy. Nonetheless, he was so ignorant of what God was doing by given His only Begotten Son. He misestimated and Jesus Christ was crucified.

Surely, Jesus Christ died on the cross to conquer Satan, death and grave. The shedding of His blood, His suffering, His death on the cross and His resurrection are part of God's strategy to bring total redemption, and then restore dominion to man. God strategized and concealed His plans from all creatures until the appointed time. Paul confirms this in 1Corinthians 2:7-8:

"But we speak the wisdom of God in a mystery, which God has hidden, predetermining it before the world for our glory; which none of the rulers of this world knew (for if they had known, they would not have crucified the Lord of glory)."

1 Corinthians 2:7-8 MKJV

Thus,

"...For this purpose the Son of God was revealed, that He might undo (destroy) the works of the Devil."

1 John 3:8 MKJV

Genesis 3:15 Judgment Executed

So, at the first advent of Jesus Christ before He went to the cross, He categorically said that this time around, *'the judgment'* would be executed on Satan. Which judgment was He referring to? It was God's judgment on Satan stated in Genesis 3:15.

Indeed, Jesus Christ executed the judgment on Satan and his host. He stripped them of all illegal authority they had over any mankind. Thus, Satan does not have any authority over any mankind anymore, except those that allow him in their life.

"Jesus answered and said...Now is the judgment of this world. Now shall the prince of this world be cast out. And I, if I am lifted up from the earth, I will draw all to Myself. But He said this, signifying what kind of death He was about to die."

John 12:30-33 MKJV

Jesus Christ has risen from the dead, and Satan works have been destroyed. The heritage dominion he stole from the first Adam, by which he ruled over the world of man, has been retrieved from him, by Jesus Christ and restored to you. Do not let him have any inch of your heritage again, no matter how little it may be.

In John.12:30-33, Jesus Christ did not state Satan's crimes, why? It is because He knew He was sent by the Father to execute the judgment earlier on passed on Satan in Genesis 3:15. Already the judgment had been declared to Satan. The mission *'now'* is to first strip Satan of the stolen 'Adam's dominion' and destroys his works.

The word *'now'* in John 12:30-33 was derived from the Greek word *'noon.'* It means present or immediate. 'Immediate', from English dictionary is referring to something to be done with little or no delay. It is an urgent matter that must be executed.

What Jesus Christ meant was His death and resurrection when Satan would be dealt with. Indeed, Jesus Christ dealt with him, and He took the dominion back from him on the resurrection day. Satan was overwhelmed by the resurrection power of Jesus Christ, and he relinquished everything he stole from Adam. Now, Satan does not have access to God again, even though he may attempt. He has been cast out forever, and you have been engrafted in, everlastingly.

Satan Cannot Escape The Lake Of Fire

At the first advent of Jesus Christ, while He died and resurrected on the third day, He only stripped Satan, 'principalities', 'powers' and the host of darkness of the stolen dominion that Satan took from Adam. In a short while, Jesus Christ would return to establish His millennium kingdom, Satan will be bound and be cast out into the abyss for a thousand-year season, and then be released.

Finally, afterwards, Satan shall be bound again and be cast into the Lake of Fire and Brimstone. He and his hosts are doomed and cannot escape it. They shall be no more forever and ever. Therefore, rejoice!

"And I saw an angel come down from Heaven, having the key of the abyss and a great chain in his hand. And he laid hold on the dragon, that old serpent, who is the Devil and Satan, and bound him a thousand years. And he cast him into the abyss and shut him up and set a seal on him, that he should deceive the nations no more until the thousand years should be fulfilled. And after that he must be loosed a little time."

Revelation 20:1-3 MKJV

"And the Devil who deceived them was cast into the Lake of Fire and Brimstone, where the beast and the false prophet were. And he will be tormented day and night forever and ever."

Revelation 20:10 MKJV

Now let us advance to the next chapter and examine the hierarchies and assignments of the principal officers and demonic spirits of Satan's kingdom.

Chapter 4

Hierarchies Of Satan's Kingdom

As explicated in the immediate two previous chapters, forthwith after God's judgment came upon Satan and the angels that took part in his insurrection, God cast him out of Eden and destroyed the whole earth that then was. Satan and his host would not escape their eternal fate.

In earnest Satan manifested his original objective for opposing God, which was to have sovereignty as *'God'* over all other creatures, including angels and mankind, and establish them as the hosts of his kingdom. He struck the angels that joined his rebellion with spiritual blindness and presented himself as the ultimate 'god' and demanded absolute worship.

Subsequently, Satan set up a kingdom of Terror by deceit with the help of his hosts to oppose with evil everything that is of God. They are the host of darkness of today.

As stated by Prophet Ezekiel, the attributes of Satan's kingdom are terror, curses, troubles, affliction, and death.

"...you shall be terrors, and you will not be forever."

Ezekiel 28:19 MKJV

The word translated *'terrors'* in *Ezekiel 28:19* is a Hebrew word *'Ballawhaw'*, also interpreted as alarm. The Greek word is further translated as destruction calamity, dreadful event.

Since Satan's rebellion, horror and nefariousness always emanate from him and his demonic angels; their primary aim is to corrupt everything that is of God, including mankind. By his kingdom of Darkness, he causes trouble and affliction to make the world tremble; and he drags anything that associates with him into eternal death.

Prophet Isaiah says:

"... Is this the man who made the earth to tremble; who shook kingdoms; who made the world as a wilderness, and destroyed its cities; who did not open the house for his prisoners?"
Isaiah 14:16-17 MKJV

Let us ponder a little on some words from Isaiah 14:16-17 to shed more light on the attributes of his kingdom. These words are 'tremble', 'shook', 'destroyed' and 'not open'. All these words characterize his kingdom and its spiritual manifestations.

The word 'tremble' was interpreted from a Hebrew word *'Rawgaz.'* It is also reded as 'tremble, quake, rage, quiver, be agitated, be excited and be perturbed.'

The word *'shook'* was also construed from the Hebrew word *'Rawash.'* It has other interpretations like fear; make afraid and quake.

The word *'destroyed'* was rendered from the Hebrew word *'Hawras.'* Other translations are 'to pull down or in pieces, break and destroy'.

Lastly, let us look at the word *'not open'*. The two words were also translated from the Hebrew words *'lo'* and *'Pawtha'* respectively.

The first word *'lo'* means 'no or never' and the other one *'Pawtha'* means 'to open wide and particularly to loosen'.

If these words are put together to obtain a definition, it can be said that the manifestation of the satanic kingdom is to cause rage among people, instill demonic fear in people and bring destruction to every good thing on earth, keep people in captivity and never let them go. They reveal how terrible Satan, and his hosts of darkness are.

Divisions and Assignments of Satan's Kingdom

Satan's kingdom is a highly organised realm, beyond what a natural man can comprehend. Their networks are orderly connected as they go about their core assignments against God and His people, especially. Regardless, God's kingdom reigns with ultimate prowess and infinite power that no kingdom of darkness can withstand.

Let us now break down Satan's kingdom into divisions and assignments.

"For we do not wrestle against flesh and blood, but against principalities, against powers, against the world's rulers, of the darkness of this age, against spiritual wickedness in high places."
Ephesians 6:12 MKJV

In the above scripture, Apostle Paul says that a Christian warfare is not with flesh and blood. Indeed, he means every Christian is engaged in an invisible fight. It is ages' struggle that goes beyond natural man's comprehension. It is a real that battle takes place in the spirit realm and manifests on earth through mankind.

The kingdom of darkness can be summarised into 5 hierarchies as Paul stated in Ephesians 6:12. From these positions, Satan rules over his subjects and delegates responsibilities.

These levels are listed as follows:

➢ Satan, The Supreme Head Of The Kingdom Of Darkness
➢ Principalities
➢ Powers
➢ World Rulers Of This Darkness
➢ Spiritual Host Of Wickedness In The Heavenly Places

Satan, The Supreme Head Of The Kingdom Of Darkness

Satan is a Cherubic angelic being called the 'anointed Cherub that covers'; besides, he is a warrior angel like Michael; equally by proxy, he belongs to the rank of princely angels that safeguard nations of the world spiritually. He is the head of the kingdom of darkness. According to the scripture, he is the *'prince of the power of the air.'*

"...according to the prince of the power of the air, the spirit that now works in the children of disobedience"
Ephesians 2:2 MKJV

From the other renditions derived from the Greek word *'Archon'*, he is *'first'* in rank of power in his kingdom; the chief 'ruler' and magistrate; the overall kingly prince. From his corrupted esteemed position of authority, he dominates his subjects with terror, makes decisions in evilness and delegates responsibilities to steal, kill and destroy.

Satan's subjects and hosts include all the fallen angels of all ranks, lesser demonic spirits, and human beings. Human beings are in the lowest ranks in his kingdom. His subjects and the hosts of his kingdom see and place him in a revered position above others; he is their 'all in all.' But is he truly the All in All? Certainly not! He is an infinite faker, a busted babbler.

Satan is not a disembodied spirit being. He has a body as indicated earlier. Because of his nature, Satan cannot come out of his form to possess anyone. Since he has myriads of demons within, as his possession and under his dominance, he takes over and control people or anything through them.

He does his control in these two ways; firstly, by releasing lesser demons that he possesses within and other ones without, which are the disembodied spirits to accomplish his intentions in a person or anything. These disembodied spirits are the ones that manifest the 'works of the flesh' in and through their victims. An example is in the case of Ananias and his wife in Acts 5. Even though Satan is the father of all lies, but he did not possess them directly, but lesser demons of lie were sent to *'fill'* them. Having filled them, the demons took control of their spirits, souls and bodies and used them to deceive the Church because of their lust for material gains.

*"But Peter said, Ananias, why hath Satan **'filled'** thine heart to lie to the Holy Ghost, and to keep back part of the price of the land?"*
Acts 5:3 KJV

Secondly, he can do it by mind-heart-manipulation (thoughts and imaginations) as he capitalises on anyone's unconquered strong desires, especially the lusts for earthly things. When there is an uncontrollable strong desire for earthly things, especially outside the will of God, the mind and heart could become vulnerable, and doors could be opened for Satan to control and perpetrate evilness.

The mind-heart-manipulation (thoughts and imaginations) through uncontrollable strong desire, especially the lust for money was what Satan used to make Judas Iscariot betrayed the Lord Jesus Christ. Judas Iscariot had uncontrollable lusts for money. Consequently, Satan used the lust through mind-heart-manipulation (thoughts and imaginations) and made him the son of perdition that betrayed the Lord Jesus Christ.

"And Satan entered into Judas, surnamed Iscariot, being of the number of the Twelve. And going, he talked with the chief priests and captains, how he might betray Him to them. And they were glad and they agreed to give him silver. And he fully consented, and he sought opportunity to betray Him to them, away from the crowd."
Luke 22:3-6 MKJV

He used the same mind-heart-manipulation (thoughts and imaginations) technique to bring down Eve and Adam in the

Garden of Eden. It is for the above reasons a Christian must guard his mind and heart diligently with the Word of God by the Holy Spirit and stay within the perimeters of grace and God's will, to keep themselves away from lusts and demonic attacks.

Satan's Earthly Thrones Locations

Because Satan is the supreme head of his kingdom of Darkness, he reserves the prerogative power to determine where he establishes his domain on earth against God and His people. He always does it by proxy, through a pseudo-human king or paramount rulers and political leaders to make his presence known. A reference is from Ezekiel 28:

"Son of man, say to the ruler of Tyre. So says the Lord Jehovah: Because your heart is lifted up, and you have said, I am a god, I sit in the seat of God, in the midst of the seas; yet you are a man and not God, though you set your heart as the heart of gods...Therefore so says the Lord Jehovah: Because you have set your heart as the heart of gods...Will you yet say before him who kills you, I am of the gods? But you are a man, and not God, in the hand of him who kills you."

Ezekiel 28:2-9 MKJV

As declared by Ezekiel in the above scripture, the word of God came to him concerning the human king of Tyre. Ezekiel narrated how the of Tyre proudly claimed to be a god. However, the identity of the personality behind his throne and pride was revealed in Ezekiel 28:12-19; he was Satan personified.

"Son of man, lift up a lament over the king of Tyre, and say to him, So says the Lord Jehovah: You seal the measure, full of wisdom and perfect in beauty. You have been in Eden the garden of God; every precious stone was your covering, the ruby, topaz, and the diamond, the beryl, the onyx, and the jasper, the sapphire, the turquoise, and the emerald, and gold. The workmanship of your tambourines and of your flutes was prepared in you in the day that you were created. You were the anointed cherub that covers, and I had put you in the holy height of God where you were; you have walked up and down in the midst of the stones of fire. You were

perfect in your ways from the day that you were created, until iniquity was found in you. By the multitude of your goods they have filled your midst with violence, and you have sinned. So I cast you profaned from the height of God, and I destroy you, O covering cherub, from among the stones of fire. Your heart was lifted up because of your beauty; you have spoiled your wisdom because of your brightness. I will cast you to the ground; I will put you before kings, that they may behold you. By the host of your iniquities, by the iniquity of your trade, you have profaned your holy places; so I brought a fire from your midst; it shall devour you, and I will give you for ashes on the earth, before the eyes of all who see you. All who know you among the peoples shall be astonished at you; you shall be terrors, and you will not be forever."

Genesis 28:12-19 MKJV

From the description in Ezekiel 28:12-19, Satan was the spiritual king-ruler of Tyre reigning through human king.

Another instance is in the Book of Revelation, chapter 2. Satan had established his throne in Pergamum. Similarly, he ruled over the land through the human king to persecute and perpetrate evilness against the Church; as a result, Antipas was martyred for his Christian faith.

"And to the angel of the church in Pergamos write: He who has the sharp sword with two edges says these things. I know your works, and where you live, even <u>where Satan's seat is</u> . And you hold fast My name and have not denied My faith, even in those days in which Antipas was My faithful martyr, who was slain among you, where Satan dwells."

Revelation 2:12-13 MKJV

From the two examples above, although the physical person on the throne of Tyre was a human being, and it was human beings that persecuted the Church of Pergamum in the Book of Revelation, but the force behind their actions was Satan and his hosts. His spiritual thrones were established in Tyre and Pergamum.

How Satan Establishes His Thrones In The World

Satan is the most deceitful being in existence, and he is the father of all lies. If he was able to deceive first Adam successfully, who at the initial stage was full of life of glory and was given the dominion by God to reign over the earth, then great care must be employed by everyone not to be deceived by him, no matter their status.

Now, how does Satan always manage to establish his throne physically in the world? He always does it through the people that are in the paramount positions of authority within a nation and regions; most especially through kings and princes and those that have the prerogative leadership power--the main decision makers of a nation. He hardly goes directly after those in lesser positions of authority. If he goes after anyone in a lesser position of authority, it is to promote and place them in the supreme human authority positions in the land and manifest his evilness by them.

Nations are ordained by God, and at their beginnings, holy princely angels are placed in charge of them. As nations sacrosanctly submit to God and continuously do His will, His holy angels will still be in charge spiritually. However, if they turned away from God, He would abandon them to worship whatever they desire, and His holy angels will depart, and Satan and his hosts will take over.

"Think about past generations. Ask your parents or any of your elders. They will tell you that God Most High gave land to every nation. He assigned a guardian angel to each of them."
Deuteronomy 32:7-8 CEV

Hence, by all manners of deceitfulness, he sways away the hearts of the supreme leaders of nations from God and makes them surrender their authority to him, as he rules over them by proxy. By those in the paramount positions of authority, he introduces hellish regular laws and decrees against God's interests. An example is the king of Tyre. The king of Tyre had surrendered his authority to Satan in exchange for spiritual powers and earthly glory.

"With your wisdom and with your understanding you have made riches for yourselves, and have worked gold and silver into your treasuries. By your great wisdom and by your trade you have multiplied your riches, and your heart is lifted up because of your riches."

Ezekiel 28:4-5 MKJV

Every person on earth needs some measures of spiritual backup-power to fulfil his purposes and destiny on earth. The spiritual back-up-power can be either sourced from God or Satan, depending on whom they are inclined to. In order to have spiritual backup-power, total surrender is demanded from whom the power is sourced.

The Lord Jesus Christ's encounter with Satan during His temptation is an example of how Satan deceives leaders to surrender their authority to him. During His temptation in the wilderness, Satan knew that Jesus Christ was the Son of God, the very God appearing bodily. He knew, Jesus Christ was the sovereign King in heaven and on earth, and He must be worshiped by all creations.

Regardless, he demanded an absolute surrender from Jesus Christ in exchange for worldly affluence and glory. In other words, he demanded the total surrender of Jesus Christ's authority. If he were able to deceive Jesus Christ, everything that is of God would have been under his control. Nonetheless, glory to God, he failed woefully in all his attempts; Jesus Christ, the Lord triumphed.

"And the Devil, leading Him up into a high mountain, showed Him all the kingdoms of the world in a moment of time. And the Devil said to Him, All this power I will give you, and the glory of them; for it has been delivered to me. And I give it to whomever I will. Therefore if you will worship me, all shall be yours. And Jesus answered and said to him, Get behind me, Satan! For it is written, "You shall worship the Lord your God, and Him only shall you serve.""

Luke 4:5-8 MKJV

In *Luke 4:5-6*, Satan claims all power of the kingdoms of the world has been surrendered to him. Who surrendered the power of the world's kingdoms to him? Adam did first; then the successive paramount kings and leaders of nations also surrendered their authority to him in exchange for some measures of spiritual backup-power and world's affluence and glory.

Christian, you can know who oversees the affairs of your country or city or a region by the style of leadership and the laws in operation. Any law that allows the welfare of the people and God's interests in the Church and anywhere in your country to flourish is free from Satan's control.

Kingdom Of Darkness' 'Principalities' Angels

Next in hierarchy to Satan in his kingdom are the 'Principalities' angels. Like Satan their master, they are invisible to the naked eye. There are one or two other views that claim that the 'Principalities' angels are the least in the kingdom of Darkness, however, I hold a different view due to these following reasons.

1. If they are not next to Satan in hierarchy, Apostle Paul would not have listed their ranks in the sequence they appear in the Bible. The leadership hierarchies that are listed in his epistles are always in chronological orders according to the pattern in his writings.

2. The root-word of the Greek word translated into 'principalities' is used for Satan in *John 14:30* and *John 12:31*.

3. According to the word 'principalities', Satan is not the only fallen princely angel in his kingdom of Darkness. There are several others.

"For our wrestling is not against flesh and blood, but against the principalities..."

Ephesians 6:12 ASV

The word, *'principalities'* was reded from the Greek word *'arche'*. Its other translations were 'origin, principle, beginning, corner, magistrate, power and rule'. *'Arche'* was derived from a Greek root-word *'Archomai'*, which was rendered as precedence and commencement (as in order of time, place, and ranks) and beginning. They derived their titles and positions from meanings of their rankings in the kingdom of Darkness.

Considering these translations, principalities of the kingdom of darkness have the power to rule and take decisions on behalf of Satan. They are 'princely' fallen angels vested with rulership over nations or regions; however, they are Satan's subordinates. Like Satan their master, they are not disembodied spirit beings; therefore, they cannot possess humans or anything directly.

Furthermore, 'principalities' are the principal or chief ruler angels, the main columns, and the *'corner'* —cornerstones of Satan's kingdom. They are the backbones and commencement of the power of Satan's reign on earth. Without them, Satan's activities in the nations of world would be extremely limited and eventually extinguish.

They are powerful, but not as powerful as Satan. Regardless, the whole of the hosts of darkness are no match to the Church of Jesus Christ and an individual Christian that knows who he/she is in Christ.

Now, what do *'principalities'* rule and take decisions over? They rule over from the immediate lesser subjects of the kingdom of darkness, and spiritually they rule over territories of the earth as princes. Their territories are spiritually demarcated areas under the jurisdiction of a sovereign state in the world of man.

Apart from Satan, *'principalities'* are the chief satanic princely spirits contending with the God's destinies for the entire nations of the world. They always rise against God's intentions from the heavenlies to prevent God's princely angels from taking control of any nation for God. They also attempt to stop God's princely angelic messengers from breaking through their territories to whoever they are sent to, especially to God's people.

'Principalities' of the kingdom of darkness can make wars and prevail, especially where God's people give up their intercessions and do not engage in spiritual wars for their land. Like Satan, they can have direct control over a paramount king and foremost leaders of a nation to direct their affairs in evilness. They do this by delegating their satanic powers to such leaders.

Daniel in his book reveals this truth.

"...Daniel: for from the first day that thou didst set thine heart to understand, and to chasten thyself before thy God, thy words were heard, and I am come for thy words. But the prince of the kingdom of Persia withstood me one and twenty days: but, lo, Michael, one of the chief princes, came to help me; and I remained there with the kings of Persia..."
Daniel 10:11-14 KJV

In the above scriptures, the prince of the kingdom of Persia mentioned in Daniel 10:11-14 was not a human being. He was one of the princely angels, a chief in the kingdom of Darkness that was assigned by Satan to rule over and defend the territory called, Persia. He takes orders directly from Satan and passes them down to the immediate lower ranking angels.

Another example of princely angels is the prince of Greece as stated in *Daniel 10:20* below.

"Then said he, Knowest thou wherefore I come unto thee? And now will I return to fight with the prince of Persia: and when I am gone forth, lo, <u>the prince of Greece</u> shall come."
Daniel 10:20 KJV

All nations of the world have princely angelic beings controlling their spiritual realms in the heavenlies. They can be God's or Satan's. They have responsibility to spiritually preserve a state or nation for the rule of God's or Satan's kingdom in the spiritual realm. The earth is of the Lord, giving to man to possess; however, satanic princely angels can prevent God's angels from carrying out their holy assignments within their controlled territories.

Consequently, there is a battle to establish sovereignty between God's hosts and the satanic hosts over a nation.

If you want God's destiny for your nation to be fulfilled, then, you must wrestle by spiritual warfare and overthrow the satanic forces. Surely, they can be overthrown if you wrestle them rightly.

Let me digress a little and use the conflicts involving Israel and some nations in the Middle East today as an example. They are not just conflicts over lands and regions, and no political or military powers of the world can never resolve them.

The conflicts are more of generational and spiritual in nature between God's kingdom and the kingdom of darkness, as they unfold materially on earth. They are battles for territorial control to establish sovereignty by angelic princes to establish their rules for God or Satan. The battles are between God's and Satan's princes. However, the earth is of the Lord, and God's counsel must stand on earth through Israel.

Therefore, United States of America, the Western nations, Arab nations, and the rest of the world should seek the living God, through Jesus Christ for real solutions. They must be careful and ensure they do not mess around with God's plan for Israel, because the consequences are grievous.

How To Defeat Satan's 'Principalities' Angels

"And having spoiled principalities and powers, he made a shew of them openly, triumphing over them in it."
Colossians 2:15 KJV

"Having stripped rulers and authorities, He made a show of them publicly, triumphing over them in it."
Colossians 2:15 MKJV

As stated above in Colossians 2:15, *'principalities'* in the kingdom of darkness are already defeated foes and can be overthrown from reigning over any nation in the world; surely you can overthrow them for God's princely angels to take control. You have matchless enormous powers in God, through Jesus Christ to defeat the host of darkness reigning over your nation.

Every one of the satanic principality angels have been wholly divested of their stolen dominion by Jesus Christ on the cross; although they still possess their angelic powers, by which they tend to control the spiritual ambiance of their conquered territories. By their angelic powers, they engage holy angels of God in conflicts. However, they are illegal occupants in any territory that is under God.

Angel Gabriel's narratives to Daniel recorded in the book of Daniel 10 confirm how 'principalities' tend to passionately control their territories. The prince of Persia recognized the regional area of Persia as his possession and fought to prevent Gabriel from coming through to Daniel, until Michael came to help. Also, Revelation 12:7-11 accounts for a similar incident while Satan led the hosts of darkness to invade heaven.

Satan and his *'principalities'* had legal control over the Persian region because the citizens of Persia had handed their nation and region to the satanic hosts through idolatry. However, Jesus Christ has died on the cross, buried and raised on the third day; He has all power in His possession. Even though 'principalities' are princely angels and are powerful, notwithstanding, they are already defeated and can be overthrown from any territories today.

Every nation of the world is under the heavenlies on the earth. Therefore, to defeat a 'principality' of the kingdom of darkness, firstly, you must know beyond any doubt that you are tackling an already defeated being that could be illegally occupying the region of your country spiritually.

Secondly, you cannot do it alone, even though you have an authority that is mighty through the Name of Jesus Christ. God must be invited, and His chief or princely angels must be involved, as in the case of Daniel, Gabriel, Michael, and the prince of Persia. Also, corporate anointing of faithful Christians can be engaged.

"For the weapons of our warfare are not carnal, but mighty through God..."

2Corinthians 10:4 KJV

God's princely angels are not assigned to defend any nation at the command of human beings, no matter their relationship with God or how highly anointed they may be. They do not respond to human commands, but to God's. Angel Michael is a reference to this, as recorded in *Daniel 10:11-13* below.

"...for unto thee am I now sent...for from the first day that thou didst set thine heart to understand, and to chasten thyself before thy God, thy words were heard, and I am come for thy words. But the prince of the kingdom of Persia withstood me one and twenty days: but, lo, Michael, one of the chief princes, came to help me..."

Daniel 10:11-13 KJV

Michael is a princely warring angel of God. When Gabriel, another princely angel could not alone overcome the principality called, the 'prince of the kingdom of Persia', Michael was sent to help him tackle his oppositions, and Daniel and Gabriel prevailed together. Therefore, Gabriel was able to reach Daniel and delivered answers to his prayers.

Daniel was not aware of the territorial spiritual battle that happened until he was told by Gabriel; he never commanded angels Gabriel and Michael to come from heaven to give answers to his prayers; God sent His princely angles appropriately to Daniel's prayers.

Michael is the princely warring angel that is always rising to defend God's interests over the nation of Israel and the Church against any satanic hosts' invasions. He always leads other God's warring angels against the host of darkness. However, he only takes commands from the Godhead, and not from human beings.

"But I will shew thee that which is noted in the scripture of truth: and <u>there is none that holdeth with me in these things, but Michael your prince.</u>"

Daniel 10:21 KJV

"And there was war in heaven: Michael and his angels fought against the dragon; and the dragon fought and his angels, and prevailed not; neither was their place found any more in heaven. And the great dragon was cast out, that old serpent, called the Devil, and Satan, which deceiveth the whole world: he was cast out into the earth, and his angels were cast out with him."
Revelation 12:7-9 KJV

In other to make God's princely angel arise to defend your nation against any satanic principality, you must call on God in continuous earnest prayers, at least, as Daniel did. Then, God can send any princely warring angel, as necessary to tackle the satanic principality. The satanic principality would be defeated, and possibly be overthrown. It could be instant or later, according to God's will.

You must realize that God will not send a lesser angel to engage a higher-ranking angel in battle; He will send an equal-ranking or a higher-ranking angel to engage the enemy angel, as narrated in the above scriptures. However, after a satanic 'principality' is defeated from a particular spiritual region, they could relocate to another spiritual region or nation or domain that has not fully yielded to the Lord.

Furthermore, you must know that you belong to God's kingdom and all authority belongs to Jesus Christ. Hence, use the 'authority of Christ', which you possess by His Name. As God's princely angels are engaging the satanic principalities in battle spiritually, you must also use your authority in Christ here on earth decisively.

"And Jesus came to them and spake unto them, saying, All authority hath been given unto me in heaven and on earth."
Matthew 28:18 ASV

"And I heard a great voice in heaven, saying, Now is come the salvation, and the power, and the kingdom of our God, and the authority of his Christ: for the accuser of our brethren is cast down, who accuseth them before our God day and night."
Revelation 12:10 ASV

Additionally, satanic princely angels can rise against themselves to steal a regional territory from each other. It is the reason ungodly nations rise against themselves to annex territories. It is what happened during the Babylonian Kingdom era, Medio-Persian Kingdom era, Grecian Kingdom era, Roman Empire era and other eras.

A recent modern-day example is China's annexation of Taiwan and Hong Kong territories. The world may perceive China's move as political, however, it is more than mere political moves; it is spiritual. Neither China, Taiwan nor Hong Kong are Christian nations totally dedicated to God, even though they have may have many Christians in them. It is the demonic princes that are rising against one another through people in authority for spiritual territorial control.

China's spiritual principality is the most powerful satanic princely angel among the spiritual princes of the East Asian countries; he is the one behind the move, as he attempts to annex and control more territories spiritually, to become more powerful and enforce his demonic rule over Hong Kong and Taiwan territories. If the demonic principality in charge of China is spiritually defeated, their annexed territories will be physically free from their control.

The demonic prince of China knows that his defeat can only happen by God's intervention; and it is only Christians that can move God to intervene. It is one of the reasons why Christianity is suppressed in China and its annexed territories today and Christians are severely persecuted.

A True Night Vision From God

In 2009, God showed me the scenes narrated below in a night vision. I am using it to support what I stated above on how to defeat a satanic kingdom's 'principalities.'

It was like a starry night, and everywhere was dark, but brightened up by the moonlight and my path was illuminated by glorious beaming lights. I was wearing a dazzling white robe. Suddenly, I saw a man-like being in an ordinary white robe descended from the sky, stood in my path to challenge me in a fight. He looks like an angel with big wings. His height reaches to the sky, and I was before him like when 'David was before Goliath' in the battle.

Hence, a battle ensued, raging between both of us. It was a fierce wrestling battle between us to claim a territory. He was like an enemy fighting to prevent me from achieving God's intention. He was very powerful, but by the Holy Spirit, I was infused with an extraordinary strength to withstand and fight him off.

Then suddenly I heard a loud voice came from heaven and said to me: *"Angel Michael has been sent to fight for you."* The voice came like the sounds of a trumpet and rent the atmosphere. Immediately after I heard the voice, I saw heaven opened. I heard great thunderous sounds and saw great lightnings flashing down from the opened heaven, from beyond the sky in form of straight lines and touched down at the place where I was standing.

The thunder and lightnings came in between me and the gigantic creature and struck him, and no strength was left in him anymore to wrestle. As he was falling, he disappeared into the thin air and I saw him no more. Then I continued following the illuminated path.

I believe the angelic being that I contended with in the vision was a princely angel, because it was the princely angel, Michael that I heard would come and fight for me; God will send an equal-rank angel to fight an enemy angel. Notwithstanding, I am not certain of the spiritual territory the angelic enemy was contending for, but he was defeated, and I saw him no more. Glory to God, glory to Jesus Christ. Hallelujah!

Humans Are Not Satanic 'Principalities' Angels

I have heard from some Christians as they claim that some powerful and wicked leaders in their nations are incarnates of principalities from the kingdom of darkness. It is a great misconception of what a satanic principality angel is and an excessive exaggeration of wicked leaders' essence.

'*Principalities*' are chiefly angelic beings that are heavenly based, although, just like Satan, the 'anointed Cherub'; they can choose to work behind the seat of power in a nation if allowed. Notwithstanding, they are mainly rulers over their conquered spiritual territories in the heavenlies. As nations are physically demarcated on earth, they are spiritually too, in the heavenlies.

In the heavenlies, individual satanic principalities angels always legally or illegally form defenses against the holy princely angelic beings to stop them from gaining access into their perceived conquered territories, depending on whose side the human kings or leaders are.

Satanic principalities are not the main satanic spirit beings that directly control human leaders in the nations of the world. It is the satanic angelic beings that are in the hierarchy of 'powers' that are assigned to do this; although, they belong to the well-connected and organised network of the kingdom of darkness.

Kingdom Of Darkness' 'Powers' Angels

""*For our wrestling is not against flesh and blood, but against...the powers...*"

Ephesians 6:12 ASV

'*Powers*' in the kingdom of darkness are also fallen high-ranking princely angels, and they are not disembodied spirit beings. Likewise, they have been defeated and stripped of their powers and authority by Jesus Christ on the cross, just like any other hosts of darkness; albeit they still possess their angelic prowess and strength. With their angelic powers, they perpetrate their evils and wickedness.

The word '*powers*' is stemmed from the Greek word '*exousia.*' Other words reded from '*exousia*' are authority, mastery, force, jurisdiction, liberty power, right, strength, magistrate and token of control'.

All the above renditions reveal that *'powers'* angels' main assignments are in the places of authority and decision-making where they control the affairs of a nation, city, towns, villages and other places and force their will on their leaders. Also, the interpretations show the attributes of the kings, queens, politicians, and other human authorities of the world. They have liberty power of authority and token of control over their jurisdictions.

In other words, the above translations of *'exousia',* apart from *'powers'* show that the high-ranking angels in the offices of 'powers' in the kingdom of darkness report and receive instructions from the constituted authority above them; from Satan and possibly from *'principalities',* which they are next to in hierarchies whenever necessary. Although they are spirit beings, but 'powers' angels have physical controls over the territories already conquered by the angelic *'principalities'* of the satanic kingdom hierarchies.

'Powers' are the chief among Satan's terrestrial hosts. Although they are invisible, however, they are the chief of the satanic unseen 'angelic-foot soldiers' in the world of man. While 'principalities' are heavenlies based and take charge of the firmaments of conquered geographical territories, and rule and contend to prevent God's angels from carrying out their assignments, *'Powers'* are spiritually earthly based high-ranking satanic angels. Although they can work in the heavenlies, however, they are the main spiritual authorities over the surfaces of the territories that 'principalities' have already conquered in the heavenlies.

Although a *'principality'* may control a region of nations or a single country's spiritual firmament area, such as in 'princes of Persia and Greece' cases -- Daniel 10, satanic 'powers' angels are always more than one within a nation. They extend and exert their individual controls over villages, towns, cities and nations where ungodly kings, queens, politicians, and other human authorities are present as paramount rulers.

'Powers' angels in the kingdom of darkness are kingly and powerful spiritual figures, but not as powerful as *'principalities.'* They are kingly because they work mainly through main seat of power, monarchs, political and unconventional government

leaders/rulers of their domains. They rule from behind the thrones or seats or political offices all the time, to perpetrate evil against God's interest, especially His Church. If they were the spiritual force behind a throne, their names could be known by the monarchy's traditional titles or areas they occupy.

Locations Of Satanic Kingly 'Powers' Spirits On Earth

Even though satanic kingly *'Powers'* beings are high ranking fallen angels and surface-based to rule over nations through leaders, their epitomized locations can be physically located and found in places like rivers, as in the case of Pharaoh king of Egypt as stated in Ezekiel 29:2-6.

"Son of man, set thy face against Pharaoh king of Egypt, and prophesy against him, and against all Egypt: Speak, and say, Thus saith the Lord GOD; Behold, I am against thee, Pharaoh king of Egypt, the great dragon that lieth in the midst of his rivers, which hath said, My river is mine own, and I have made it for myself..."
Ezekiel 29:2-6MKJV

In *Ezekiel 29:2-6*, God unmasked the real personality called Pharaoh. He is not human, but a great spiritual dragon living amid rivers of Egypt. Of many rivers in Egypt, he specifically chose river Nile as his spiritual base, while simultaneously by proxy the spiritual power behind the human king that everyone knew as Pharaoh.

The other places of satanic kingly *'Powers'* can be located on mountains, hills, rocks, special stones, groves, underneath trees, dry places, temple, and other unimaginable places dedicated to them by abstract symbols and images.

And because leaders like kings, queens, presidents, prime ministers, etc. are under their controls while they are involved in idolatry, idol worshipping could become part of a national or regional traditions or cultures or religions of their places as they are in many nations today.

In some cases, leaders of such places could lead or enforce rules on their subjects, to worship the fallen angels as deities from the strategic places in their lands. This is the genesis of all modern-day religious practices, and many of them have been from ancient times and gone through modernisation.

"Manasseh was twelve years old when he began to reign...he did the evil in the sight of Jehovah...he built again the high places which Hezekiah his father had broken down, and he reared up altars for the Baals, and made Asherahs, and worshiped all the host of heaven, and served them...he built altars for all the host of heaven in the two courts of the house of Jehovah...Manasseh made Judah and the people of Jerusalem to err, to do worse..."
2Chronicles 33:1-9 MKJV

"And also he even removed his mother Maachah from being queen because she had made an idol in a grove. And Asa destroyed her idol and burned it by the torrent Kidron."
1King 15:13 MKJV

"And the sons of Israel secretly did things that were not right against Jehovah their God. And they built high places in all their cities for themselves...they set up images and Asherahs for themselves in every high hill, and under every green tree. And they burned incense in all the high places, like the nations whom Jehovah had removed from before them; and did evil things to provoke Jehovah to anger. For they served the idols, of which Jehovah had said to them, You shall not do this thing.
2Kings 17:9-12 MKJV

"And Judah did evil in the sight of Jehovah, and they provoked Him to jealousy...for they also built high places for themselves, and images, and Asherahs, on every high hill and under every green tree."
1King 14:22-23 MKJV

Solomon is another example of leaders that built abstract symbols and images for powers angels as gods.

"Now king Solomon loved many foreign women, together with the daughter of Pharaoh, women of the Moabites, Ammonites, Edomites, Sidonians, and Hittites; of the nations concerning which Jehovah said unto the children of Israel, Ye shall not go among them, neither shall they come among you; for surely they will turn away your heart after their gods: Solomon clave unto these in love...For it came to pass, <u>when Solomon was old, that his wives turned away his heart after other gods; and his heart was not perfect with Jehovah his God</u>, as was the heart of David his father. <u>For Solomon went after Ashtoreth the goddess of the Sidonians, and after Milcom the abomination of the Ammonites.</u> And Solomon did that which was evil in the sight of Jehovah, and went not fully after Jehovah, as did David his father. Then did <u>Solomon build a high place for Chemosh the abomination of Moab, in the mount that is before Jerusalem, and for Molech the abomination of the children of Ammon.</u> And so did he for all his foreign wives, <u>who burnt incense and sacrificed unto their gods</u>.

1Kings 11:1-8 ASV

In today's modern day, one of the epitomized references is the statue of 'Europa Riding The Bull' that is set up in front of the European Union Parliament complex in Brussels and in some other places like Strasbourg in France and its drawing on the Berlin Wall in Germany. It is also engraved on the Two-Euro coin. The statues, drawings and etching on the Two-Euro coin are all spiritual symbols linking Europe to Satanism.

Directly or indirectly, the European leaders have approved Satanism and encourage an average ordinary European citizen to accept the 'Europa Riding The Bull' as the 'spirit of Europe.' Hence, in their ignorance, they have rejected God and accepted idolatry in His place throughout the continent. It is no surprise Europe is forcefully opposing Christianity and fast embracing worldliness. May God mercifully touch the hearts of the Europeans before the Day of Rapture.

Similarly, in the nearest future after the rapture of the Church, Satan will demand mandatory worship from the people of the world through the beastly image of the Antichrist that will be set up in every place as he, the Antichrist emerges from Europe. By proxy, Satan will rule most parts of the world as 'king of nations' through the 'Beast' and other world leaders, especially by the European leaders —Revelations 13:11-15.

Satanic Kingly 'Powers' Angels Have Great Mastery

Additionally, the *'Power'* angels in the kingdom of darkness have masteries in swaying the hearts of people in authority, especially the main leaders like kings, princes, presidents, head of states, prime ministers, and their key decision makers in unrighteousness, to perpetrate evilness.

Besides, they act as spiritual magistrates, with primary responsibilities to enforce, administer and influence the spread of fiendish laws through people in government positions, by manipulations, mostly through important decision makers of a nation. In many cases, they also work through the 'deep state' agents.

An example of how *kingly 'Powers'* angels in the kingdom of darkness can influence people in authority occurred in Exodus 1:9-11 at the time the children of Israel lived in Egypt. Pharaoh said:

"And there arose a new king over Egypt, who did not know Joseph. And he said to his people, Behold, the people of the sons of Israel are many and mightier than we. Come, let us deal slyly with them, lest they multiply, and it will be when there comes a war, they join also to our enemies, and fight against us, and get out of the land. And they set taskmasters over them to afflict them with their burdens. And they built treasure cities for Pharaoh, Pithon and Raamses."

Exodos 1:9-11 MKJV

The emergency rule instituted by Pharaoh in *Exodus 1:9-11* was a Draconian decree to perpetrate evil and wickedness, and suppress, afflict, and enslave the children of Israel. Even though the decree was introduced and enforced by Pharaoh and the Egyptian authorities respectively, however, demonic *'Powers'* angels, were the main forces behind their actions. They were the kingly spiritual authority in the land.

Another example of the activities of satanic *kingly 'Powers'* angels through those in authority was the enactment and execution of a demonic exigency law during the birth of the Lord Jesus Christ in *Matthew 2:1-15.*

The decree was issued by Herod, the king. He ordered that every male child under two years old must be killed in order to kill the little boy, Jesus Christ. Glory to God the exercise to kill Jesus Christ failed. The enforcement was carried out by government's representatives in security positions, under the control of demonic spirits.

Matthew recorded in his gospel:

"Then Herod, when he saw that he was mocked by the wise men, was greatly enraged. And he sent and killed all the boys in Bethlehem, and in all its districts, from two years old and under, according to the time which he had carefully inquired of the wise men."

Matthew 2:16 MKJV

Likewise, king Ahab and his wife Jezebel were controlled by the satanic 'power' spirit called Baal to enact a death decree against Naboth because he refused to give his inherited vineyard to king Ahab.

"And Ahab came to his house heavy and displeased because of the word which <u>Naboth the Jezreelite had spoken to him...I will not give you the inheritance of my fathers</u>...And his wife Jezebel came to him and said to him, Why is your spirit so sad that you are not eating food? And he said to her, Because I spoke to Naboth of Jezreel and said to him, <u>Give me your vineyard for silver</u>...And his wife Jezebel said to him, <u>Do you now rule over Israel?</u>...I will give you the vineyard of Naboth of Jezreel. And <u>she wrote letters in Ahab's name, and sealed them with his seal, and sent the letters to the elders and to the nobles in his city, dwelling with Naboth</u>...saying, Proclaim a fast and set Naboth on high among the

people. And set two men, sons of Belial, before him to bear witness against him, saying, You blasphemed God and the king. <u>And carry him out and stone him so that he may die.</u>

1Kings 21:4-10 MKJV

As seen in the scriptures above, the reigns of Pharaoh, Herod and Ahab and many other leaders as constituted authorities had liberty power of authority and token of control over their jurisdictions as they were ruled by satanic high ranking 'powers' angels remotely. Thus, in turn, these leaders designated the authorized representatives of their lands to enforce their demonic decrees.

In every generation of man, and today's generation is of no exemption, despite the defeat of satanic hosts by Jesus Christ on the cross, these demonic angels still control people in the positions of authority, especially leaders in the nations of the world that have not given their hearts to Jesus Christ. Regardless, satanic 'powers' angels can only gain access where a leader has not surrendered to the Holy Spirit to control his heart.

Furthermore, you must understand that satanic *kingly 'Powers'* angels can be defeated without the defeat of their satanic *'Principalities, angels'* cohorts in the heavenlies and vis-à-vis. While they are all satanic spiritual beings, working in well-connected networks, still, they possess and operate on different spiritual realms against God and man.

Additionally, while satanic *'Powers'* angels are defeated, God's holy angel that is equivalent to satanic *kingly 'Power'* angel in rank will be dispatched to take charge.

How To Defeat Satanic 'Powers' Angels?

"For the weapons of our warfare are not carnal, but mighty through God..."

2Corinthians 10:4 MKJV

Although, the *kingly* angels in the hierarchy of *'Powers'* in the kingdom of darkness are powerful, however, they cannot match the spiritual power of a Christian warrior that wants their nations delivered from satanic controls. Since all satanic hosts have already been defeated by the Lord Jesus Christ, the victory can be exerted by you today. Notwithstanding, exerting the victory of Jesus Christ over the satanic *kingly 'Powers'* angels, sometimes, are not always easily attainable, as can be seen in many cases in the Bible.

Although, as a Christian, because you have power so mighty through God, does not mean that you can independently of God defeat a satanic *kingly 'Powers'* angel. Remember, God ordains, according to His predetermined plans and engrafted into His plans human kings to be in their positions despite the evilness of many of them, as influenced by satanic host, as can be seen very often today.

The victory over the satanic 'Powers' angels that are ruling through the hearts of the leaders of your nation must always starts with you, through consistence spiritual warfare and obtained divine instructions.

Receiving divine instructions from God is always preceded by your holy acquaintanceship and then being of service to Him. Acquaintanceship with God is a continuous total dedication and fellowship with Him, where divine instructions are sought and obtained. By divine instructions, you can receive either private or opened strategies for winning spiritual battles, especially against the high-ranking angels of the satanic kingdom.

If you want to exert the victories of Jesus Christ over satanic 'powers' angels, do not just pray some religious prayers that give you goose pimples, as in the attitude of some Christians today. While you pray to God about the evilness of the leaders in your country, ensure you pray to receive divine instructions on what to do and lay those instructions in your spirit. Pray to receive God's next plan of action for execution.

"Now be of service with Him, and be at peace. Good shall come to you by them.

Job 22:21 MKJV

"Receive instruction from his mouth, and lay up his words in your heart."

Job 22:22 ESV

Now, having received instructions of steps to take from God, do not pray them back to Him, because they are divine strategies for winning. There is no place in the Bible where warriors of God receive instructions from Him on what to do, and then fold their arms and ask Him again to do the work. They follow the instructions through with actions. God has placed you here on earth to do the work. You are well equipped; you are up to the task.

Therefore, follow up the divine instructions with actions, as directed. Turn the instructions you have received into prophetical decrees when necessary and initiate the battle. Use the gift of prophecy to decree things into manifestations.

Spiritual warfare is a war of words, and gift of prophecy is a powerful weapon. Whatever you prophesy or decree is what you will have. They will prosper as sent by you, and not fall to the ground. It is one of the reasons you have power with God as His child and prince.

Another crucial thing needed to defeat a satanic kingly 'Powers' angel is your possible physical presence where you feel they are located or epitomized by images or symbols. As led by the Holy Spirit, go to where they are located physically or embodied by their symbols. Prophesy the words you have received from the mouth of the Lord against them.

The words coming from your mouth are as if they are coming from the mouth of the Lord; they are sharper, quicker, and powerful than any two-edge sword. Make decrees with those words, and they shall come to pass.

Moreover, take other necessary steps as God instructs against the enemies of your nation, and then continue to give praise and thanks to God for the manifestations of victory. Victory always manifests from the place of execution of divine instructions, followed by praise with thanksgiving.

"Let the high praises of God be in their mouth, and a twoedged sword in their hand; To execute vengeance upon the heathen, and punishments upon the people; To bind their kings with chains, and their nobles with fetters of iron; To execute upon them the judgment written: this honour have all his saints. Praise ye the LORD.

Psalms 149:6-9 MKJV

Whenever victory of Jesus Christ is exerted over satanic kingly 'powers' angels or any of their host of darkness, there will definitely be negative impacts on them and their human hosts. At times, their human hosts could repent of their wickedness, or be dethroned and lose their positions, or be consumed by their evils and die. Pharaoh, Herod, Nebuchadnezzar are few examples of these.

Moreover, a repentant leader could take the first step by leading the rest of his nation into repentance and prayers of forgiveness before God. Let them hand over to God the affairs of their country and rededicate their nation to God by covenant, based on the Blood of Jesus Christ. These steps will totally stop the reign of satanic 'powers' angels in the land and God's angels will take control.

Realizing The Satanic 'Powers' Warfare Capability

One other thing you must know about the satanic 'powers' angels is their capabilities in spiritual warfare. Like satanic principalities, they also have the capability to fight in the heavenlies. Among the creations of God, what depicts superiority is the weight of glory and the natural prowess they possess individually. Angelic beings are not exempted; therefore, fallen angels still possess glories, even though their glories have been corrupted with 'darkness.'

By their weight of glory and prowess, angels are grouped into ranks for battles. It is the reason a lesser angel will dare not engage a principality or power angel in battle, it does not matter if the lesser angel is of God or not. Angels engage one another in battles in equal ranks and prowess. It is the basis for which it is angel Michael that is always engaging satanic princely angels like Satan, the Princes of Persia, Greece, etc. in battle on behalf of God's people.

As stated earlier, an average 'powers' angel rules over their conquered nations by proxy, through the prime leadership, while satanic 'principalities' angels rule directly in the heavenlies, and sometimes by human leaders physically on earth. The satanic 'powers' angels have the capability to fight in the heavenlies with God's angels while they move their human kings and leaders of nations under their controls to engage in physical battles. By their actions, they give necessary spiritual supports. Moreover, they can fight with help of satanic 'principalities' angels.

An example is when the kings of Canaan fought with the children of Israel in Judges 5. While the battle was underway physically on earth, the satanic kingly angelic stars simultaneous engaged in battles in the heavenlies. Who were the satanic kingly angels? They were the kingdom of darkness kingly 'powers' angels that were ruling the land of Canaan by proxy through their human kings, and God's angels of equal ranks fought against them.

"Kings came and fought. Then the kings of Canaan fought in Taanach by the waters of Megiddo. They took no gain of silver. They fought from heaven; the stars in their courses fought against Sisera."

Judges 5:19-20 MKJV

The above incident is a different scenario from what happened in Daniel chapter 10. In Daniel chapter 10, no earthly king or satanic 'powers' angels were involved. The battle was only between higher-ranking princely principality angels, God's angels, Michael and Gabriel and the satanic Prince of Persia. God's princely angel, Michael came to help angel Gabriel against the Prince of Persia. The Prince of Persia on this occasion was defending his territories against Gabriel and Michael's invasion.

A True Revelation

Some decades ago, as a member of the 'Nigeria Youth Corps', I observed my mandatory one-year graduate service in one of the northern states in Nigeria. After I had completed my orientation training at the camp situated at a University in the state capital, I was posted out to another city within the state with some other Nigerian Youth Corps colleagues for primary assignments. Then, I was a fully dedicated member of the Nigerian Christian Corper Fellowship ('NCCF').

Prior to my posting, I was moved by the Holy Spirit to pray and fast for some days concerning my stay in the city of my primary assignment; I prayed intensely in those days. Therefore, on the day I arrived in the city for the first time for my primary assignment, while I slept at night, I had a dream. The entire scenes in the dream were warfare.

In the dream I saw myself walking through a street in the city. As I continued walking, I observed a monument of ram with big horns erected at a certain place on the street. I was amazed by the sight because I had never seen any image like it before.

While I stood watching the image, thinking of what to do, I noticed that the image started turning into a real-life ram. When it fully transformed, it became a huge beastly angry ram, rushing furiously with a speed, while he galloped towards me for a fight. As he wanted to gore me with his horns, a supernatural strength came upon me from nowhere (surely from the Holy Spirit) and I held him by his horns and cast him off.

He got up on his four legs, stepped backwards a few yards, and then came galloping furiously to gore me with his horns again. I held him by his horns the second time and cast him off.

Again, the ram got up on his four legs, took some few yard-steps backwards, and started galloping towards me with a greater force, possibly with his greatest strength. I held him by his horn again wanting to cast him off, then a fierce struggle commenced between us.

Finally, I wrestled him down, by now I was on his top. Instantly a force (surely from the Holy Spirit) stretched forth my right hand forward to receive something, and a shining golden fiery sharp-edged sword came into my hand. With the sword, I slaughtered the beastly ram and started cutting off his head.

While cutting off his head, as he dies, I noticed that the beastly ram started transforming into a human being, lying lifeless. He was wearing a typical full traditional kingly-royal attire, like one of the tribes of the northern people of Nigeria. He had a big kingly-royal turban on his head. Having been sure that I got my victory over him, I got up and started walking away from him. Then I woke up from my dream.

After I woke up from the dream, I asked Holy Spirit the meaning of the dream. He said to me, "You have just conquered the satanic kingly 'power', the spiritual king of this city." I did not fully understand the interpretation of the dream until years later.

The Satanic Kingdom 'World-Rulers of This Darkness'

""For our wrestling is not against flesh and blood, but against...<u>the world-rulers of this darkness</u>..."
Ephesians 6:12 ASV

From the above scripture, Apostle Paul directly linked the hosts of darkness with the global affairs. The *'World-Rulers Of This Darkness'* can be grouped into two: Demonic Beings and Demonic Possessed Human Beings.

As there are rulers in the kingdom of darkness, there are also rulers among human beings that are part of the satanic networks. These *'World-Rulers of This Darkness'* are the demonic spirits that manifest through people of the world in every generation, to manifest ungodliness in all global affairs settings. They are lesser fallen angelic spirits to 'principalities' and 'powers' of the kingdom of Satan. Additionally, they function terrestrially and in the heavenlies as well.

"And you hath he quickened, who were dead in trespasses and sins; Wherein in time past ye walked according to the course of this world, according to the prince of the power of the air, the spirit that now worketh in the children of disobedience: Among whom also we all had our conversation in times past in the lusts of our flesh, fulfilling the desires of the flesh and of the mind; and were by nature the children of wrath, even as others."

Ephesians 2:1-3 MKJV

The *'World-Rulers of This Darkness'* are the spirits that work 'in' people and make them disobey and blaspheme God and oppose anything godly. Part of their assignments is to promote sinfulness among people in all walks of life and make an average person manifest detrimental unfruitful works of darkness to their souls and attack God's interests in all places on earth.

The *'World-Rulers of This Darkness'* work by unleashing spiritual darkness on an average person that are in any quarters assigned to them by Satan and the angelic *'Principalities'* and *'Powers.'* Beginning from the unbelieving leaders of such places to the least of their elites, they control and rule their hearts, minds, and bodies against God's will, openly and secretly. Due to their presence in different locations, there are variations in ungodly lifestyles around the world.

By their titles, names, and fruits, you can know them and their assignments. From *Ephesians 6:12*, let us consider certain words to understand better this next hierarchy to 'powers' in the kingdom of darkness. The words are 'world', 'rulers' and darkness.

The word translated *'world'* is the Greek word *'Aion.'* It has other interpretations like universe, period of time, age, eternity, and perpetuity of time.

'Rulers' is the next word. This was translated from the Greek word *'Kosmokrator.'* Other translations are 'lord of the world, prince of this age, Satan and demons.

The word *'darkness'* was construed from the Greek word *'Skotos.'* It has other construals like shadiness and obscurity. The meaning of 'shadiness' is something that is of 'questionable honesty or legality.'

Nonetheless, let us also consider the Hebrew word for *'darkness'* as stated in *Genesis 1:2*. It is the word *'Choshek.'* As stated earlier, *'Choshek'* means darkness, ignorance, misery, sorrow, destruction, death, wickedness, waste, desolations, etc.

"And the earth was without form and empty. <u>And darkness was on the face of the deep</u>. And the Spirit of God moved on the face of the waters."

Genesis 1:2 MKJV

If these words are fused, it can be said that the *'World's Rulers of Darkness'* always execute their assignments through the global societal lords or rulers or leaders or elites to unleash misery, sorrow, destruction, death wickedness, waste, desolations, etc. on people, while they make those leaders and elites become ignorant of the will and plans of God for them.

As *'Powers'* angels of the kingdom of darkness rule through the main leaders of a nation to enact and execute satanic laws to afflict and oppress people, the *'World's Rulers Of Darkness'* have demonic prowess to work in and through the lords or leaders or rulers or elites to release misery, sorrow, destruction, death wickedness, waste, desolations, etc. on their societies.

The *'World-Rulers of This Darkness'* also, are part of the demonic spirits that control human vessels to introduce and execute works of the flesh and lusts and other ungodly lifestyles that cause misery, sorrow, destruction, death wickedness, waste, desolations, etc. They work from the global authority and through higher influencers of global affairs, down to the lowest facets of life.

Additionally, they are responsible for the generational global new age wickedness, miseries, sorrows, destruction, waste, desolations, unjustly deaths, and other moral decadence. There is no generation since Adam and Eve that do not have the manifestations of the new age spirits and the manifestations of their works only differ from generation to generation.

Out of the many attributes of the *'World-Rulers of This Darkness'* of the Satan's kingdom, a cogent one that must be well understood is that they mainly operate through human influencers of a country and its societies.

Satan is their commander in chief and can be anywhere on earth to set up his base as deemed fit for him. *'Principalities'* are mostly heavenly based contending over the heavenlies atmosphere of nations under their conquered territories. *'Powers'* also can be heavenlies based, but they are mainly working through paramount monarchies and central governments of a country and their cities, towns and villages by proxy.

However, the *'World-Rulers of This Darkness'* spirits have their rule through an average human elite or lord or leader in the world. Because these people are influencers, they could directly or indirectly be part of a government as satanic cult's members, controlling its affairs.

Many of the world's lords, elites and celebrities in various societies and fields of endeavours, including governmental structures are approximately, directly, or indirectly leaders in their various classes. They rule, lead, and subtly influence their followers and the affairs of their nations in their respective quarters for the satanic kingdom.

Nonetheless, these world-class elites, lords and celebrities are always influenced by the disembodied spirits under the hierarchy of the *'World-Rulers of This Darkness'* demonic spirits to introduce and showcase assorted ungodly lifestyles and trends into the world. Consequently, whatever lifestyles they introduce, their fans tend to imitate, knowingly or unwittingly to promote satanic cultures. The semblances are visible in every society of the world today. For instance, various fans of the world's celebrities always imitate their fashion craze.

It is also the *'World-Rulers of This Darkness'* spirits that are behind many of the 'Deep State' fraternities in many countries of the world. The 'Deep State' agents are cabals that dictates the affairs of a nation and if they are global, they generally control the world's affairs by proxy to unleash *'works of darkness'*—wickedness, miseries, sorrows, destruction, waste, desolations and unjustly deaths all over the world. The 'Deep State' members are clique of people that have sold their souls to Satan for worldly gains. Hence, they can reach for any length of evilness to accomplish their goals against God's interests on earth, especially His Church,

How To Defeat The Satanic Kingdom World-Rulers Of This Darkness

Because the *'World-Rulers of This Darkness'* are a part of the satanic hosts that have already been defeated by Jesus Christ on the cross, their activities can be defeated. Nevertheless, they will continue to influence world's affairs if the Church does not rise in spiritual warfare to tackle them.

Now, how can Christians overcome the activities of the *'World-Rulers of This Darkness'* in their nations, cities, towns, villages, and general societies? The Church will definitely overcome from the place of 'knowing' and through spiritual warfare and sharing gospel of Christ.

Overcoming from the place of knowing requires that an average Christian should recognize the root cause of the ungodly activities in their nations, cities, towns, villages, communities, and general societies. The origin is always in the spirit realm, as satanic hosts battle for mastery and control of global affairs through humans. Also, by letting human influencers of satanic policies and activities know that they are the under the control of the *'World-Rulers of This Darkness'*, being used by Satan and his hosts.

Every human is sold out into the hands of the *'god of this world'* and they are under the slavery to sin and death. However, all humans have been saved by the works of Jesus Christ on the cross and his resurrection. Hence, no person is supposed to be lost to Satan if what Jesus Christ did for them is appropriated. However, many have been prevented by the satanic hosts having been mind-blindfolded by Satan, *the 'god of this world'* to prevent them from receiving Jesus Christ as their Lord and Saviour. He prevents them by employing the weapon of ignorance.

"But also if our gospel is hidden, it is hidden to those being lost, in whom the god of this world has blinded the minds of the unbelieving ones, so that the light of the glorious gospel of Christ (who is the image of God) should not dawn on them."
2Corinthians 4:3-4 MKJV

What is mind-blindfoldedness? Mind-blindfoldedness is the spiritual ignorance created by the worldly lusts as a veil on people's minds. What are the components of the worldly lusts? The components are the lust of the flesh, lust of the eyes and pride of life. These components are possessed by people to obtain the pleasures of this life by ungodliness. They are all working in an average lost soul by the satanic weapon of deceit. They are the same weapons Satan used against Adam and Eve by deceit, and they fell. Satan engaged similar weapon against Jesus Christ as he tempted Him in the wilderness, and he failed woefully, while Jesus triumphed.

Now, how can you remove the spiritual mind-blindfoldedness? You can by shinning the light of gospel of Christ Jesus into their hearts to give them *'enlightenment'* and clear away ignorance. In other word, Jesus Christ must be witnessed to them. Nonetheless, it must be amid spiritual warfare.

In the case of spiritual warfare, the corporate Christian authority in the Name of Jesus Christ and by the anointing of the Holy Spirit must be employed. The satanic hosts must be placed in their class; they belong to the class of the defeated and outcast creatures, and victory will manifest.

"Truly I say to you, Whatever you shall bind on earth shall occur, having been bound in Heaven; and whatever you shall loose on earth shall occur, having been loosed in Heaven. Again I say to you that if two of you shall agree on earth as regarding anything that they shall ask, it shall be done for them by My Father in

Heaven. For where two or three are gathered together in My name, there I am in their midst."
Matthew 18:18-20 MKJV

"And I also say to you that you are Peter, and on this rock I will build My church, and the gates of hell shall not prevail against it. And I will give the keys of the kingdom of Heaven to you. And whatever you may bind on earth shall occur, having been bound in Heaven, and whatever you may loose on earth shall occur, having been loosed in Heaven."
Matthew 16:18-19 MKJV

'Kingdom Of Darkness" Spiritual Hosts Of Wickedness In The Heavenly Places

"For our wrestling is not against flesh and blood, but against...the spiritual hosts of wickedness in the heavenly places.
Ephesians 6:12 ASV

After Apostle Paul had listed the fallen angels in their chronological ranks, he concluded their hierarchies by mentioning another class. This class is the *'Spiritual Hosts Of Wickedness In The Heavenly Places.'* The demonic spirits in this class, even though are also in the heavenlies are in the lowest subordinate rank to Satan (the commander in chief) and principalities, and powers and the world-rulers of darkness. They are the demonic spirits that are always at the disposal of the demonic angels and spirits above them as couriers of wickedness. They are the messengers of any type of evilness that can manifest in or through anyone.

The higher-ranking demonic angels of the kingdom of Darkness are embodied spirits. They do not have the capability to possess humans or animals or any object directly, regardless, they are master minders. Thus, to achieve their goals against God's interest through humans, disembodied demonic spirits must be employed. This is how the *'Spiritual Hosts Of Wickedness In The Heavenly Places'* become an integral part of their activities.

The *'Spiritual Hosts Of Wickedness In The Heavenly Places'* are the grass roots 'spiritual foot soldiers' of the satanic kingdom; the last of the demonic connection with people, animal or object for possession to perpetrate wickedness or spiritual attacks. They are the common demonic spirits always at the battlefront with an average person, irrespective of their status. They battle directly or through their human agents invisibly.

For instance, in Genesis, chapter 3, when Satan wanted to deceive Eve in the Garden of Eden, even though he deceived her by serpent, however, he would not have succeeded without the employment of the *'Spiritual Hosts Of Wickedness In The Heavenly Places.'* He would have hatched his sinful plots through the *'Spiritual Hosts Of Wickedness In The Heavenly Places'* that possessed serpent while he (Satan) spoke through him, to deceive Eve. After Eve had succumbed and opened the doorway to the *'Spiritual Hosts Of Wickedness In The Heavenly Places'* by her disobedience, they were able to control her to deceive Adam too.

To have a better understanding of their activities, we need to consider some words from *Ephesians 6:12* above. These words are spiritual, wickedness and high places.

The word *'spiritual'* was translated from the Greek word *'Pneumatikos.'* It was interpreted as ethereal, spirit, supernatural, religious. Another meaning is, ***one who possesses souls***. These renditions summarise everything about their nature.

The next word is *'wickedness'*. This was translated from the Greek word *'Poneria.'* Other renditions from it are depravity, plots, and sins. Also, it was reded as evil purposes and desires. These interpretations reveal their intentions.

The last word for consideration is *'high-places.'* It was translated from the Greek word *'Epouranios.'* It was also interpreted as sky and heavenly region. These renderings show that they are from the heavenlies.

From the different interpretations above, the *'Spiritual Hosts of Wickedness in The Heavenly Places'* are depraved spirits that have their origins in the heavenlies. They plot sins and desire to possess unobservant souls to accomplish their evil purposes against God's interests in all places on earth.

The *'Spiritual Hosts Of Wickedness In The Heavenly Places'* are the spirits that empower and embolden people that are in both secular and religious cults to plot sins and wickedness. They corrupt the minds of their victims to manifest evil purposes and desires at higher and lower levels of life. They are in every generation of man, and their activities are apparent in every society of the world.

Moreover, they are the satanic spirits behind secret arts, enchantment, divination, sorcery, incantation, stargazing, demonic soothsaying, mysticism, astral projection, crystal ball gazing, etc. They also, along with other satanic hosts in the heavenly places influence sinful works of wickedness that Apostle Paul stated in the book of *Galatians 5:19-21.* Their perverse workings are apparent in the world today.

"Now the works of the flesh are clearly revealed, which are: adultery, fornication, uncleanness, lustfulness, idolatry, sorcery, hatreds, fightings, jealousies, angers, rivalries, divisions, heresies, envyings, murders, drunkennesses, revelings, and things like these; of which I tell you before, as I also said before, that they who do such things shall not inherit the kingdom of God."

Galatians 5:19-21MKJV

The main fact about spirits; whether it is the Spirit of God or Satan's is that they love to control their vessels 100 percent. When any satanic spirits gain access into their victims, they control their bodies, and souls absolutely and become the lord of their souls and control their spirits, to plot and execute sins and decadence. During the time of their manifestations, they control their victims autocratically, evilly.

Additionally, *'Spiritual Hosts Of Wickedness In The Heavenly Places'* can possess and control their victims under the instruction of other higher-ranking spirits of the kingdom of darkness, depending on their assignments and the victim's status.

Pride is one of the attributes of the satanic kingdom. For instance, a fallen angel in the hierarchy of 'principalities' in the kingdom of darkness will not descend so low to execute the assignments of the *'Spiritual Hosts Of Wickedness In The Heavenly Places.'* Although, 'principalities' 'powers' and 'rulers of darkness' tend to work evilness by the elitists or people in the positions of rulership or leadership or lordship directly, but they can only achieve their wickedness when those leaders are already possessed by the *'Spiritual Hosts Of Wickedness In The Heavenly Places.'*

As revealed in *2Chronicles 33:1-9*, King of Judah, Manasseh, the son of Hezekiah is also example of people that were controlled by Satan through 'Powers', 'World-Rulers Of This Darkness' but possessed by the *'Spiritual Hosts Of Wickedness In The Heavenly Places.'*

"Manasseh was twelve years old when he began to reign...he did the evil in the sight of Jehovah, like the abominations of the heathen whom Jehovah had cast out before the sons of Israel. For he built again the high places which Hezekiah his father had broken down, and he reared up altars for the Baals, and made Asherahs, and worshiped all the host of heaven, and served them. And he built altars in the house of Jehovah, of which Jehovah had said, In Jerusalem shall My name be forever. And he built altars for all the host of heaven in the two courts of the house of Jehovah. And he caused his sons to pass through the fire in the valley of the son of Hinnom. He also practiced secret arts, and used fortune-telling, and used witchcraft, and dealt with mediums, and with soothsayers. He did much evil in the sight of Jehovah in order to provoke Him to anger. And he set a carved image, the idol which he had made, in the house of God, of which God had said to David and to Solomon his son, In this house, and in Jerusalem, which I have chosen before all the tribes of Israel, I will put My name forever...And Manasseh made Judah and the people of Jerusalem to err, to do worse than the nations whom Jehovah had destroyed before the sons of Israel.

2Chronicles 33:1-9 MKJV

In the above scriptures, Manasseh reared up altars for Baal and epitomised Asherah and made people worship the hosts of heaven. How did he find himself in such state? The genesis of his move into such state was his being possessed and controlled by the *'Spiritual Hosts Of Wickedness In The Heavenly Places'* to practice secret arts, and use fortune-telling, and witchcraft, and have a relationship with mediums, and soothsayers. He opened himself to them by associations, and then the *'Spiritual Hosts of Wickedness'* started to control him to give his royal worship to the satanic 'powers' and 'world-rulers of this darkness' instead of God, Subsequently, he perpetrated much wickedness before God and provoked Him to anger.

Today, the *'Spiritual Hosts Of Wickedness In The Heavenly Places'* are at work in and through the lives of unsaved people of all ages across the world. They control their lives and make them practice depraved and ungodly deeds and sin against God and people.

'Spiritual Hosts Of Wickedness In The Heavenly Places' are also the demonic spirits that are responsible for all spiritual attacks of all degrees that people suffer here and there in all areas of life. The spiritual attacks could be afflictions of any kind, which may include mysterious disability, sickness, misfortunes, maladies, and oppressions of all kinds.

A True Story

A few years ago, a girl narrated how she was initiated into witchery and other practices of occultism by her grandmother. Eventually, she worked against her father.

After her attacks on her dad, her dad who was a senior professional banker in one of the leading banks in Nigeria suddenly suffered many setbacks in his career; subsequently, he lost all his possessions and became a pauper. The man wondered why he suddenly became unprosperous.

One day he was advised to receive Jesus Christ into his life and go for deliverance; possibly, God would turn things around for him. He did and received Jesus Christ as his Lord and Saviour.

Hence, he was empowered and enlightened by the Holy Ghost and began the most intense spiritual battle of his life. The battle was between the decisions of the host of darkness and what he believed God has created him to be. These were the two hands working behind the scenes of his life: one for his good and the other for evil.

A few days after this, his daughter told him that she was responsible for all his predicaments. She told him how she was introduced into witchcraft by one of her grandmothers. Since then, a spirit has been controlling and working through her to perpetrated evils and wickedness against human beings at any level. Eventually her dad became one of her victims.

The only people she could not spiritually confront and perpetrate her evils against were Christians who were filled with the Holy Ghost.

To cut a long story short, she was brought for deliverance, she confessed her sins and accepted Jesus Christ into her heart and the 'spirit of wickedness' was cast out of her. After this, things began to turn around for good for her dad once again. Let God be glorified.

How To Defeat The 'Spiritual Hosts Of Wickedness In The Heavenly Places'

There is no satanic host in any of their hierarchies that a Christian cannot defeat; the *'Spiritual Hosts Of Wickedness In The Heavenly Places'* are of no exception. You must remember that every satanic host, whether they are spirits, or their human beings have already been defeated triumphantly by the Lord Jesus Christ. As a 'son' of God in Christ Jesus, the challenges you may face could be how to identify their works in and through a person and exert your authority and appropriately obtain your victory over them.

As stated repeatedly in this chapter, satanic hosts have organised powerful networks. Regardless, a true Christian in the Church of Jesus Christ belongs to a greater formidable network with the hosts of God—angels and saints; the Lord Jesus Christ is the Captain of the hosts. A Christian also owns weapons that are mighty through God; Satan's kingdom arsenals are no match to them.

"For though we walk in the flesh, we do not war after the flesh: (For the weapons of our warfare are not carnal, but mighty through God..."

2Corinthians 10:3-4 MKJV

What are the weapons of warfare available to defeat the *'Spiritual Hosts Of Wickedness In The Heavenly Places'?* Among many, let us consider a few as enumerated below.

Using The Gospel As A Weapon: Witnessing Jesus Christ To Souls

There is no soul that does not need Jesus Christ to obtain eternal life; every soul needs the Redeemer, Jesus Christ. As said earlier, all souls have sinned and come short of God's glory. The first weapon that must be employed is 'witnessing Jesus Christ' through the gospel.

If a victim of demonic possession realises what Jesus Christ has done for them and receives Him as their Lord and Saviour, they will not want to belong to Satan anymore; they will refuse to be used by him to perpetrate wickedness again. Moreover, the afflicted soul will desire to be free from any demonic afflictions. The lasting solution they need is the Lord Jesus Christ; therefore, give Him to them.

Ask them if they truly believe in Jesus Christ with all their hearts, and sincerely confess with their mouth He is the Lord of their life. The ownership of their soul will change hands, and they will be saved.

Weapons Of Holy Ghost's Power And A Christian's Authority

Moreover, you must use your Christian-Believer's authority in the Name of Jesus Christ and the anointing of the Holy Spirit that is on you to engage the *'Spiritual Hosts Of Wickedness In The Heavenly Places'* in spiritual warfare. One of the things they fear most is an anointed Christian that knows their authority and can place a demand on their anointing and use them effectively against the hosts of darkness.

"And he said unto them, I beheld Satan as lightning fall from heaven. Behold, I give unto you power to tread on serpents and scorpions, and over all the power of the enemy: and nothing shall by any means hurt you."

Luke 10:18-19 KJV

"But as many as received him, to them gave he power to become the sons of God, even to them that believe on his name: Which were born, not of blood, nor of the will of the flesh, nor of the will of man, but of God."

John 1:12-13 KJV

"And these signs shall follow them that believe; In my name shall they cast out devils; they shall speak with new tongues; They shall take up serpents; and if they drink any deadly thing, it shall not hurt them; they shall lay hands on the sick, and they shall recover."

Mark 16:17-18 KJV

If you use your authority and anointing effectively, you will become a terror to all the hosts of darkness; they can never withstand you anymore—as in the cases of Jesus Christ and Paul in Acts 19:14-16. Hence, use your anointing and authority in the matchless Name of Jesus Christ to cast *'Spiritual Hosts Of Wickedness In The Heavenly Places'* out of their victims—whether they are human agents or afflicted persons. They will flee, and their victims shall be free to serve Jesus Christ and acquire divine goodly heritage and enjoy God's providence ordained for them.

Weapons Of Righteousness

Every spiritual weapon at our disposal is a weapon bestowed by God in righteousness. If employed in righteousness, they would accomplish the purpose of their provisions, and the Name of Jesus Christ will be glorified. Hence, using the 'Weapons of Righteousness' against the hosts of satanic kingdom will fulfil the corporate intentions of God and the Church.

Indeed, the 'Weapons of Righteousness' should be engaged to defeat the *'Spiritual Hosts Of Wickedness In The Heavenly Places.'* As stated, beforehand, human vessels are their main target for possession to manifest their nature of wickedness through them, even though they can possess animals and objects for similar purpose.

"In the Word of Truth, in the power of God, through the weapons of righteousness on the right hand and on the left."
2Corinthians 6:7 MKJV

The 'Weapons of Righteousness' can be used as both defensive and offensive weapons. They include the 'Power of Truth'; the 'Breastplate of Righteousness'; the 'Gospel of Peace'; the 'Helmet of Salvation'; the 'Shield of Faith; 'Prayer and Supplications in the Spirit'; the 'Sword of the Spirit' and 'Persistent Spiritual Watchfulness.'

"Stand therefore, having your loins girt about with truth, and having on the breastplate of righteousness; And your feet shod with the preparation of the gospel of peace; Above all, taking the shield of faith, wherewith ye shall be able to quench all the fiery darts of the wicked. And take the helmet of salvation, and the sword of the Spirit, which is the word of God: Praying always with all prayer and supplication in the Spirit, and watching thereunto with all perseverance and supplication for all saints."
Ephesians 6:14-18 MKJV

All satanic hosts, including the *'Spiritual Hosts Of Wickedness In The Heavenly Places'* work to oppose the Truth; the Righteousness; the Peace; the Salvation of souls; the Prayerfulness; and tempt Christians in diverse ways.

In the place of Truth, the *'Spiritual Hosts Of Wickedness In The Heavenly Places.'* cozen people and make them live by falsehood and become treacherous in all their dealings.

In the place of righteousness, they move people to exhibit impiety, blasphemy, and irreverence towards God; they are perverted in all their ways and become enemies of God.

Instead of peace, they unleash terror, and cause strife and hostility among people everywhere; equally, the Church is not spared.

They replace Salvation with damnation, as they oppose the spread of the gospel and prevent people from hearing it. Equally, they stop unbelievers from accepting Jesus Christ as their Lord and Saviour.

In the place of Faith, they influence people to doubt God, His works and reliability. They make people discredit all things about God.

In the place of fervent and effectual Prayer and Supplication, they render Christians lukewarm and prayerless and make unbelievers channel their worship and prayers towards false gods.

In the place of Persistent Spiritual Watchfulness, they make Christians become loathsome. They control all people to be insensitive to other people plights and display apathy for all.

As they work and manifest their evilness through their human agents, an average person, including many Christians, are adversely affected. Nevertheless, if all weapons of righteousness are engaged as both defensive and offensive weapons by an average Christian, all hosts of darkness, including *'Spiritual Hosts Of Wickedness In The Heavenly Places'* will be put to flight. Their works will be destroyed, and their victims will be totally set free for Jesus Christ.

Weapons Of Charismatic Gifts, Living In The Spirit And Cluster Fruit(s) Of Love

The next available weapons are the *"Charismatic Gifts of the Holy Spirit"* as listed in 1Corinthians 12:8-10, the *"Power of Living in the Holy Spirit"* in Galatians 5:16-17 and the *"Gifted Cluster Fruit(s) Of Love"* stated in Galatians 5:22-23. Many Christians are not aware that they are indeed for spiritual warfare against the hosts of darkness.

"For through the Spirit is given to one a word of wisdom; and to another a word of knowledge, according to the same Spirit; and to another faith by the same Spirit; and to another the gifts of healing by the same Spirit and to another workings of powers, to another prophecy; and to another discerning of spirits; and to another kinds of tongues; and to another the interpretation of tongues."

1Corinthians 12:8-10 MKJV

"This I say then, Walk in the Spirit, and ye shall not fulfil the lust of the flesh. For the flesh lusteth against the Spirit, and the Spirit against the flesh: and these are contrary the one to the other: so that ye cannot do the things that ye would."

Galatians 5:16-17 KJV

"But the fruit of the Spirit is: love, joy, peace, long-suffering, kindness, goodness, faith, meekness, self-control; against such things there is no law."

Galatians 5:22-23 MKJV

All the spiritual gifts listed in the above scriptures are essentially for your profit. They are for you to gain advantage over any situation to get a specific desired result, as translated from the Greek word, *'Sumphero.'*

"But to each one is given the showing forth of the <u>Spirit to our profit."</u>

1Corinthians 12:7 MKJV

What specific result do you desire over the host of darkness, including the *'Spiritual Hosts Of Wickedness In The Heavenly Places.'*? I believe it is ***'All-Round Victory'*** by Jesus Christ, whereby Satan and his hosts should not again have any inch of your life's territory—spiritually, martially, financially, socially, emotionally, etc.

Every one of these gifted weapons must be employed to defeat any satanic hosts, especially the *'Spiritual Hosts Of Wickedness In The Heavenly Places.'*

If you use the 'gift of 'discerning of spirits' as a weapon, you will be able to differentiate between godly and satanic spirits that are operating by deception in any place and life.

By the 'gift of word of knowledge', you can know their activities in anyone and place.

By the 'gift of faith, you can move against them by spiritual warfare having great confidence in God and exert your authority over them and obtain victory.

By the 'gift of word of wisdom', you can make known to all hosts of darkness the manifold wisdom of God; teach their human hosts and victims the mysteries of the unsearchable knowledge of God.

By the 'gift of working of powers', you can display authentic divine signs, wonders, and miracles, to counter their deceits to make people believe in Jesus Christ, the Lord.

By the 'gifts of healing', you can unleash God's power of deliverance on their victims, set them free and put the demons of affliction to shame.

By the 'gift of prophesy', through the power of your tongue and sword of the Spirit, you can declare the outcome and what their ends would be.

By the 'gift of kinds of tongues', you can speak mysteries to God to confound the networks of the hosts of darkness and assault them unaware.

By the 'gift of interpretation of tongues', you can reveal their secrets and show that God's power at work in you is not limited to a language and natural knowledge, but God is the Creator of all nations and languages; He is Omniscient.

By living in the Spirit, you are always aware of God's presence, which is the Holy Ghost in you. With Him, you have the power of union by the righteousness of Christ with Him; He is a better and invincible Partner to work with.

By the gift of love, you can conquer their wickedness in and through people with forgiveness and love.

I will teach more on gifts of love and charismatic along the pages of this book.

Christian, know that Satan and his hosts are already judged; they will never escape their anticipated eternal fate. To conserve your victory, you should continue to live in the consciousness of the fact that you are tackling already defeated foes. They can never triumph again. Praise the Lord!

Despite Satan's organise kingdom and their strategized schemes, God remains the greatest Strategian of all times. In earnest, God arose and manifested His next strategy, while Satan and his hosts were scattered. Now, let us see how God's next stratagems against the satanic hosts unfolded in the next chapter.

Chapter 5

God Is The Greatest Strategian

Eternally, God is Love. His love and care for mankind is unfathomable; it is constant and everlasting. At all time, as necessary, He has never been restrained from proving His love for mankind, even though he does not condone their sinfulness.

God's love is explicitly stated throughout the pages of the Bible and showcased across the ages by His works. Momentarily, He wants the radiation of His glory to be revealed in man, so that all mankind can be encapsulated by His resplendent presence.

God is the Creator of all things, and everything He creates is made for His will and pleasure. God has never created anything without a purpose in mind, and He always expects all creations to fulfill their divine purposes in Him.

As stated in chapter two, Satan was created for certain purposes by God, and while he abused and departed from his divine purposes, he became the originator of sin and death. Any evil manifesting through anyone in the world today is an indirect result of Satan's activities everywhere. Consequently, he fills almost every place in the world with his horror.

At the time he conceived sin, he pitched his tent against God, and afterwards against humanity; he becomes an arch enemy forever. Despite God's wrath upon him and the inevitable divine judgment that will determine his fate, yet he goes about working viciousness among nations.

Holy Ghost Took Charge By His Ultimate Force

After God destroyed the world of Satan, He sent forth His Holy Spirit to take control of the earth. Bible makes us understand what happened afterwards.

"...And the Spirit of God moved upon the face of the waters."
Genesis 1:2 KJV

To get to the depth of what happened when Holy Spirit took charge, let us look at some words from the above scripture. They are 'move', 'upon', 'face' and 'waters'.

The word *'move'* was derived from the Hebrew word *'Rachaph.'* It has other interpretations like to relax, brood, flutter, move and shake.

The next word is *'upon.'* It was translated from the Hebrew word *'Al.'* Other translations are above, over, upon, against, had the charge of, etc.

The word *'face'* also came from a Hebrew word *'Paniym.'* Other renditions from it are over against, anger, battle, etc.

The last word is *'waters.'* It came from the Hebrew word *'Mayim.'* It was also reded as waters as of danger, violence, transitory things, refreshment.'

What is the deduction from these interpretations? It could be said that, immediately Satan sinned and turned the earth into a place of violence and God's judgment came upon him, God sent forth the

Holy Spirit in full force of violence to brood, shake and flutter against him.

Holy Spirit came and took charge by warfare and raised His standard against what Satan might stand to symbolize. And by anger and violence, Holy Spirit prepared the ground for divine transition and replenishment.

In earnest, the work of cleansing commenced as Holy Spirit purged and restored the earth. Holy Spirit's action shows us that God does not restore anything or anyone that has come short of His glory without cleansing. After cleansing, then restoration and blessings are released. This has been His way with all humanity since the fall of Satan.

Universally, Holy Spirit was all over the face of the waters and continued to be on earth until the days of Noah. His presence manifested God's judgments upon Satan and the other fallen angels. Then, God's preconceived plans for man became apparent on earth, as He rolled out His strategic plans, to create man as His prototype to live on earth.

God Severed Light and Darkness

It should be noted that, while Holy Spirit was on the face of the waters, the satanic presence was no longer mentioned as God commenced His works to create and renew the earth. Satanic presence and activities were utterly dispelled.

"You send forth Your Spirit, they are created; and You renew the face of the earth."

Psalm 104:30 MKJV

So, God said:

"...Let there be light. And there was light."

Genesis 1:3 MKJV

Once again, let us look at the other words translated *'Let there be light'* for us to know what happened better.

The words translated *'Let there be'* were from a Hebrew word *'Hayah.'* It has other renditions like to be, become, come to pass, exist, happen, and fall out.

Also, the word translated *'light'* was derived from a Hebrew word *'Ore.'* Its other interpretations were illumination or light, lighting, happiness, etc. In other words, what God said was, let 'light' exist.

We should remember that after God's judgment came on Satan and the angels that took part in his rebellion, darkness, which signifies sorrow, misery, destruction, death, and ignorance became the symbols of their self-chosen purposes. Then, God called forth light (happiness) by the power of His Word, and it existed and started manifesting as He intended.

What is happiness? Happiness is expression of intense joy. God brought into existence light--happiness, intense joy--to overcome the spiritual darkness--sorrow, misery, destruction, death, and ignorance that originated because of His judgment on Satan.

"And God saw the light that it was good. And God divided between the light and the darkness."
Genesis 1: 4 MKJV

Once more, let us look for other renditions from the words translated *'saw'* and *'good.'* The word *'saw'* was derived from a Hebrew word *'Raah'*. It also rendered as 'advise self, appear, approve, behold.'

The word *'good'* was construed from another Hebrew word *'Tobe.'* The other translations are 'good, pleasant, agreeable, prosperity', etc.

Therefore, when the *'light'* appeared, God gave His approval that the 'light'--happiness--intense joy was pleasant and agreeable with His purpose and prosperity of mankind on earth.

Now, God moved on to the next level of His plans. He drew a line of separation between light--happiness--intense joy and darkness--misery, destruction, death, and ignorance. The word *'divide'* was translated from a Hebrew word *'Badal.'* It has other interpretations like 'to divide, separate, distinguish, differ, select'.

God, at sundry times uses natural things to explain His spiritual agendas on earth, so everything God was doing here has spiritual connotations. From Genesis 1:4b, we can see that God was pointing to something that will distinguish the present from the past. He was speaking about an emblem of separation between Satan and his fallen angels and His new creation, called 'Man.' He was speaking of the breakup between reverence for God and rebellion, and rectitude and unrighteousness and sanctity and evilness.

Now, God was laying a new foundation for godliness that His new 'creations' would be fashioned after. Proverbially, he was saying that He did not want His new 'creations' that were coming into manifestation to have any form of agreement with rebellion and 'darkness'--misery, destruction, death, and ignorance.

Satan and his hosts and their rebellion belong to the past; God has now utterly severed His new 'creation' from them. It was His clear message to the new 'creation' that were about to manifest.

Likewise, God is extending this message to Christians in every generation, including you. We are God's children, His new creations in Christ Jesus. We are the light of the world, created to express His intense joy during the world's severe darkness.

There must be no agreement between us and the works of darkness of this world. In other words, totally, we must consciously reject 'darkness'--misery, destruction, death, and ignorance through the expressions of our light's supernatural intense joy.

You may ask, why didn't God take out the darkness completely so that light would be everywhere? Some people have asked me this question many times before now. God could have, if He wanted; but, possibly, in His wisdom He decided not to because He wanted

His new creatures to know the differences between light and darkness, and godliness and evil, and submission and rebellion and make free choices. In His wisdom, He always allows us to learn from the past to make wise decisions about the future.

"Behold, I set before you today a blessing and a curse."
Deuteronomy 11:26 MKJV

"Behold! I have set before you today life and good, and death and evil"
Deuteronomy 30:15 MKJV

I believe if Satan were able to catch a glimpse of what God was doing, he would have wondered what He was up to. However, he never had the opportunity; God kept him in ignorance.

You and I should know that our God, the Holy One of Israel, the Most High and the God of Abraham, Isaac and Jacob is the greatest Strategist. He is full of surprises to beat the enemies at their games.

All strategies for winning every battle of life are in His hands. If you must win, you must receive, follow, and obey His instructions. Then you shall have all the good things He has already ordained for you; then His plans for you would be fulfilled. Thus, He said to us and everyone:

"For I know the purposes which I am purposing for you, says Jehovah; purposes of peace and not of evil, to give you a future and a hope."
Jeremiah 29:11 MKJV

Creation of Man: The Manifestation Of God's Strategy

God manifested His stunning strategy and created everything by the power of His Word as Holy Spirit continues to move upon the earth. Behold, at last *'MAN'* was created to replace Satan. This last action gave Satan and his host the greatest humiliation and shocks of their existence. They never envisaged the creation of 'Man.'

Beforehand, Satan should have known that wisdom emanated from God, and there is no wisdom that can outwit His infinite hallowed wisdom. Satan had seen how God had used His wisdom to lay the foundation of the earth, created everything in it and all angels shouted for joy – Job 38:1-7.

However, he never had any idea of what God would do next, because he has already been cursed with ignorance.

"Who has directed the Spirit of Jehovah, and what man taught Him counsel? With whom did He take counsel, and who instructed Him and taught Him in the path of judgment, and taught Him knowledge, and made known the way of understanding to Him?"
Isaiah 40:13-14 MKJV

Man Is A Resemblance Of God

In earnest, God demonstrated the prowess of His master creative skill by extraordinary wisdom, and the power of His wisdom was accentuated to debase Satan and his hosts. Therefore, He created *'MAN'* in His image.

"...Let Us make man in Our image, after Our likeness...And God created man in His image; in the image of God He created him. He created them male and female."
Genesis 1:26-27 MKJV

Now, let us continue with the pattern of this book and look at some words from the above scriptures to have a good picture of what God was doing here. These words are 'make, image and likeness.'

The word translated *'make'* came from the Hebrew word *'Asah.'* It is also translated as 'to do, fashion, accomplish, make, be industrious, etc'.

The next one is the word *'image.'* It was reded from the Hebrew word *'Tselem.'* It has other translations like images, likeness, and resemblance.

Lastly the word *'likeness'* was construed from the Hebrew word *'Demuth.'* It was also interpreted as resemblance, model, and shape.

From these meanings, we can conclude that when God wanted to make man, He did not fashion him to resemble any other creature He had already made. He did not make Adam or Eve to look like an angel or any other creations, but they were a thorough replicated process of His image.

Let us also see Genesis 2:7:

"And Jehovah God formed man of the dust of the ground, and breathed into his nostrils the breath of life; and man became a living soul."

Genesis 2:7 MKJV

Again, let us look at some words from the scripture above. They are 'formed, dust, breathed, breath and living'.

The word translated *'formed'* was derived from a Hebrew word *'Yatsar.'* It has other renditions like squeezing into shape, to mould into a form like a potter and purpose.

The next one is *'dust.'* It came from the Hebrew word *'Aphar.'* Other translations are 'dry earth, powder, ashes, earth, ground, mortar, rubbish'.

Also, the word *'breathed'* was construed from the Hebrew word *'Naphach.'* It is also reded as 'puff, inflate, kindle, expire, blow hard and scatter.

The word *'breathe'* was interpreted from the Hebrew word *'Neshamah.'* Its other translations are puff, wind, vital breath, divine inspiration, intellect'.

Lastly the word *'living'* was derived from the Hebrew word *'Chay.'* Other renditions are alive, fresh; strong, life, quick, etc.

The idea is that when God was creating man, He took what was regarded as so insignificant and considered as 'rubbish.' He caused it to go through a process of squeezing and shaped it to be His model.

God looked at the frame of man lying helplessly without life, and He breathed the breath of life through its nostril. He puffed man with divine inspiration and intellect and gave him the wind of life that is vital to his existence on earth. Finally, something good, great, and glorious manifested. Man became a quickened fresh and strong living soul, bubbling with God's life.

Now, out of what Satan has trampled upon when he was in Eden and counted as rubbish, God created something that is much more glorious than all angels. From something inconsequential if equated with the precious stone material that Satan was made of, God revealed a mind-boggling surprise and abased Satan and his hosts forever.

God poured contempt on all of Satan's pride. Out of worthless stuffs, He made something beautiful and wonderful. He glorified His holy Name then, and now, and forever. It is written:

"But God has chosen the foolish things of the world to confound the wise; and God has chosen the weak things of the world to confound the things which are mighty; and God has chosen the base things of the world, and things which are despised, and things which are not, in order to bring to nothing things that are; so that no flesh should glory in His presence."
1 Corinthians 1:27-29 MKJV

You Are A Force To Be Reckoned With

Dear reader, you are the one Genesis 1:26-27 is all about. Carefully look through the process of your creation by God. He spent a considerable time on your entire being, He caused your being to go through a process and brought you out as the most important creature on earth.

You became an intelligent creation, full of creative acumen and wisdom. Satan thought it was over for the earth; however, it was just the beginning of God's display of His manifold wisdom for all creations to know that, indeed, He is God over all.

Satan, through people might have rubbished you; they claim that nothing good could come out of you. You might have been despised and considered a cipher. Hear this, and let it continuously reecho in your consciousness: *"You Are A Force To Be Reckoned With In Your Generation."*

What makes the difference in anyone is the life of glory in them. If you have not received Jesus Christ as your Lord and Savior, you are depriving yourself of life of glory. If you already have Jesus Christ in you, then, the place of glory is your limit.

Today, you can tell your critics and those that have despised you that, God has not yet finished with you. He is taking you through a process of glory. When He completes His good works in you, He will display you for the world to see His glory in your life.

Your society might have rejected you because of your yesterday, your low status, your complexion, your race, and your background. Yet, God wants to celebrate you before your ostracisers. He wants to use you to taunt Satan and the world of wickedness.

Have you been ridiculed by the world because of your imperfections? Are you at your wits end and hopeless? Look up to Jesus, there is hope in your end. He will lift you up and showcase your outstanding qualities the world has never seen before and you will manifest His glory. Where you have been rejected, they would accept and fete you, and Jesus' Name shall be glorified. Amen.

You Are Distinctively Unique

By God's sovereign will, man is uniquely made as God-kind creature besides other creations. There is no other creature that carries God's striking resemblance than mankind; they are God-specie.

God's plans and thoughts for man are very deep and greater than what any mind can comprehend. No creature ever occupies such a special place in the heart of God more than mankind. I will expatiate more on this in the next chapter. However, David said:

"For You have possessed my inward parts; You have covered me in my mother's womb. I will praise You; for I am fearfully and wonderfully made; Your works are marvelous and my soul knows it very well. My bones were not hidden from You when I was made in secret and skillfully formed in the lowest parts of the earth. Your eyes saw my embryo; and in Your book all my members were written, the days they were formed, and not one was among them. How precious also are Your thoughts to me, O God! How great is the sum of them!"

Psalms 139: 13-17 MKJV

Surely, because you are unique God has given you unequaled purpose to fulfill in this life. In your uniqueness, you carry the similitude of no other being, except God's. Nevertheless, you may say, "But I look like my biological parents." Look at your parents; you would notice they carry the very God's image. They may not have Holy Ghost's power, but they are in His image.

Image is other representation of the real object; so, you are a miniature look-alike of God and not of the devil. It does not matter what the world calls you and how they see you according to your complexion--black, green, red, or white, you are still a physical image of God. Do not fall by Satan's weapon of racism; its action-field is in the mind, to create complex issues.

Anyone that wants to know what God looks like should look at you. It is the real reasons Jesus Christ did not come in any other form but in the likeness of man. When He came, He declared anyone that had seen Him had seen the Father - *John 14:8-9*. He is exactly God's replicate, God manifestation in a tabernacle of flesh.

Whether your complexion is black or white, or yellow, you are a carrier of God's skin color. The complexion of your image is God-type because God is Light, and light reveals various colours. Now is the right time for you to jump for joy, shout aloud and proclaim everywhere: *'I am 'UNIQUE'; I am 'Created in the Image of God; I am Godkind."*

I wish every man on earth, including Satan's worshippers would realize that God has created them to greatly humiliate Satan. Therefore, Satan is not supposed to be worshipped by any person or any creation of God, but he should be greatly abhorred and held in complete contempt in every sphere of life.

A True Life Story

In 1993, I was a minister of God at Faith Clinic Ministries in Lagos, Nigeria; a girl of about 16 years was brought for deliverance.

On this fateful day, as I and other ministers were ministering to her, she began to confess so many things that were too difficult for a natural human being to comprehend. She claimed she was initiated into an occult group at the age of 6 years and recruited as a part of Satan's foot soldiers, having been possessed by demonic spirits.

She became the leader of the occult group at the age of 10 having people that were older than her under her control. She confessed that before she could become the leader, she entered a covenant to be a worshipper of Satan and promised to marry him. As part of her assignment, as early as age 10, she had started having sexual relations with Satan. By the time she turned 16; she had recruited and initiated so many males, both adults and minor into the occult group through sex.

She stated that Satan always changed into a beautiful man whenever he wanted to meet with her. She claimed that he has never seen a beautiful man like him. At times, he would take her in the spirit, by water to India for meetings and introduced her to other cult members as her only bride.

When the facts were stated from the Word of God, she found it so difficult to believe that Satan was just a creation and not a creator like God. She had been greatly deceived to believe that Satan is 'God.'

As she was being delivered from occultism during ministrations, she was made to know that she was not the only one Satan has been going about deceiving; he has deceived so many people across the globe in every generation, beginning from Adam and Eve.

Glory to God; at the end, by the help of the Holy Spirit and the power in the Name of Jesus Christ, she broke her covenant with Satan, renounced her marriage relationship and accepted Jesus Christ as her Lord and Savior and became a born-again Christian.

The girl in the above testimony never knew that she was made in likeness of God and was unique in His sight, to fulfill His purposes in this world. Until the weapon of enlightenment was used to remove satanic ignorance from her life, and she became enlightened, she did not know that Satan and his followers were deceivers, and Satan should not be worshipped.

Please say it again *'I AM UNIQUE. I am a worshipper of God. I wholly belong to Jesus Christ.'* You are unique indeed.

Man Is Genetic Expression of God's Life And Glory On Earth

During man's creation, God did not just puff him with intellect and inspiration, He also gave him unending divine genetic life; a type of life of glory that only Him has. God never intended that His life of glory would depart from man, and any mankind would die and be eternally separated from Him. He made them a little lower than Himself and crowned them with glory and outstanding honour.

"For thou hast made him a little lower than the angels, and hast crowned him with glory and honor."

Psalms 8:5 KJV

In the above scripture, the word translated *'angels'* is a Hebrew word *'Eloheem'*, meaning Gods. Other renditions are 'magistrates; great, judges, mighty.'

Also, the word *'glory'* was reded from the Hebrew word *'Kabod.'* It has other translations like weight, splendour, honour, glorious, abundance, riches, dignity, reputation, and reverence.

And the word *'crown'* was derived from the Hebrew word *'Atar.'* It has other derivations like encircle for protection and compass.

So, God created man to be great, mighty and have, dignity, reputation and to be reverenced with honour among His creations. Inclusively, He put him in the magistrate position to judge the earth; consequently, He encircled him with weight of glory for protection and blessed him with abundant riches.

What other creatures were in the earth then? They were Satan and his fallen angels roaming about the earth and other creations that were created before Adam, including animals.

For your life to reflect the originality of God, you must see yourself as a creation of glory and honour. You are not a weakling that the falling nature of man has revealed, but a mighty man for and of God. You have been made to rule over your world and the forces of darkness.

Therefore, carefully behold yourself more and more in the mirror of these revelations and shake off the devils and circumstances they have created to demean you. By the virtue of the position that God has accorded mankind, no angels were made better than you. You are the best of God and the best you can be is yet to manifest; live in anticipation of it.

Step out of those situations that have belittled you now and declare continuously, *"I AM THE BEST OF GOD, AND MY BEST MANIFESTATION IS YET TO COME."*

Adam Was The King And Lord Of The Earth

In today's world, there are kings and lords, even though God is the overall KING and LORD, the Ruler over all things. However, when God created man, He made them the king and lord of the earth; an extension of God's LORDSHIP, to rule and judge other creatures under his jurisdiction.

A lord is not just an ordinary person, he has power above those in his class, and they submit to him. Likewise, a king reigns over the affairs of his jurisdiction. Adam, indeed, was one of the creations of God; regardless, as earth is concerned, he had power above all other creations that inhabited the sphere, Satan and his host were not excluded. All things were made to be under his control, in total submission.

Even though the first Adam lost his kingship and lordship to Satan, however, now that you are in Jesus Christ, you have regained your kingship and lordship. By Him, you are a king and lord over all things. You are an extension of His Kingship and Lordship that encompasses all jurisdictions of life on earth. You are a manifestation of the heavenly kingdom's authority on earth.

Therefore, never let any situation diminish you. Whatever they are, you must rise above them. Hence, arise now and assume your kingship and lordship positions. Now, assert and declare *"I AM A KING AND LORD OVER ALL THINGS. I RULE OVER MY WORLD. SATAN AND HIS HOSTS ARE UNDER MY SUBJECTION, IN THE NAME OF THE LORD JESUS CHRIST."*

Man Was Blessed Without Curse

As God breathed the breath of life into man, and encircled him with His glory, He did not just stop there. He did something that established His intention for him; He 'BLESSED' him. While Satan and his fallen angels were cursed, eternally, God pronounced everlasting blessings upon man. We shall see more on this in the next chapter.

The Best Position Of All

After God finished the work of His creation on man, not only did He crown him with glory and blessing, but He also placed him in the best place of all on earth. It was a peculiar place of beauty where God could step down into the world of man for fellowship. It was a place where His glory would encapsulate man, and he would be rhapsodically elated to a level beyond his imagination. The Bible says:

"And Jehovah God planted a garden eastward in Eden. And there He put the man whom He had formed...And Jehovah God took the man and put him into the garden of Eden to work it and keep it."
Genesis 2:8-15 MKJV

Let us continue with the pattern of this book to have a good picture of what God was up to in *Genesis 2:8-15* and analyze the word *'Eden.'*

Having compassed man about with His glory, He blessed and put him in Eden. The word *'Eden'* was construed from the Hebrew word *'Eden.'* Other inferences are pleasure, delicate, luxury, dainty, delight, and finery.

These interpretations reveal part of God's original plan for man. God surely wanted man to have a delightful life of godly pleasure and luxury. God never intended that man would spend his life in sorrow, sickness, lack and poverty.

If God did not want mankind to have delightful life of godly pleasure, luxury, and dainty, He would not have created and positioned Adam in Eden, a place of abundance and pleasance. God wanted Adam to enjoy life at maximum luxury to reveal his material glory. God, in a limitedly degree demonstrated this type of life before in the lives of Job, Abraham, Joseph, Solomon and so many people that had Him as their God.

Dear reader, Satan does not want an average man in the world, particularly you, Christian to know this divine truth; it is the fact that he was once in Eden before his rebellion, and he fell without obtaining mercy and restoration afterwards. Now, he is condemned and doomed for all eternity; he would never be redeemed.

He knows what life at the maximum godly pleasure indicates, and he wants to deprive all mankind on earth, including you from possessing it. Because of this, he goes about, deceiving mankind to submit and worship him to have a pleasurable luxurious life that originally belonged to the first Adam.

Carefully note, Satan is not the giver of life. God is the source of life and true blessings. Whatever pleasure of life Satan gives will always end in unrighteousness, tragedy, and eternal condemnation. You can count many worldly rich people that have embraced him, and his illusive glory and their lives have ended in tragedy. Subsequently, they missed God and the true life for all eternity.

God in His faithfulness does not bless and add sorrow to it. Sorrow is an emblem of satanic darkness in the soul, and it belongs to Satan and his hosts.

"The blessing of Jehovah itself makes rich, and He adds no sorrow with it."
Proverbs 10:22 MKJV

Part of Satan's agenda is to steal, kill and destroy whatsoever God has endowed man with to have godly pleasurable, luxurious, dainty, and abundant life as heritage. They include your peace, health, finances, marriage, children, ministry, flourishing, etc.

"The thief does not come except to steal and to kill and to destroy. I have come so that they might have life, and that they might have it more abundantly."
John 10:10 MKJV

However, *"...For this purpose the Son of God was revealed, that He might undo the works of the Devil."*
1 John 3:8 MKJV

Man's Divine Heritage Outlined

Everything God empowered Adam to have at his creation, which included the earth and its fullness, the striking likeness of God, the divine genetic life and nature that God puffed into him to make him an inspirational and intellectual living soul. The glory he was crowned with to make him a force to be reckoned with among other creations. The power of procreation to replenish the earth with holy offspring. His inheritance of the best place of all--the Garden of Eden and the remaining blessedness that God unleashed on all mankind through him are his entire divine heritage.

*"Ye are blessed of the LORD which made heaven and earth. The heaven, even the heavens, are the LORD'S: **but the earth hath he given to the children of men.**"*

Psalms 115:5-6 KJV

Every component of Adam's divine heritage was given to him to showcase his dominion and reign in life on earth. Therefore, he must jealously guard and maximally protect them. Now, let us move on to the next chapter to further examine his dominion.

Chapter 6

Dimensions Of Adam's Dominion

As seen in the previous chapter, after God created man, He gave him a heritage. He did not only form him in His similitude and prototype, but He also encircled him with protection of glory, blessedness and placed him in Eden, the best place of all on earth.

Indeed, Eden was a place of attraction, beauty, and glory to be admired by all other creatures of God. All of these and more are the components of Adam's divine heritage.

From the beginning of their creation, God loved man with endless and selfless love. It is the kind of love that can never be compared with any other. It is the type of love that sins cannot quench; it supersedes all the upshots of temptation that Satan can lure man into. It is love at the peak of its demonstration that made God condescended into man, to rescue all mankind from sin and all its consequences.

God's affection for man is uncomprehendingly extraordinary and makes Him long for mankind despite their short comings and abuses of His purposes of their existence. It is a peculiar love that makes God reaches out to humanity, irrespective of their depravity.

"Jehovah has appeared to me from afar, saying, Yea, I have loved you with an everlasting love; therefore with loving-kindness I have drawn you."

Jeremiah 31:3 MKJV

Satan Lost Eden And Man Gained It As A Heritage

As aforesaid in chapter two, God created Satan and placed him in Eden for a purpose, to rule over the earth before Adam and gave God glory moment by moment. As soon as Satan, the 'son of the morning' and his fallen angels overstepped the boundaries of their assignments and abused the purpose of their creation, they lost the glorious Eden-heritage. Afterwards, they were chucked out of Eden. Bible says about Satan:

"You have been in Eden the garden of God."

Ezekiel 28:13 MKJV

So, Satan lost his glory; he lost Eden-Heritage and the power to reign forever on earth. God refreshed and replanted the same Eden and earth where Satan was and gave it to Adam as a heritage to fulfill His purpose for him. Fulfillment of God's purpose was the vital objective of Adam's creation.

Adam's primary purpose was to worship and glorify God moment by moment on earth by his inherited *'DOMINION'*, and then reign from Eden. By his heritance dominion he would subdue every contrary force, and righteously become fruitful (reproduce offspring after his likeness), multiply and replenish the earth. Consequently, all generations of man would bear his likeness and likewise become worshippers of God, by their dominion.

"And God said, Let Us make man in Our image, after Our likeness. And let them have dominion over the fish of the sea, and over the fowl of the heavens, and over the cattle, and over all the earth, and over all the creepers creeping on the earth."

Genesis 1:26 MKJV

Indeed, dominion is another component of Adam's heritage. From the above scripture, God's primary heritage assignment for Adam's' was to *'have dominion over everything on earth.'* After God created them, He blessed, empowered, and gave them a blueprint to fulfill the divine assignment of their creation. I called it, **'the blueprint of Adam's fivefold divine undertakings on earth.'**

God's Blueprint For Adam's Fivefold Undertakings

"And God blessed them, and God said unto them, Be fruitful, and multiply, and replenish the earth, and subdue it: and have dominion over the fish of the sea, and over the fowl of the air, and over every living thing that moveth upon the earth."

Genesis 1:28 KJV

Let us examine Adam's fivefold divine heritance mission on earth as stated in Genesis 1:28 above. We will consider the following words:

- ➢ Be Fruitful
- ➢ Multiply
- ➢ Replenish
- ➢ Subdue
- ➢ Exert Dominion

Be Fruitful

The words translated *'be fruitful'* were from the Hebrew word *'Parah.'* It also referenced as to bear fruit, branch off, bring forth, grow, and increase.

In the Bible, fruitfulness symbolises many things. However, two of its symbolism are 'childbearing' and 'character'—in the sense of godly attributes.

"Rejoice, O unfruitful one that never bore; break out a song and shout, you who never travailed. For more are the sons of the desolate than the sons of the married woman, says Jehovah."

Isaiah 54:1 MKJV

"Lo, children are the inheritance of Jehovah; the fruit of the womb is a reward."

Psalm 127:3 MKJV

"But the fruit of the Spirit is: love, joy, peace, long-suffering, kindness, goodness, faith, meekness, self-control; against such things there is no law."

Galatians 5:22-23 MKJV

"Therefore by their fruits you shall know them."

Matthew 7:20 MKJV

By decree that man should be *'fruitful'*, God's plan for Adam and Eve was to bring forth children that would have distinct inherent godly attributes after their kind; and all successive offspring would also possess godly attributes as heritage. Subsequently, they would increase by procreation and fill up everywhere on earth with their godly species. They would be distinguished as Godkind by their righteous character and fruits.

From Eden, which is Adam's dominion's headquarters, God, by him would give instructions to all successive heritage offspring's generations. Thus, every man on earth would be holy to God and righteously obey and serve Him. Hence, Adam and his descendants would rule over the earth, in reverential subjection to God's sovereign authority.

Multiply

The word *'multiply'* was derived from the Hebrew word *'Rabah.'* It has other renditions like, to increase, be or become great, be or become many, be or become much, be or become numerous.

The above renditions state another God's decree on Adam. He wanted him to increase greatly and become numerous.

God's multiplication formula is not like man's natural mathematics. Man counts numbers in natural sequences and multiplies indexed numbers in logical orders. God increases things in super-hyper multiples, too illogical for man to comprehend. God's decree of Multiplication on Adam was a divine accelerated increase, whereby Adam would fill the face of the earth with godly species quickly.

"And I will make your seed as the dust of the earth, so that if a man can count the dust of the earth, then shall your seed also be counted."

Genesis 13:16 MKJV

"As the host of the heavens cannot be numbered, nor the sand of the sea measured, so I will multiply the seed of David My servant and the Levites who minister to Me."

Jeremiah 33:22 MKJV

Adam was indeed supernaturally empowered by God for the assignment.

Replenish

Also, the word *'replenish'* was derived from the Hebrew word *'Mala.'* Other translations from the word are, to fill, be full of, presume, replenish, satisfy etc. From the English dictionary, the word 'replenish' means to 'fill something that had previously been emptied.'

In other words, if God instructed to Adam to refill the earth, then His decree suggested that the earth was formerly inhabited before it became empty. Who previously inhabited the earth before Adam? It was Satan and other angels. Satan and one third of the angels filled up everywhere on earth with iniquities before God's judgment came on them.

So, the earth that Satan filled with iniquities was destroyed and refreshed by God and gave it to Adam and his successive offspring. Part of the heritance duties of mankind was to fill up the earth with God's type of righteousness and reign in life.

When the generation of people that built the Tower of Babel did not obey God and refused to spread abroad to replenish the earth as God commanded, He came down and scattered them. He caused confusion in their camp and divided their one language into many languages that are spoken on earth today—*Genesis 11:4-8.*

Subdue

Besides, the word *'subdue'* was derived from the Hebrew word *'Kabash.'* Other interpretations from it are, to tread down, to disregard, to conquer, subjugate and violate.

To make a more sense out of the above interpretations, God decreed that Adam should use force to subdue and keep the earth under him and bring it in subjection to His will. The decree did not permit any excuses; it was the highest and binding command.

God would not just instruct Adam to subdue the earth if there was nothing to subdue. Satan's posture is the reason; he had already drawn a battle line against God. Satan and his fallen angels had already pitched their tents against every good thing God has made; Adam was created as the principal being on earth to tackle Satan.

In addition, note that Satan and his hosts were not destroyed after they were judged. They were still very much around and had their angelic powers. Therefore, the conflict to fully regain control of the earth was about to start. God created the earth and willed it to man as a heritage that must be preserved.

God knew Satan has not given up on his intrigues and wiles to be what he was not created to be. He wanted worship from God's other creations. Thus, Adam and his offspring in every generation were assigned to conquer, subjugate, and keep under, every opposing force that might rise against the will and counsel of God on earth. Satan's insurrections must not be allowed.

The use of force is the answer to bringing all things into subjection if Adam would reign as God intended. All mankind are Adam's offspring, and they too are created to assert and establish God's purpose on earth.

Adam Unfolds His Dominion

The word *'dominion'* was first mentioned in *Genesis 1:26* in relation to Adam, as God considered his creation and purpose. Adam would be empowered with dominion, to reign in life on earth—*Genesis 1:28.*

The word *'dominion'* was translated from the Hebrew word *'Radah.'* It is also translated as, to tread down, subjugate and crumble off.

Another word we should consider is *'have.'* It means to possess something. If the word *'have'* is examined in the context it was used by God, it would reveal that the most important aspect of God instruction and blessings upon Adam and his offspring is to *'possess dominion.'*

God, having decreed, and blessed Adam with inherent ability to be fruitful, multiply, and replenish the earth, the word *'have'* actually gave Adam the privilege to be a custodian of *'dominion'* to subdue everything on earth and reign over them. As a creature created after the similitude of God, reigning in life is part of his divine heritage. God is the eternal reigning KING; He reigns over all things in heaven and on earth; hence, He wanted Adam to take control of the earth and reign as well.

Adam's Dominion Defined His Position

What is dominion? The English dictionary meaning of the word 'dominion' is sovereignty over something, power through legal authority, dominance, supremacy, stewardship, kingdom, nation, governed territory.

From these meanings, it could be established that, when God decreed that Adam should *'possess dominion'*, He gave him the whole earth as his sovereign kingdom, nation, and governed territory. Simultaneously, He gave him legal supremacy over other creations on earth to be their king, lord, and chief steward officer. He occupied the position of 'The Possessor of Earth.'

In a nutshell, Adam inherited a divine sovereign government; an extension of heaven's kingdom on earth, where God would be His only Instructor. In this position, he had the privilege to take decisions on God's behalf and reign over anything on earth. Satan too had this type of government on earth until he rebelled against God. He was then ruling from Eden over angels and other things on earth.

Hence, whatever decision Adam takes in line with God's instructions is binding on heaven to permit. God gave him the absolute delegated power to rule and reign over the earth. He displayed his delegated power in Genesis 2:19-30.

"And out of the ground Jehovah God formed every animal of the field and every fowl of the air, and brought them to Adam to see what he would call them. And whatever Adam called each living creature, that was its name. And Adam gave names to all the cattle, and to the birds of the air, and to every animal of the field..."

Genesis 2:19-20 MKJV

Adam's Dominion In Action

In earnest, Adam occupied his position and activated his dominion by naming other creations on earth, and God allowed Adam's decisions and decrees to stand. By this, God attested that He had given Adam absolute dominion over everything He had created that exist on earth. So, as He ascertained, He watched how Adam demonstrated his divinely gifted legal authority righteously.

Another example was when God created Eve and brought her to Adam, as explained in *Genesis 2:22-25*. Having seen Eve, Adam said:

"And Jehovah God made the rib (which He had taken from the man) into a woman. And He brought her to the man. And <u>Adam</u> <u>said, This is now bone of my bones and flesh of my flesh. She shall</u> <u>be called Woman because she was taken out of man. Therefore</u> <u>shall a man leave his father and his mother, and shall cleave to his</u> <u>wife and they shall be one flesh.</u> And they were both naked, the man and his wife; and they were not ashamed."

Genesis 2:22-25 MKJV

Some intriguing and wonderful things happened here as Adam's displayed his dominion. Let us examine them.

Firstly, Adam, by his prerogative decision differentiated between himself, (the male specie) and his female helpmeet, and called her, 'Woman.' God did not call Eve 'Woman', Adam did.

Secondly, while God called both 'Adam' as stated in Genesis 5, the Male-Adam took a prerogative decision again and called the Female-Adam, Eve—*Genesis 3:20*.

Furthermore, God did not tell Adam that Eve, his woman *'Helpmeet'* was his wife. God did not pronounce them husband and wife, but Adam did on God's behalf. Once again, Adam used his prerogative heritance dominion to formally declare that both 'Man' and 'Woman' Adam were husband and wife.

Please note, marriage is a holy institution, ordained by God and very sacrosanct in His sight. It was His godly idea that He manifested at beginning for the good of mankind. However, Adam was the one that made the decision, as God's representative to unfold the mystery of marriage; therefore, in his decision, he set his marriage apart for God as a sacred institution between him and Eve (a man and a woman) on earth. He said:

"...Therefore shall a man leave his father and his mother, and shall cleave to his wife and they shall be one flesh."

Genesis 2:23-24 MKJV

While human beings live on earth, marriage institution stands between a man and woman, and not between human beings of the same sex; and it is one marriage a lifetime. By his heritance dominion, Adam took charge and made all decisions in righteousness, and they were approved and eternally established by God. Despite his fall, things did not change as decreed by him prior his fall. Everything he decreed and called by names stands the same today just as they were then.

The Lord Jesus Christ in *Matthew 19:3-6* answered His critics concerning the institution of marriage. He said:

"...Have you not read that He who made them at the beginning "made them male and female", and said, For this cause a man shall leave father and mother and shall cling to his wife, and the two of them shall be one flesh? Therefore they are no longer two, but one flesh. Therefore what God has joined together, let not man separate."

Matthew 19:3-6 MKJV

Jesus Christ took every one of His critics back to the beginning of things before Satan's interfered in the affairs of mankind. He emphasized God's intentions and then quoted what Adam had established through his heritance dominion regarding the institution of marriage. God has not changed His mind concerning them; they remain the same and binding on all generations of man.

Apart from the fact that Adam had heritance dominion to make decisions on God's interest on earth, he also had the Spirit of God to direct him to exercise his dominion within the ambits of God's will. He took every decision by the Holy Spirit, and did whatever was in the mind of God, as intended.

Although Adam sinned by Eve's influence, and Eve sinned through Satan's deception, and the life of glory left them. Since then, Adam could not exercise his dominion as before. Regardless, God did not leave Adam and his successive generations alone. He continued to plead with him and his progenies by His Spirit to restore humanity back to Him—*Genesis 6:3 MKJV*. He still does today.

Adam Was Created An Adult Man

As revealed earlier, immediately Satan rebelled against God and sinned, he drew a battle line between him and God. Consequently, the battle of mastery to dominate the earth and heaven began between him and God.

God was aware that Satan was very much around before He created Adam; notwithstanding, He wanted Adam to use his dominion against every opposing force that might rise within his earthly jurisdiction and subdue and put them in perpetual bondage. Therefore, He never created Adam a child-man, but an adult-man.

There is a difference between a child and an adult-man. An adult-man is a matured being, considered to be proficient in taking right decisions, whereas a minor is inept.

Right from the first day of Adam's creation, he was a mature person puffed with impeccable heritage deific intellect, to be sensitive to everything happening within his environment, physically and spiritually. Adam was never created to be tamable by Satan, or being incapable of handling Satan's invasions, whatever their forms.

God gave Adam the highest heritage authority and power any of His creatures could possess, and no creature should be able to resist his spiritual prowess. As far as the earth is concerned, Adam's sovereign power was only next to God's, and his decrees were God's commands. His volition would be permitted by God on earth, as long he walked and worked responsibly in line with God's commands. It is like what the Lord Jesus Christ says to the Church in *Matthew 18:18*

"Truly I say to you, Whatever you shall bind on earth shall occur, having been bound in Heaven; and whatever you shall loose on earth shall occur, having been loosed in Heaven."

Matthew 18:18 MKJV

Features Of Adam's Dominion

It has now been established that Adam had a heritance dominion with responsibility to exercise sovereign power over the earth. Without dominion, he would never fulfill God's original purposes and be everything he was predestined to be. Let us examine the features of his dominion.

It is a Kingdom Dominance

When God considered that Adam should 'possess dominion' and subdue everything on earth, He had in mind a 'kingdom dominance.' God gave him a heritance earthly kingdom whereby Adam would have royal rule over everything that God created to live on earth.

As outlined earlier, dominance speaks of a country under governance. The whole earth was supposed to be a state under Adam's jurisdiction and governed by God's law of the Spirit of life. Then, Adam would reign as God intended.

By dominance, God wanted Adam and his offspring to replenish the earth while the whole world would be under 'One World Theocratic Government', and the living God would be the overall supreme KING and All in All that reigns over all in all. Although God gave Adam the permission to exercise dominion, it must be according to His commandment, applying heavenly principles to issues on earth.

It Is A Dominion With Blessed Providence

Indeed, God blessed Adam and ordered him to manifest his heritance blessings. The first order He gave him was a command of provision whereby He said:

"And God blessed them. And God said to them, Be fruitful, and multiply and fill the earth, and subdue it. And have dominion over the fish of the sea and over the fowl of the heavens, and all animals that move upon the earth. And God said, Behold! I have given you every herb seeding seed which is upon the face of all the earth, and every tree in which is the fruit of a tree seeding seed; to you it shall be for food. And to every beast of the earth, and to every fowl of the heavens, and to every creeper on the earth which has in it a living soul every green plant is for food; and it was so."
Genesis 1:28-30 MKJV

God gave the order so that the *'bestowed blessings'* on Adam and his offspring would manifest. Even though God has blessed him with fruitfulness, multiplication, replenishment of the earth, power to subdue and privilege to possess of dominion, they were blessings with an attached order that created some limits on how far Adam can go. The command must be obeyed for Adam's heritance blessings to be evidence. The command was given for Adam's good.

God started a new world through Noah and his children. After the death of Noah, instead of spreading all over the earth to replenish it as God intended, Noah's progeny reached an accord to remain at the plain of Shinar, and they built the Tower of Babel—***Genesis 11:1-9***.

God saw the deeds of Noah's descendants as noncompliance to the command He gave to Adam, and then to Noah. For the blessing of *'Replenishment'* to manifest, He confused their ideas, divided their language, and scattered them abroad, all over the earth.

The incident in *Genesis 11:1-9* reveals that, even though God had blessed Adam and Noah in *Genesis 1:28-30* and *Genesis 9:1*, regardless, His command must be obeyed, to evidence man's heritage on earth. Without compliance, the blessing of replenishment would not manifest.

The issue of noncompliance was not only limited to the generation of man that built the Tower of Babel at Shinar, it all started from Adam and Eve and becomes the norm in many generations; present generation is not exempted. Mankind, in their depraved nature always despise God's commands, to gratify their lustful souls; thus, they procure condemnation as gains.

Healthy lifestyle, blessed marriage and holy offspring, power to subdue, and defeat every enemy and exert your dominion are heritance blessings that God has bestowed on you. If you must evidence them, you must follow divine principles as gazette in God's holy creed.

Adam's Dominion Has The Potential To Establish His Perpetual Life's Blessings

As stated earlier, Satan lost his Eden, and Adam gained a new one that he was supposed to keep as an earthly heritage, to be the headquarters of his sovereign reign. Now, as Adam was basking in the glory of his heritage and enthralled with the beauty of Eden, God bestowed another heritance blessing on him. By a decree, it was the heritance blessing of perpetual life.

Unlike the first bestowed blessing, the second commanded blessing came with some stringent conditions attached to it. This demanded a non-dissension posture from Adam, if he wanted to be what God had created him to be and possess his heritage forever.

It was an order that would have either positive or negative impact on all generations of mankind. It was an order that could make man in every generation retain or lose their bestowed heritance blessings from God. It was a prescription that could pitch God and man against each other and provoke heavy punishments on many generations if violated.

Therefore, God said:

"And Jehovah God took the man and put him into the garden of Eden to work it and keep it. And Jehovah God commanded the man, saying, You may freely eat of every tree in the garden, but you shall not eat of the tree of knowledge of good and evil. For in the day that you eat of it you shall surely die."

Genesis 2:15-17 MKJV

From the above scripture, the word 'but' carries weights of consequences for Adam and his kind. It summarized exclusions and set the boundaries of his freedom. If he would preserve his bestowed heritage forever, a full compliance to the given instruction is required, and he must live within the limits of his freedom.

Furthermore, it is an expression of God's objection to any alternative idea to His laid down executive orders. It is a condition that spells out severe consequences of doom for the whole humanity if there is any disobedience to the laid down orders.

On earth, every sovereign country has its dos and don'ts under their laws that their citizens must comply with. Violation of the 'don'ts would ignite punishment, so it was with the wholly earthly kingdom that God gave to Adam.

Appropriately, God gave Adam a kingdom, and a territory called earth, and principles to enable him to know his limits within God's will, and the 'dominion' to implement God's will on earth. Adam's obedience and decisive use of his dominion will establish him and future generations in perpetual blessings as God intended.

Adam's Dominion Manifested His Divine Ageless Royal Heritage

As seen above, the intention of God for Adam was to make the whole earth his kingdom, whereby, it would be an extension of God's theocratic state under Adam's leadership. As stated earlier, dominion means 'dominance or power through legal authority'; and the authority of a kingdom always flows from the supreme head to his subjects. Various examples in the Bible and around the world confirm this fact.

For instance, whenever the Queen of England addresses the parliament at the beginning of the financial year, she always refers to the reign of government of England as 'My Government.' If there is a new Prime Minister, he must first receive the Queen's approval to form a government on her behalf. The prime sovereign authority in the United Kingdom is the monarch, politicians only become part of the government as representatives.

The word 'kingdom' is a combination of two words which are 'King' and 'Dom'. The word 'king' means 'crowned ruler of a kingdom, monarch and powerful or majorly influential person' and 'Dom' means a 'domain, dominant and dominion'. 'Domain' means 'land governed by a ruler or government'.

Again, the meanings of 'king' and 'Dom' give us an idea of what God wanted for Adam. God made Adam to be the king and lord over all the earth. Then, his successive descendants would be kings and lords under his rulership. It is the reason Christians are kings and lords under the rulership of our Lord and King Jesus Christ, the Son of God.

Kingship is about power of dominance to manifest rulership. There is no king that can rule without dominion. If Adam did not possess dominion, he would not manifest his kingship and lordship over his world, to fulfill God's purposes. He would be a mere powerless man on earth.

Satan was fully aware of the above facts, while Adam regarded his dominion as worthless and handled things with levity. Satan knew the degree of Adam's dominion before he moved to deceive Eve, then, Adam by Eve to usurp Adam's dominion. As soon as Satan seized Adam's dominion, he legally arrogated the whole earth under his rulership, as if it were divinely given. Hence, Adam was unable to govern as God intended.

Now, everything has turned into a mess, and things could no longer hold together for mankind's benefit. Adam watched as he and his wife became mere persons, totally stripped of their divine powers and glory, and there was nothing they could do to retrieve what they lost. The divine goodly heritage dominion he needed to exert his authority is no longer in his possession; it is now in the hands of his arch enemy. May God deliver us all Satan's wiles.

Dominion Manifested Adam's Glory

Satan knew what the dominion that Adam possessed could accomplish; he schemed to take it away from him, and he succeeded.

As stated previously, Adam was created a spiritual adult-man, puffed with higher intellect. He was fully aware of God's principles and consequences of noncompliance to His orders. He was supposed to perceive everything going on within the Eden that God gave to him as a home and his operational base. However, he became indifference and permit Satan to gain an upper hand. God had said to him:

"And Jehovah God commanded the man, saying, You may freely eat of every tree in the garden, but you shall not eat of the tree of knowledge of good and evil. For in the day that you eat of it you shall surely die."

Genesis 2:16-17 MKJV

Naturally, quantity and quality of materialism reveal the different levels of glory of man, to distinguish classes. Likewise, in spiritual matters, glory has various grades, to depict hierarchies and superiority. After Adam was created, he was crowned with glory as heritage. The weight of his glory was more than the glory of any angelic beings; it encompassed all the earth. The beam of his glory dispensed rays of power that no creation could withstand at the fullness of its radiation.

Before now, Satan and his fallen angels had lost their true glory after they rebelled and sinned against God. What they have been manifesting since then is no longer true light but an aura of utter darkness. Wherever they are, they mete out nimbus of darkness and fullness of deceit to bring forth wickedness.

So, Adam was placed in the best position to be aware of what Satan was doing and take decisive control of his heritage. The dominion that Adam possessed was for him to manifest his glory all over his given sphere and glorified God.

Satan was in cognizant that without dominion, Adam would not manifest his glory, and truly, he did not want him to reveal his glory. Because of this, he schemed Adam, shortchanged, and dispossessed him, only of his dominion.

Dominion Speaks of War

Adam had a nature that he took for levity and refused to stir it up. He was created a warrior like God to tackle Satan and his hosts. He knew that possession of dominion speaks of war, to subdue whoever the enemy may be.

How did he know this? The answer is, would God have left him in ignorance of what Satan could do? The answer is NO, God did not! God ordered him to subdue anything that could work contrary to divine principles given to him.

Similar things are happening today. God has never left any man in confusion of whom the real enemy is. An average person knows who Satan is, and they chose to ignore him, while he steals their heritage.

Adam had the option to comply with what God had said or did not say, after Eve oversubscribed Satan's idea to him. God did not give Eve any direct instruction, but he gave it Adam. He was the one that passed the principle of God to his wife and other creatures within his domain.

While Eve suggested the idea of disobeying God, Adam should have discerned and know the personality at work, rebuked the devil and delivered his wife. In addition, that was the first time Adam had the opportunity to 'subdue', however, he failed to use his dominion to subdue Satan and put him where he belongs.

Nowhere on earth, never, within his domain should Satan raise his ugly head and manifest through an acquaintance—the serpent for that matter.

Primarily, Satan no longer belonged to the circle of the righteous creations of God. Adam had the prerogative means to unravel the mystery behind Eve's idea, discovered Satan's intention and chucked him out eternally by using the power of his authority, to put the situation under control. Satan should not have a foot in Adam's heritage; he did not deserve any. He had already lost his own Eden; he lost it forever and ever. Amen!

Adam was supposed to know that when God instructed him to subdue, He was referring to conquering anything and anyone that might rise contrary to His order. Whatever he executes within the boundaries of the order, it is heaven's authority that is at work by him. Whatever his decision might be in relation to subduing Satan and his host, it was as good as God had taken the decision. Satan knew this as truth, but Adam did not.

Moreover, Adam should have known that it is through spiritual warfare that he would be able to fulfill other righteous assignments of fruitfulness, multiplication, and replenishment that God gave to him, and his dominion speaks of that. Therefore, he had the dominion as a weapon of war.

Adam's Dominion Was Designated To Subdue

Moreover, the terms *'subdue'* and *'dominion'* work hand in hand to conquer any rising oppositions. If Adam had wanted to subdue without any legal authority, he would just be an empty barrel that makes nuisance noises before other creatures of God. Thus, his actions would have been sin. Therefore, his heritance dominion was designated to subdue and avenge every disobedience to God's command.

It is just like someone wearing a police uniform without the approval of the recognized legal authority of the land and wants to arrest somebody. Immediately the person he wants to arrest realizes that he is not appointed to do so, he would scornfully laugh at him. He would see him as an impostor and intruder into his privacy. He would either tackle him directly or call the bona fide authority to arrest the situation.

Adam was not an intruder on earth, he was the unquestionable owner, the holder of the bona fide authority. Satan was the intruder, the thief. Adam possessed heaven's authentic heritage dominion designated to exhibit his real position in God's governance on earth.

Primarily, he possessed dominion to subdue Satan in all his maneuvers and then govern the earth. Having conquered Satan, then godly fruitfulness, multiplication and replenishment of the earth would commence without any satanic interference, as God has destined things for him.

When Jesus Christ came the first time, He came as the Second and Last Adam. He possessed the legal authority of heaven just as the first Adam possessed dominion. He knew that His authority was designated to dispossess Satan and his host and dislodge them out of His territory, which He did. After He disposed Satan and his host, then, godly fruitfulness, multiplication and replenishment started springing up all over the earth. God now has offspring He can call His own in us; we Christians are His people. Hallelujah!

Dominion Justly Exercised Brings Peace

Dominion rightly used will bring peace. As dominion speaks of war, if justly utilized will bring peace and tranquility at the end. If Adam had used his dominion as God intended, peace would have been all over the earth today. Satan would have been defeated and peace and orderliness could have been in the world of man.

Solomon the King of Israel, in the early part of his reign is an example on this. Bible testifies of him in 1King 5:12.

"And Jehovah gave Solomon wisdom, as He promised him. And there was peace between Hiram and Solomon. And the two of them made a treaty together."

1 Kings 5:12 MKJV

What is responsible for peace during the early part of Solomon's reign? It was a dominion justly exercised with wisdom in the fear of God. As a result, there was peace. He inherited the kingdom and dominion from his father and knew how to use his dominion justly, by the fear of God. While the fear of God ceased, and he went after other gods, there was no more peace left in his kingdom.

Many kings after Solomon had the kingdom and dominion too but did not rule in the fear of God, and they did not have peace. As their punishment, they were carried away into captivities and afflicted by the satanic hosts through human vessels. Dominion exercised in the fear of God is dominion justly used; and it would bring peace in all facets of life.

Do you have any challenge in your life? You are a man of kingdom and dominion in Jesus Christ. Your life is the first place to use your dominion. Use your authority in the Name of Jesus Christ to put any circumstances you may be facing under control. You can overpower them, and now is the best time to utilize your dominion.

Exercise your dominion justly in the fear of God; root out the devils and their works. You will overcome and have peace in all territories of your life. As Jesus Christ triumphed, you shall, too.

Chapter 7

Where Adam Failed Jesus Triumphed Conclusively

In the previous chapter, Adam's dominion was outlined and defined. We learned where, why and how he failed to tackle Satan to establish his heritage earthly kingdom once and for all. However, glory be to God that where the first Adam failed, Jesus Christ, the Second and Last Adam was victorious.

Scriptures from Genesis *1:27-28* and *Psalm 8:4-5* clearly reveal to us that after Adam was created by God, He blessed and crowned him with power and glory. He placed him in Eden as the super-human-overseer of everything on earth. He did not send him to Eden without maximum and necessary empowerment with legal authority to rule.

"And God created man in His image; in the image of God He created him. He created them male and female. And God blessed them. And God said to them, Be fruitful, and multiply and fill the earth, and subdue it. And have dominion over the fish of the sea and over the fowl of the heavens, and all animals that move upon the earth."

Genesis 1:27-28 MKJV

"What is man that You are mindful of him, and the son of man, that You visit him? For You have made him lack a little from God, and have crowned him with glory and honor."

Psalms 8:4-5 MKJV

Before Adam could exclusively use the power of his authority to subdue the earth, Satan manifested. There are striking similarities in the manner Satan moved against the first Adam and Jesus Christ, the Second and Last Adam.

Having received the Holy Spirit, before Jesus Christ could commence His public ministry, He encountered Satan's fierce battle in the wilderness. Satan quoted and used scriptures, the sword of the Spirit inappropriately to attack Jesus Christ.

In the wilderness, after Jesus Christ had fasted for forty days and nights, Satan appeared. He challenged Jesus Christ from the position of His heirship.

"And the Devil said to Him, <u>If you are the Son of God</u>, speak to this stone that it might become bread. And Jesus answered him, saying, It is written that 'man shall not live by bread alone, but by every Word of God.' And the Devil, leading Him up into a high mountain, showed Him all the kingdoms of the world in a moment of time. And the Devil said to Him, All this power I will give you, and the glory of them; for it has been delivered to me. And I give it to whomever I will. Therefore if you will worship me, all shall be yours. And Jesus answered and said to him, Get behind me, Satan! For it is written, "You shall worship the Lord your God, and Him only shall you serve." And he brought Him to Jerusalem and sat Him on a pinnacle of the temple and said to Him, <u>If you are the Son of God</u>, cast yourself down from here. For it is written, "He shall give His angels charge over You, to keep You; and in their hands they shall bear You up, lest at any time You dash Your foot against a stone." And Jesus answering said to him, It has been said, "You shall not tempt the Lord your God."

Luke 4:3-12 MKJV

Satan's motives behind his attacks on Jesus Christ were attempts to rob Jesus Christ of His kingdom heritage. He knew that Jesus is the God's only begotten Son, the authentic deific Heir of God. He is the Second and Last Adam that would restore whatever has been stolen from first Adam to mankind.

Satan knew that Jesus Christ was the Lord God Almighty that created all things, including the satanic hosts. God's love for mankind constrained Him to become a Man, to redeem and restore mankind to their original position in God. Satan knew if Jesus Christ could fail this time around, humanity has failed forever to regain the lost sovereignty; there will be no hope left.

If Jesus Christ were unable to conquer him, who else could? Thank God, thank the Lord Jesus Christ; He did not fail like the first Adam. He did not disappoint the Father and whole humanity. He triumphed in the wilderness and put Satan where he belonged. He said:

*"...**Go, Satan! For it is written**, "You shall worship the Lord your God, and Him only you shall serve." **Then the Devil left him**. And behold, angels came and ministered to Him."*
Matthew 4:10-11 MKJV

Lust And Pride Are Satan's Arsenal's Fireball

By Satan's words against Jesus Christ in the wilderness, he spoke as someone that knew Jesus Christ and His heritage beforehand. In all his three-ways inducement on Jesus Christ, by deceit he persuaded Him to assent to pride and lust. Pride and lust are the two major fireballs in his armoury at any point in time.

While he used the phrase, *"if you are the Son of God"*, he was insinuating Jesus Christ to pridefully display His glory against the will of the Father. Note, at this point in time, Jesus Christ had humbled Himself and left His glory in heaven and became a Man to save humanity.

Again, Satan used the second fireball of his weapon. It was the fireball of 'lust.' As he tried to entice Jesus Christ from his assignment, he led Him to a high mountain. He showed Him the glory of this world, which he had corrupted after he stole it from Adam, *"...the Devil, leading Him up into a high mountain, showed Him all the kingdoms of the world in a moment of time."*

Then he spoke from the position of lawful ownership, as he wanted to deceive Jesus Christ. He claimed, *"...All this power I will give you, and the glory of them; for it has been delivered to me. And I give it to whomever I will."*

Subsequently, by the display of the fireballs of pride and lust again, he told Jesus Christ the condition for the release of *"...power...and the glory..."* of this world to anyone that desires it. The condition was, "Give Worship To Satan." He said to Jesus Christ: *"Therefore if you will worship me, all shall be yours."*

All creatures know that only God deserves their worship, and all glory should be ascribed to Him momentarily. However, Satan demanded it from Jesus Christ, the Lord God.

Now, what power and glory did Satan refer to in Luke 4:6? It was the inherited glory and dominion that Adam got from God, and Satan cunningly took them from him. He claimed, they were delivered to him to keep, use, and rule over Adam's world.

From whom did Satan receive the power and glory? Not from God, certainly, he got them from Adam. He stole it by weapon of deceit he unleashed on Eve, and then on Adam.

The word *'deliver'* was derived from the Greek word *'Paradidomi.'* It was also translated as to surrender, yield up, intrust, and transmit.

Immediately after he deceived Adam by Eve, as they both disobeyed God, the dominion was lawfully surrendered to Satan. The dictionary meaning of the word 'surrender' is to relinquish possession or control of something over to someone else.

Through Satan's deception, Adam deviated from God's command, he yielded up his goodly heritage in God—his godly offspring and their future generations, his godlike dominion, personal glory, all earthly blessings, and the glory of his world. He surrendered them all to Satan. Satan annexed them, and since, he has been keeping them as his lawful possession until Jesus Christ triumphed over him and all his hosts.

Satan's main objective was to be as 'God' on earth, have total control over Adam's heritage, and make people to worship him. While tempting Jesus Christ, he presented himself as the overall owner, controller and the god of the world that was supposedly Adam's, and then, he demanded worship.

Deception Is Satan's Greatest Weapon

While Satan wanted to get at Adam, he did not appear directly to him but through Eve. Equally, he did not deceive Eve directly, he did it by using a pseudo-vessel, the serpent.

Satan knew the place of Adam among God's creatures; He was in the best glorious position than all in God; a little lower than God. Adam was higher than Satan in glory and could not access him directly. So, by pseudo force, he gained access to Eve, and then to Adam, while he used familiar insiders and their gifts--Genesis 3:1-6.

"Now the serpent was more cunning than any beast of the field which Jehovah God had made. And he said to the woman, Is it so that God has said, You shall not eat of every tree of the garden? And the woman said to the serpent, We may eat of the fruit of the trees of the garden. But of the fruit of the tree which is in the middle of the garden, God has said, You shall not eat of it, neither shall you touch it, lest you die. And the serpent said to the woman, You shall not surely die, for God knows that in the day you eat of it, then your eyes shall be opened, and you shall be as God, knowing good and evil. And when the woman saw that the tree was good for food, and that it was pleasing to the eyes, and a tree to be

desired to make wise, she took of its fruit, and ate. She also gave to
her husband with her, and he ate."

Genesis. 3:1-6 MKJV

From the narration in above scriptures, Eve had the heritage power
of influence, and by pseudo force, Satan used her gift of influence
to make Adam disobeyed God. Serpent had power of wisdom, and
Satan also used its wisdom to deceive Eve, even though Adam and
Eve were supposed to know better.

Satan used his corrupted wisdom to beguile Eve by Serpent and
engaged her in illusive discussions that confused on her. Finally,
he seduced her by lies to rebel against her husband and God.

Eve permitted Satan's move without due consideration of the
consequences of her decisions, even though her purpose in God
and posterity might be adversely affected. She succumbed to pride
and lust by Satan's deceit. Her righteous power of influence was
corrupted as she used it, possibly with power of emotions to
prevail over Adam, while she convinced him to embrace Satan's
lies.

Indeed, Serpent was very shrewd, but flawless until Satan
possessed his being. After Serpent was created, God looked at its
nature and confirmed, 'it is good.' However, Adam and Eve were
maximally loaded with everything they needed to overcome
evilness. Especially Adam, he had everything to discern Satan's
schemes and speedily avenge all disobedience.

The Hebrew word translated *'cunning'* is *'Arum.'* It was also reded
as 'crafty, prudent, subtle and sensible'.

From the above translations, 'Serpent' was created by God to be
full of righteous wisdom and skill, appealing and sensible; hardly
can an ordinary person tracks his path of wisdom when in use.
Nonetheless, was Adam created an ordinary person? The answer is
no. Adam was created a supernatural being, supposed to be wiser
than 'Serpent' and Satan.

The played-out scenario in the garden of Eden was that Serpent allowed Satan to use his inheritance righteous gift of wisdom to confuse and deceive Eve. If God said everything He created in the days before Adam was good, invariably, they were good indeed, thus, everything about Serpent before its fall was good.

Creations Of God Were Flawless Before Satan Sinned

If all things that God made in the days before Adam were good, then, where did the Serpent get his perversion from? The answer is, he got it from Satan by acquaintanceship. Satan was the one that manufactured and introduced sins and depravity into the world of man.

Adam and other creatures that God made were not created with evilness. God created them flawless. He looked at them after He had finished His works on each of them and testified, **"It is good."** He was very pleased that they were good, including you; you are good in God's sight before you were formed in your mother's womb and brought forth into this world. Genesis 1:24-25 says:

"And God said, Let the earth bring forth the living creature after its kind, cattle, and creepers, and its beasts of the earth after its kind; and it was so. And God made the beasts of the earth after its kind, and cattle after their kind, and all creepers upon the earth after their kind. And God saw that it was good."
Genesis 1:24-25 MKJV

The word translated *'good'* was derived from the Hebrew word *'Tobe.'* It has other interpretations like 'good, pleasant, agreeable'.

After God created everything for Adam's world, His opinion was that they were pleasant and agreeable with His objective for Adam. One of the meanings of the word *'pleasant'* is 'beautiful.' The animal, Serpent was made beautiful and good for God's purpose for man and his world.

Similarly, in relation to Eve. The moment she accepted Satan's lies, she opened herself to be possessed with evil, and her desires to obey God were instantly corrupted. God's commandment did not matter to her anymore. Delusion by ignorance from Satan had struck her; by influence, she persuaded her husband to consent to Satan's lies. Without discerning Satan's wiles, Adam also fell for his ploy.

How can you know if your relationship with God is still amiable? You will know if the standards of His Word and Holy Spirit's leadership were the still the pivots of your life, to rule and guide at every point, no matter the challenges. If you compromise God's standards and despise Holy Spirit's gentle warnings, you should know that Satan is at work, gradually eroding away your dominion.

Because they refused to compromise, the church, in their early years, was full of Holy Ghost's heritage-power; signs, wonders and miracles testified that they had dominion to reign over their worlds. In order not to lose your divine goodly heritage-dominion like Adam, you must resist Satan's suggestions to compromise with the world.

Satan may try to unleash his ideas on you by your associates or loved ones. If you compromise and embrace such ideas, you will lose your divine goodly heritage-dominion, and your spiritual authority will no longer be effective. Then Satan and his hosts can torment you anyhow. God forbid you fall.

God created the earth for Adam, his offspring and successive generations to have life at maximum pleasure and delight as heritage. At the instant Adam lost his dominion to Satan, he became powerless, and God's punishment came on him. Then the earth becomes a place of free for all rebellion against God and godliness.

Since then, Satan's foothold has been in the world, dispelling auras of darkness in the place that is supposed to be full of goodness, pleasure, and luxury for all mankind. Auras of darkness are not supposed to be man's attributes, they are Satan's. Generations of man have had their fortunes replaced with emblems of auras of darkness—ignorance, sorrow, misery, destruction, death, wickedness, and reproach. Hence, an average man now exhibits evilness.

Ignorance Is Satan's Unnoticed Weapon

Whether you believe it or not, ignorance is a disease that everyone on earth must be delivered from. It is an illness that Satan uses continually to afflict and take advantage of everyone in the world, since the fall of Adam. You must know that after God's judgment fell on Satan and his rebellious angels, misery, destruction, death, *__ignorance,__* sorrow, and wickedness became the order of their endeavours.

Apart from weapon of deception that Satan uses to manipulate man's mind, another weapon he possesses most of the time is *'ignorance.'* He uses it to attack man's 'inherited God-like intelligence' and they always forget their Godlikeness and divine purposes for them.

It is ignorance that makes a person neglects the worth of God's purpose for his life, to pursue its shadow. It will make anyone not to be fully aware of the eternal blessings that are available should he righteously fulfill God's plans for his life.

Again, ignorance will make a man abuse the purpose for which certain systems have been put in place, either directly by man or indirectly through God for the common social benefits of mankind. It is the satanic weapon that causes the tragedies of existence.

The Church is not spared. It is the use of weapon of ignorance by Satan against Christians, that has made many 'Christians' to never consider the blessings of having personal communion with God, while they always give the highest priority to fellowshipping with the world. They chuck out the Holy Spirit and consult demonic mediums and take part in the works of darkness, to direct their paths in life. What a catastrophe caused by ignorance.

Nonetheless, Holy Spirit is given to the Church to deliver every Christian from any type of ignorance, whatever it may be. Holy Ghost is the Revealer of all things to the Church.

"But the Comforter, the Holy Spirit whom the Father will send in My name, He shall teach you all things and bring all things to your remembrance, whatever I have said to you."

John 14:26 MKJV

May God deliver all mankind from all demonic bondage.

A Conversation With A Supposedly 'Christian' Lady

One day, I was engaged in a conversation with a supposedly 'Christian' lady. In the cause, I asked how she normally goes about her daily chores. She told me many things without mentioning her communing or relationship with the Lord or studying the Bible.

Further, I asked her if she had heard the voice of the Lord at any time or felt the presence of the Holy Spirit. She did not know what I meant, and I explained things to her. She said she does not know the Holy Spirit neither has she heard the voice of the Lord at any time.

Her answer prompted me to further query how she gets inspired spiritually as a Christian. I was shocked by her response, while she boldly confessed that she always read the zodiac star signs for inspirations and directions on her daily routines.

I was flabbergasted; I have never heard such a thing since I became a born-again Christian. A Christian that is always in the Church does not read the Word of God or know Holy Spirit? Instead of reading the Bible and seek to know the Holy Spirit, she was committed to reading Zodiac signs books to be inspired and receive directions in life.

At the end, I took time to explain to her the importance of reading and studying the Word of God and having the Holy Spirit. Also, I informed her about the benefits of having communion with the Holy Spirit and being led by Him.

What a pity? What an ignorance? She did not know that Satan, by device had taken advantage of her. How ignorant she was, while being deluded by satanic mediums. Every Christian is advised by Paul to be careful in *2 Corinthians 2:11*:

"...Lest Satan should get an advantage of us: for we are not ignorant of his devices."

2 Corinthians 2:11 KJV

Wisdom For Scientific And Technological Innovations Is From God

No one came into this world without some inherent gifts that could be developed, and later in life be profitable to them. Hence, all scientific and technological inventions emanated from the inherent wisdom and intelligence given to man by God to benefit mankind. However, as usual, Satan manipulates the mind of an average carnal man and strikes them with ignorance to prevent them from knowing the good purposes of such innovations. Consequently, they are used to spreading sinfulness to pervert godliness.

For instance, today, media technological inventions that are supposed to be used to promote human wellbeing spiritually, materially, and socially all over the world are being used to promote perversions. By ignorance, inventors' primary good intentions have been manipulated to perpetrate evilness.

Should God be blamed for given such wisdom and intelligence to man? God would never be blamed; never again! Notwithstanding, God has stated clearly,

"...the wrath of God is revealed from Heaven against all ungodliness and unrighteousness of men, who suppress the truth in unrighteousness, because the thing which may be known of God is clearly revealed within them, for God revealed it to them...And even as they did not think fit to have God in their knowledge, God

gave them over to a reprobate mind, to do the things not right, being filled with all unrighteousness, fornication, wickedness, covetousness, maliciousness; being full of envy, murder, quarrels, deceit, evil habits, becoming whisperers, backbiters, haters of God, insolent, proud, braggarts, inventors of evil things, disobedient to parents, undiscerning, perfidious, without natural affection, unforgiving, unmerciful; who, knowing the righteous order of God, that those practicing such things are worthy of death, not only do them, but have pleasure in those practicing them."

Romans 1:18-32 MKJV

Money Is Good

Additionally, I will use money to illustrate another good invention that came from the wisdom and intelligence given to man by God. Money is good, and God approves its usefulness for the common benefits of all mankind. The invention and use of money spans over many generations; it is dated back to the days of Abraham-- *Genesis 13:2*; *Genesis 17:12*.

Money as a blessing is supposed to be accumulated gradually and used to evidence God's goodness momentarily. It is a great material weapon of defense that provides succor at the time of needs that it can only procure. Regardless, riches have wings; it must be tied down by wisdom in investment and prudently managed to fulfill godly intentions and build up treasures in heaven. If not prudently managed and shielded with the weapon of wisdom and discretion, it could fly away like a bird that escapes from a fowler's trap.

"For wisdom is a defense, and money is a defense..."

Ecclesiastes 7:12 MKJV

"Labour not to be rich: cease from thine own wisdom. Wilt thou set thine eyes upon that which is not? for riches certainly make themselves wings; they fly away as an eagle toward heaven."

Proverbs 23:4-5

If God blesses you with money abundantly, He has a purpose for it. The purpose can never be for ungodly ventures or for money to become your god. It is always given to fulfill His purposes; primarily to look after yourself and household, finance the gospel and diversely work righteousness in these Last Days.

Many have been deceived while they claim that abundant possession of money is evil. Such mindsets are weapons of ignorance employed by Satan to prevent them from knowing God's good intention for money. The use of money for exchange of goods is not Satan's idea. He did not devise the idea, neither did he invent any good thing for the benefit of mankind. Nothing good is in him; he is totally evil.

If being rich is evil, why have Satan and his hosts not allow you to have it abundantly? Why have they been preventing you from using money to do works of righteousness for God's glory? Do not be deceived by Satan's lies again. There is no evil in being rich if gathered by righteous means and used to work God's purposes as indicated earlier. Money is good. If money is good, then, it is not Satan's idea.

What is evil about money possession is your love for it by covetousness. Your desire to get money by crooked means will manifest your lustfulness and evilness. The amount of money you possess, small or large is not the sin, it is the love of money and covetousness that is the evil. God approves your possessing money abundantly for His glory.

"For the love of money is the root of all evil: which while some coveted after, they have erred from the faith, and pierced themselves through with many sorrows."
1Timothy 6:10 KJV

Expense Money Within The Boundaries Of Its Purpose

With God, there is a purpose for whatever He gives directly or indirectly by other means. Therefore, the use of money should be limited to the boundaries of its purposeful provision. If money comes into your hand, ask God what it should be used for. It could be your wage, or a gift or honorarium if you are a minister of God.

You can learn from the children of Israel's errors. As they were about to leave Egypt, God ordered them to demand articles of silver and gold from their Egyptian neighbors. They obeyed and collected the articles in abundance and left Egypt.

Miraculously, they got their deliverance from oppression in Egypt, crossed the Red Sea and got into the wilderness. They did not get the treasures from the Egyptians by their might or power. They got them by the power of favour that God unleashed on them. Nevertheless, before God could declare His intentions for the articles of silver and gold they had collected from the Egyptians, they called on Aaron to make them a god to worship from the articles.

They became idol worshippers and worshipped the god of silver and gold. They chose to worship what was supposed to serve them, to fulfill God's purpose. The purpose for which God had miraculously blessed them with the articles of gold and silver was abused, and they incurred His wrath—*Exodus 12:35* and *32:1-5*.

Hence, always use the money God has provided for you within the limits of its purpose. You will be blessed more and more.

Personal Testimony

Let me share a personal testimony with you. There was a time a gifted money came into my hands. It came at a time I needed money so much to attend to some pressing family needs.

As soon as I wanted to start expending the money, Holy Spirit instructed me not to spend it, but set it aside until He gives me further instructions. Without hesitations, I set it aside, waiting for His next instructions, possibly He will consider my urgent needs. Thus, I told my wife everything God had told me to do with the gift.

Barely three weeks after this, I was invited to a breakfast meeting by Rheinhard Bonkee's ministry, and Evangelist Rheinhard Bonkee of blessed memory was at the meeting preaching. At the end of his message, Evangelist Rheinhard Bonkee asked the congregation for financial support for his crusade meetings in Africa.

While Evangelist Rheinhard Bonkee was speaking, Holy Spirit spoke to me that the gifted money He had instructed me to set aside should be given to support Rheinhard Bonkee on his crusade meetings in Africa; everything should be given. Even though it was a bit of a challenge because my personal needs were staring at me, begging for urgent attentions. Notwithstanding, in absolute obedience to God, I called Rheinhard Bonkee's ministry afterwards and gave the money for the preaching of the gospel. I believe, by my giving and obedience, I laid another treasure in heaven.

A True Story

Please pause a moment and let me share another true story with you. I believe it will further illustrate the money issues I have been discussing thus far, and how you can operate within the boundaries of its purpose.

A Christian woman in Nigeria was praying to God to make her a millionaire to finance the gospel. Suddenly, God opened a door of opportunity, and she got a business contract. When she finished the work, she indeed became a millionaire after tax, by her profit margin.

In today's Nigeria, such opportunities do not just come so easily, except you are an influential person or have a god father/mother connection at the place of decision-making. For this woman, God was her connection, her Godfather.

After she finished the contract, she suddenly found herself with riches she never expected sooner. Instead of inquiring God to know the purpose for such unusual abundant blessings, she proceeded on a spending spree to gratify her mundane desires. She forgot that she had vowed to finance the preaching of the gospel.

Abruptly, she discovered that all remaining contracts she was expecting from other companies could no longer materialize. She wondered what had happened.

One day, she was in a Christian gathering and the Word of God came through His servant who did not know her before. The Man of God narrated how she prayed and vowed to God to bless her to finance the gospel. While God proved faithful, she turned out to be unfaithful. She misappropriated the blessings and abused the purpose of divine abundant financial provision.

The Man of God said that God wanted to bless her with an ocean of financial blessing but gave her just a drop to see if she would be faithful. At the point of making good her vow to God, she mishandled it to gratify her mundane desires.

The lady in this story forgot her vow and became ignorant of what God had in stock for her, as she overstepped the boundaries of purposeful divine abundant financial provision. At the end she paid the heaviest price.

Dear reader, could this be one of the reasons you are struggling financially today? When last did you take your tithe and offering before the Lord to prove Him, as He says in His Word?

Possibly, you have become an emotional giver because you are ignorant of God's reward, if you obey. It has been one percent here today and five percent there tomorrow, while you shortchange yourself.

Perchance, you have always nursed the sentiment that you have been giving your tithe and offerings to a man instead of God, because your Pastor is the person you see in charge of the Church in lieu of God.

The reason for such emotional giving and misplaced sentiments is your ignorance of how spiritual matters operate. Regardless, God says through Hosea:

"My people are destroyed for lack of knowledge..."

Hosea. 4:6 MKJV

Accordingly, from Hosea 4:6, it is the ignorance of not knowing what to do or how to go about things at the right time that brings an end-all destruction. God does not want you to be ignorant, He has provided you with a Bible, full of His promises. However, Satan wants you to be ignorant of how to receive and keep your divine goodly heritage blessings. Thus, he keeps you away from reading the Bible to know divine principles already available to you.

For instance, many people have rejected Jesus Christ as their Lord and Saviour. Do you think they merely rejected the call to accept Jesus Christ as their Lord and Saviour? No, they did not just reject the call. Satan was the one at work, using the weapon of ignorance. Ignorance is his unnoticed weapon.

"But if our gospel be hid, it is hid to them that are lost: In whom the god of this world hath blinded the minds of them which believe not, lest the light of the glorious gospel of Christ, who is the image of God, should shine unto them."

2Corinthians 4:3-4 KJV

May God, the Father and God of our Lord Jesus Christ continue to deliver us all from ignorance.

Where And How To Defeat Satan's Weapon Of Ignorance

Now, where, and how can you destroy Satan's vicious attacks unleashed on you by his weapon of ignorance? Jesus Christ has given us the answer in John 5:39. He said:

"You search the Scriptures, for in them you think you have eternal life. And they are the ones witnessing of Me."

John 5:39 MKJV

Place Of Scriptures

The first place you must be to destroy Satan's weapon of ignorance is inside the 'Bible', the Word of God. To be precise, the Holy

Bible is not just a book, but an armoury full of spiritual lethal weapons that the host of darkness cannot overcome. It is the book of enlightenment that gives you opportunities to discover who you are in God and what He has provided for you. It is the treasury of knowledge and revelation where you can acquire what you need to prevail over the hosts of darkness.

Search and investigate the Word of God to discover God's purpose for your earthly life. You will find the promises and blessings He has already showered on you. For sure, you will find answers to heart probing questions. Satan, through weapon of ignorance does not want you to have a full knowledge of the will of God for your life. His aim is to take advantage and dispossess you of your divine goodly heritage in God. Hence, ensure you are always at the 'Place of Scriptures.'

Place Of Personal Communion

The next place you can destroy Satan's weapon of ignorance is the 'Place of Personal Communion.' 'Place of Personal Communion' is the place you can be infused with the power of divine wisdom, knowledge and understanding. If you are not sure of God's will for you, during communion time, lay your concerns bare before Him. He will answer and lead you in the way everlasting.

While you are in the 'Place of Personal Communion', ask God to forgive your mistakes and give you another chance. Know that God is not watching out for your mistakes to afflict you. He is waiting to unleash more grace on you, so that you can be obedience and faithful. He wants to prosper and perfect what He has begun in you, by His grace.

If God chastises you, it would be with love and for your personal good, and for the benefit of others. On the other hand, Satan will always plot your downfall and take advantage of you when you are vulnerable. Although Satan wants you to focus on your mistakes and sins and believe God is a taskmaster waiting for you to err, but in fact, God is focusing on your expected end, which is your perfection by His Son, Jesus Christ.

When you are down, God will always stretch out His hand and lift you up. No matter how weak you may be, God's grace will be your strength. So, what are you waiting for? Move on to the place of communion and talk to God, and ignorance will disappear.

Place Of Knowing The Worth Your Heritage

Satan can only deceive a Christian that does not know who he is and the worth of what God has given him to possess as his heritage. As stated severally in this chapter, ignorance is Satan's unnoticed weapon, oftener used against many Christians and the rest of the world. He uses ignorance to lead Christians into a place of 'misplaced priority' to sidetrack them from God's primary purpose.

Nonetheless, would God keep His children in ignorance of their divine inheritance in Christ? Never! God would not keep you in ignorance of what your goodly heritage is in Him. He wants you to be aware of them. Your heritage in God is eternally enormous, greater than what any natural mind can comprehend, and He has delivered them to you by His Son, Jesus Christ.

Therefore, the 'Place of your Heritage' in God is Jesus Christ. Jesus Christ is your 'Destination Divine Goodly Heritage.' While you abide in Jesus Christ you can possess them, and by the help of the Holy Spirit, you can comprehend them all. So, abide in Jesus Christ, while He remains in you; ask Holy Spirit to reveal them to you.

"Abide in Me, and I in you...for without Me you can do nothing."
John 15:4-5 MKJV

"For in him dwelleth all the fulness of the Godhead bodily. And ye are complete in him, which is the head of all principality and power."
Colossians 2:9-10 KJV

"In whom also we have been chosen to an inheritance,"

Ephesians 1:10-11 MKJV

Place Of Occupying Of Your Position

It is not enough for you to know your position in God, but you must be willing to use the authority of your position in Christ and Satan will flee from you. He should never deceive you the again. People of the world do not understand that Satan is a creature and not God; he is not even a creature that should be respected. Therefore, he must never be worshipped or glorified.

Today, many Christians are yet to comprehend the fact that, they occupy a highly exalted position in God through the Lord Jesus Christ. God did not allow we, Christians to be in this glorious position and then be subjected to Satan again. This can only happen by satanic ignorance.

For you to fully assume your position and exercise the authority of your divine heritage position against satanic ignorance, there must be no compromise between you and the world. The world has been deceived to worship Satan, but you have been given divine authority by the Lord Jesus Christ to rule over Satan and his hosts. Thus, let the Lord Jesus Christ have His ultimate position in your life, while God reigns supreme over all things for you.

Place Of Spiritual Alertness

Jesus Christ used the weapon of 'Spiritual Alertness' to conquer Satan's weapon of ignorance in the wilderness. Satan thought Jesus Christ was ill prepared for his weapon of ignorance. In Matthew 4:9, He said to Jesus Christ that he would give Him the Kingdom of this world and their glory if He would worship him.

Thank God Jesus Christ was adequately prepared for the battle with Satan. He had already prayed and fasted for forty days and forty nights. He was spiritually fit and fully aware of His spiritual environment. As Satan came with his lies and manipulations, Jesus

Christ knew the personality at work. It is the 'arch impostor'; Satan the chief enemy of God.

If you noticed, Satan said he would give Jesus Christ the kingdom of this world and its glory, if He would worship him. In the first place, the kingdom was never his; the kingdom belongs to Adam as a gifted divine goodly heritage. Satan, a perpetually unrepentant thief stole it, but Jesus Christ came to retrieve it from him; Jesus Christ has already taken back all dominion from him.

Glory to God, Jesus Christ, our Lord used the weapon of 'Spiritual Alertness' against him. By the weapon of 'Spiritual Alertness', He identified Satan, and called him by his real name. Finally, He said to him, 'Satan Go!'...

"...Go, Satan! For it is written, "You shall worship the Lord your God, and Him only you shall serve.""
Matthew 4:10 MKJV

In the garden of Eden, Adam possessed similar weapon of 'Spiritual Alertness' but he refused to use it to identify Satan. Invariably, he fell for his tricks.

World's Kingdom Now Belongs To Jesus Christ

"...The kingdoms of this world have become the kingdoms of our Lord, and of His Christ. And He will reign forever and ever."
Revelation 11:15 MKJV

Surely, Satan and his hosts of darkness have been defeated by our Lord Jesus Christ, and the kingdoms of this world would soon be under Jesus Christ's direct majestic control.

Satanic hosts may still be able to manipulate the hearts of certain world leaders that allow him to executive evilness through them, however, their time is short. Power will soon finally change hands and King Jesus Christ and His Church will be directly in charge. Then, the Most High will rule in the affairs of men forever, Amen.

*"...until he knew that the Most High rules in the kingdom of men,
and that He appoints over it whomever He will."*
Daniel 5:21 MKJV

Now let us analyze the word *'kingdom'* and *'rule'* from the
scriptures quoted from *Revelation 11:15* and *Daniel 5:21*. We will
look at the Greek and Hebrews words that were translated
'kingdom.'.

The word *'kingdoms'* was translated from the Greek word
'Basileia.' It has other interpretations like 'royalty, rule, a realm,
kingdom, or reign.'

The word *'kingdom'* was interpreted from the Hebrews word,
'Malkoo.' It has other renditions like 'dominion, kingdom, kingly,
realm, or reign.'

The word *'rule'* was derived from the Hebrew word *'Shallyit.'* It
was also reded as rules, having mastery, having authority, ruling.'

Taking a note from the translations of 'kingdom' and 'rules', we can
conclude that Satan did not truly have possession of the kingdoms
of the earth while he battled Jesus Christ. Even though Adam and
generations of man lost possessions of their divine goodly heritage
to Satan, and cannot absolutely reign on earth as God intends,
however, God and Jesus Christ, His Son still have ultimate
ownership.

Satan is not always what he claims to be to people. He is liar and
the father of all lies. He may possess the hearts of many world's
leaders and use them to perpetrate his vicious agendas, regardless,
God is in firm control of everything. King Jesus Christ still rules in
the affairs of men and will soon retrieve the kingdoms of the earth
from their rulers.

Jesus Christ knew Satan before Adam was created; He would not
allow him to gain an inch of ground in His presence. Jesus Christ
has fought the battle that Adam failed to fight and conquered every
demonic principality and power and stripped them of stolen
dominion.

Christian, in your life, Satan has been defeated and shamed forever. Satan's reign has been overthrown and devastated so that you can have your divine dominion heritage and subdue all hosts of darkness.

By the authority in the Name of Jesus Christ, arrogate to yourself fruitfulness, multiplication, and replenishment of the earth with holy offspring as part of your divine goodly heritage. What the first Adam could not do due to his gross negligence, King Jesus Christ has done, and He overcame. Where Adam failed, Jesus Christ has indeed triumphed.

Satan Has Already Fallen

Before now, Jesus Christ has claimed the victory for you because Satan is already fallen and defeated. He said:

"...I saw Satan fall from Heaven like lightning."
Luke 10:18 MKJV

Jesus claims further:

"... All authority is given to Me in Heaven and in earth."
Matthew 28:18 MKJV

As declared in the above scriptures, Jesus Christ did not say He would see Satan fall by and by; He did not declare what did not happen. If He did, it would amount to deception and lies. Jesus Christ is eternal Truth, and He has already seen Satan fallen. Indeed, Satan is fallen, and he will rise no more; he will never be among glorified creatures of God.

The statement, *'**fall from heaven**'* in *Luke 10:18* foretells an execution of another judgment on Satan. The implication is that Satan does not have access to God's presence in heaven any longer. He has been banished. And because of Jesus Christ, dominion is yours; dominion is mine; corporate dominion belongs to the Church; dominion is ours now and forever, Amen.

Chapter 8

Dominion Is Yours Today

Now, let there be no controversy any further, Jesus Christ, the Son of God, and Son of Man possesses all power in heaven and on earth, and eternally dominion belongs to Him. Presently, you are a child of God, and He has designated to you a goodly heritage dominion to reign over your world, no matter its dimension and the weight of its glory. You are a possessor of divine dominion; Satan does not have it anymore. Hallelujah!

Understand that your world first encompasses your entire life (spirit, soul, and body), your relationship with God, your marriage, and children. It also includes your finances, material investments, social life, immediate community, village, town, city, nation, and other righteous daily chores. All the above are the components of your world's territory that Satan may want to steal, kill and destroy.

Satan is an interloper that always wants to intrude on another person's privacy or property without permission or notice. Never allows him to have an inch foothold inside your territory. If allowed, an inch could become a mile, while he claims complete ownership. You now possess dominion to fence off Satan and his hosts. So, rise to the occasion.

From here, let us begin to consider the attributes of your goodly divine heritage dominion.

Your Dominion Is A Heritage Restored In Jesus Christ

As you have seen before now, Jesus Christ has defeated Satan and his demons once and for all. He possesses dominion and all authority in heaven and in earth, and Satan has not refuted the claim, and he can never contradict the fact.

God did not send any man, or woman, or angel to conquer Satan and his fallen angels except Jesus Christ. No so-called founder of any religion across the world today could face Satan and wrest man's dominion out of his hand, only Jesus Christ did. Founders of world's religions could not, because none of them was anointed of God; none of them was the 'Seed' of the woman prophesied in *Genesis 3:15*.

Jesus Christ is the One that has successfully subdued Satan and his demonic forces. When He got the dominion back from Satan, as a heritage, He gave His Church the heaven backed authority that would manifest their dominion.

If you have exclusively received and believed in Jesus Christ, you have been automatically reconciled to God, and you have been restored to your original position in Him. You are now a son of God. Your restoration did not happen for you to become a weakling spiritual person; spiritually, you are God's living powerhouse with privilege to exhibit your heritage dominion over your world. John affirms:

"But as many as received Him, He gave to them authority to become the children of God, to those who believe on His name, who were born, not of bloods, nor of the will of the flesh, nor of the will of man, but were born of God."

John 1;12-13 MKJV

Jesus Christ has triumphed and given you and me the assurance that the dominion that Satan stole from the first Adam has been retrieved from him. It now belongs to Him; therefore, he said:

"Behold, I give to you authority to tread on serpents and scorpions, and over all the authority of the enemy. And nothing shall by any means hurt you."

Luke 10:19 MKJV

Satan Cannot Steal Your Dominion Again

Child of God, the heritage spiritual authority that has been given to you by Christ Jesus, in His Name reveals that your dominion cannot be stolen again by Satan and his demons. Not again! And never again!

Why is it impossible for the host of darkness to steal your dominion? It is because the exclusive sovereign authority in heaven and earth has now been given to Jesus Christ and it has the seal of His Name on it. Anything that has the seal of the Name of Jesus Christ cannot be claimed by Satan and his hosts.

Jesus Christ affirms that:

"All authority is given to Me in Heaven and in earth.'

Matthew 28:18 MKJV

Again, He attests that:

"...in My name..."

Mark 16:17 MKJV

Furthermore, whatever that has the seal of the Name of Jesus Christ cannot be stolen or destroyed by Satan and his demons. If they dare take it, they cannot keep it. It will be calamitous to them, and they will be consumed by it momentarily. Be assured, the authority that reveals your heritage dominion has been retrieved from Satan once and for all. He cannot have it again.

If you feel you have lost it because of sin, please get this message very clear: you did not lose it to Satan and his hosts. Demonic spirits might have influenced you to sin to lose it, but they can never possess it. Repent of your sins and live right, and you will have it again to rule over your world.

Possibly, you might have dropped it because of apathy or lack of faith, however, Satan and his demons have not taken it up. Go back to where you left it due to doubt or indifference; acknowledge your mistakes and pick it up through faith and use it for God's glory. What belongs to Jesus Christ cannot be stolen by Satan and his demons.

"For the free gifts and calling of God are without repentance."
Romans 11:29 MKJV

For instance, after Philistines stole the ark of covenant of God and kept in the house of their god Dagon (devil). Afterwards, they confessed that the hand of the God of Israel was sore upon them. They could not keep it, and they sent it back to the rightful heritage owners, with treasures.

"And when the men of Ashdod saw that it was so, they said, The ark of the God of Israel shall not abide with us: for his hand is sore upon us, and upon Dagon our god."
1 Samuel 5:7 KJV

Again, when Abimelech stole Sarah, Abraham's wife; what happened to him? The hand of God went hard against him and his entire household. What they took from Abraham became a snare to them. They returned her immediately to him with gifts.

"...And Abimelech the king of Gerar sent and took Sarah... Now therefore, restore his wife to the man. For he is a prophet, and he shall pray for you, and you shall live. And if you do not restore her, know that you shall surely die, you, and all that are yours..."
Genesis 20:1-8 MKJV

Do not let anyone deceive you that, as a child of God, Satan can take back from you the authority that manifests your dominion.

Note, it is exclusively Jesus Christ's, dominance authority. It is not possible for Satan or any of his hosts to take it back from you. Satan cannot have it. It is your exclusive divine goodly heritage, by Jesus Christ.

The truth of the matter is that Jesus Christ, the Son of Man, and the Last Adam has delegated you to use the authority in His Name to reveal your goodly heritage dominion and reign over the world He has given you on earth. So, the host of darkness has not taken your authority from you. It is still where you dropped it.

Because it has the seal of the Name of Jesus Christ boldly written on it, it is full of the fire of the Holy Ghost. Thus, Satan cannot take it! Satan cannot keep it! Satan cannot handle it! Satan cannot use it! It will be too dangerous for him to retain.

Moreover, if you are a child of God in Christ Jesus, the authority that manifest your dominion is absolutely yours, by inheritance in Jesus Christ. Understand that the dominion that Satan claimed to be his before Jesus Christ's advent was given to him directly by the first Adam in the garden of Eden. The dominion had the seal of first Adam on it, and it was given to mankind by God; it was not an angelic dominion. For this reason, Satan cannot rule anywhere in the world without the mask of man; he must use the dominion through mankind.

But the delegated authority you possess now does not have the seal of first Adam or your name on it. As stated above, it has the seal of the Name of Jesus Christ. Jesus Christ did not, and He has not handed it over to Satan. Therefore, it is still yours.

If you put the seal of your name instead of the Name Jesus Christ on it, you will be in trouble. It is because you were not the one that confronted, defeated, and took the dominion out of the hands of Satan two thousand years ago. It was Jesus Christ, the Son of the Living God that did it triumphantly.

You have not shed off your blood for the sins of the world, Jesus Christ did. You have not died on the cross, buried bodily and resurrected from the dead with a glorified body on the third day,

Jesus Christ did. Neither have you gone to the lowest part of the earth to lead captivity captive. Jesus Christ did it. You have not yet ascended into heaven and sit at the right of glory forty days after resurrection like Jesus Christ. Your hair and head are not as white as snow to reveal that you are the Ancient of Days, and your eyes are not like flame of fire.

Jesus Christ is the authentic Owner of all authority in heaven and earth. He is the Possessor of the real eternal dominion, and He has not handed it over to Satan. It will be so difficult for Satan to have it.

If Satan claims he has any authority to rule over your world, ask him what authority he possesses. What he possesses is counterfeit and his claims must not stand. It will be his great mistake to stand before you because the authority you possess has power to undo his works, if rightly used.

Supposing you think of handing it over to any host of darkness, they cannot receive it. It will be too perilous for them to take it from you. It will be precarious for them to use; they will turn down your offer instantly, because it will consume them. They clearly know this fact. John the Beloved amplifies this truth in *1John 3:8*:

"For this purpose the Son of God was revealed, that He might undo the works of the Devil."
1 John 3:8 MKJV

And Jesus Christ says:

"...concerning judgment, because the ruler of this world is judged."
John 16:11 MKJV

After Satan and his hosts were judged and Jesus Christ undid their works, no authority to rule over your world was left in their hands. They were disarmed absolutely and stripped naked of all authority.

Dominion Manifests Your Position In Jesus Christ

"And miraculous signs will follow to those believing these things: in My name they will cast out demons; they will speak new tongues; they will take up serpents; and if they drink any deadly thing, it will not hurt them. They will lay hands on the sick, and they will be well."

Mark 16:17-18 MKJV

Now, you know that Satan and his hosts cannot have your authority, not to talk of using it, because it does not belong to them. So, the challenges you may face at any time in your daily endeavors are not matters you cannot overcome. Possibly, God allows and uses the situations to lead you to point where you can use your delegated authority, assert your dominion and rule over them.

Despite what Jesus Christ did, if you still see those challenges as battles you would start all over again with Satan, you will not overcome them. Scriptures never tell us to face the satanic hosts all over again. We are instructed to only exert the authority in the Name of Jesus Christ to manifest dominion to reign over our worlds.

Satanic hosts have been defeated over two thousand years ago. Jesus Christ fought Satan and his demonic angels once and for all and discomfited them overwhelmingly and won victories for you. He did not spare any of them for another day's battles. He dealt with them utterly, while He declared, *"It Is Finished."*

Hence, you must tackle Satan and his hosts from the point of Jesus Christ's declarations on their defeat—*"It Is Finished"* and *"these signs shall follow them that believe; In my name shall they cast out devils..."* Brandish and assert the victories that Jesus has already won for you. Use your delegated authority to manifest the heritage dominion you possess in Jesus' Name.

Many Christians always miss the opportunity when they are confronted with devil's trials and temptations. They face them as if Jesus Christ has done nothing about those attacks at all. Carefully note, Jesus Christ has defeated all satanic hosts at all fronts, including the demonic spirits that may be behind your travails.

No one could take the stolen dominion back from Satan except Jesus Christ, the Son of the Living God. Look back two thousand years ago and see what Jesus Christ did to Satan and his hosts on the cross and at His resurrection. They were all beaten hands down and defeated like stubbles before fire. No authority to rule over any mankind belongs to them any longer, they have been stripped of all; never to regain them.

"Having stripped rulers and authorities, He made a show of them publicly, triumphing over them in it."
Colossians 2:15 MKJV

To manifest yourself in your new position as a son of God in Jesus Christ, it must be through your authority to reveal your dominion. It is by dominion that you can manifest yourself in Jesus Christ. It is the reason Jesus Christ gave you the authority in His Name. Therefore, arise from the abased position the circumstances of life have placed you. Stand and confront the enemy with your authority in the Name of Jesus Christ; then your supremacy will manifest.

All power and dominion belong to Jesus Christ, and equally, they are yours in Him; they belong to you as a heritage. Your dominion has the seal of the Name of Jesus Christ on it. It is the only Name that has authority with the heavenly seal, and the satanic hosts recognize this fact.

Many times, I have heard some Christians while they said that a Christian could lose a battle in certain areas of life to Satan. I found it so difficult to believe. Which battles are they referring to? The battles that Jesus Christ has already fought and won, and Satan and all his demons know that they have been already defeated overwhelmingly?

Please note, Jesus Christ has not relinquished his victory to Satan and his hosts to take over, and He would never abandon His victory to Satan. Since you are still in Him as a member of His Body by faith, your victory is continuously guaranteed.

A Christian may engage in many battles in this life, and be overwhelmed, and possibly becomes weak in faith, but that does not mean that he has been defeated. He may be attacked with all sorts of Satan's weapons and becomes sick or lack certain things at a point in time. He may be discouraged and faints on the journey of life. All these things do not mean that he has lost the battle to Satan. For,

"Nay, in all these things we are more than conquerors through him that loved us."

Romans 8:37 KJV

The Church, at the early stage fought so many battles at many fronts, but they never lost any of them to Satan. The only time a Christian can lose his victory is when he stops believing in Jesus Christ and His finished work at Calvary. If your faith in everything Jesus Christ is and what He has accomplished still stands, then you constantly possess the weapon that overcomes Satan and the world; your 'FAITH' is the undefeatable weapon!

"For whatsoever is born of God overcometh the world: and this is the victory that overcometh the world, even our faith. Who is he that overcometh the world, but he that believeth that Jesus is the Son of God?"

1 John 5:4-5 KJV

Child of God, no true Christians that have before gone through what you are presently passing through lost to Satan, you too cannot be defeated by him; never again! Hold on to your faith, arise in the strength of the Holy Ghost, and by your dominion, manifest yourself in Christ Jesus.

Your Dominion Is a Spiritual Legal Entity

Dear Christian, understand that Jesus Christ has given you an authority backed by heaven's spiritual law, so that you can reveal your divine goodly heritage dominion, to genuinely reign in life. It is your heritage from the Godhead—God the Father, God the Son and God the Holy Spirit.

What spiritual law makes your authority legitimate? It is 'the Law of Spirit of Life in Christ Jesus', instituted by God, released in the Name Of Jesus Christ and powered through the Holy Spirit towards His Church.

"For the law of the Spirit of life in Christ Jesus hath made me free from the law of sin and death."

Romans 8:2 KJV

Under the Law of the Spirit of Life in Christ Jesus, every Christian is entitled to claim the benefits of the law. The authority of your reign by Jesus Christ is founded upon the law. Therefore, the heritage dominion that will be revealed by your authority is legal and free to use against the host of darkness to reign in life.

Give attention to this fact again, your dominion to rule over every facet of your life is no longer in the hands of Satan and his hosts, it is your 'now' possession, although the host of darkness may sometimes raise their already crushed heads.

Any satanic venture into any area of your life is not based on the Law of the Spirit of Life in Christ Jesus. So, they are illegal moves that must be stopped and avenged appropriately until your reign over every facet of your life is established on the victories of Jesus Christ.

Only you, as part of the Church, under the authority of Jesus Christ have the legal authority over your world. You are no longer under Satan's world; thus, Satan does not have authority over you.

Consider what the following scriptures say about you as part of the Church:

"But you have come to Mount Zion and to the city of the living God, the heavenly Jerusalem, and to an innumerable company of angels, to the general assembly and church of the first-born who are written in Heaven, and to God the judge of all, and to the

spirits of just men made perfect, and to Jesus the Mediator of the new covenant, and to blood of sprinkling that speaks better things than that of Abel."

Hebrews 12:22-23 MKJV

From the above scriptures, you and I are integral parts of the council of heaven, the decision-making body of the Godhead, holding forth the rule of God on earth. God's rule must be upheld over your life without fear and intimidation of any enemy. Never retreat, never surrender.

Also, Paul said:

"Now therefore you are no longer strangers and foreigners, but fellow citizens with the saints, and of the household of God."

Ephesians 2:19 MKJV

So, when you use your authority to reveal your dominion for the purpose it is given and according to the blueprints of the Law of the Spirit of Life in Christ Jesus, there is no way victories will not manifest. You will have favourable results. You will evidence that you have overcome all demons of hell, indeed.

Your Dominion Is Invisible and Mighty

Your dominion in Jesus Christ is unlike the powers of the kingdoms of this world. Perhaps you have been searching for it, thinking you will tangibly lay hold of it. Possibly, you think it emanates from the worldly realm, and can be enforced materially. If you are of such mindsets, then you are mistaken. The heritage dominion you have in Jesus Christ is spiritual, therefore, invisible; however, its works are manifest when it is in use. Jesus Christ said:

"...My kingdom is not of this world: if my kingdom were of this world, then would my servants fight, that I should not be delivered to the Jews: but now is my kingdom not from hence."

John 18:36 KJV

In this world, 'the powers that be' take their physical ammo weapons here and there and destroy lives, especially the guiltless in cold blood. Regardless, with all their weapons, they have never tackled the real culprits and enemies.

The question is, are they aware that the real culprits and enemies are Satan and his hosts? Verily, they do not know; they have been struck with ignorance by Satan to destroy one another, while he laughs and drags them to hell.

By now, you and I know the arch enemies and surely, they are the satanic hosts. They are spiritual beings, engaging in spiritual battles of supremacy over man's divine goodly heritage. So, you do not expect the authority that reveals your dominion to be visible; yet its works are apparent in the realm of man if you rightly engage it.

Apostle Paul, an experienced Christian spiritual warfarer shares his experience with us, as inspired by Holy Spirit. He says in *2Corinthians 10:4-6.*

"For the weapons of our warfare are not fleshly, but mighty through God to the pulling down of strongholds, pulling down imaginations and every high thing that exalts itself against the knowledge of God, and bringing into captivity every thought into the obedience of Christ; and having readiness to avenge all disobedience, when your obedience is fulfilled."
2Corinthians 10:4-6 MKJV

God is a Spirit, likewise, your weapons through Him in Jesus Christ are spiritual. You may be wondering how you could find your spiritual weapons. You do not have to walk through the earth or materially travel to heaven to get them. They are already supplied, and they are within you. They are the words of God and the anointing supplied by the Holy Ghost, by the authority in the Name of Jesus Christ.

The words are the Holy Spirit inspired Words that you speak and the gifts of the Holy Spirit that evidence His anointing in your life. The words of God are the substance of the constitution of God's kingdom, given to His Church. By it, you must assert your authority in line with its provisions, to reveal your dominion over your world.

While the Word you speak by the authority in the Name of Jesus Christ is backed up by the anointing of the Holy Spirit, the impact is always unprecedented, as you exert both the Word and anointing, to reveal your dominion over your world.

"But what does it say? "The Word is near you, even in your mouth and in your heart"; that is, the Word of Faith which we proclaim."
Romans 10:8 MKJV

There is power in the tongue and the words you speak carry weight. They are spirits while they proceed from your mouth; as a result, they are invisible. Even though they are within you, they are voices that speak within you before they are uttered audibly, as you release them at will. When they are spoken, they have either positive or negative impacts on anything and people. Frequently, actions are weighed by them.

Likewise, the Word of God is the two-edged sword. It is powerful with positive and negative impacts over any situation, depending on how it is used as it proceeds from your tongue. The Word of God must abide within your heart and come forth from your mouth as a declaration of your authority, to reveal your dominion over your world.

"For the word of God is quick, and powerful, and sharper than any two edged sword, piercing even to the dividing asunder of soul and spirit, and of the joints and marrow, and is a discerner of the thoughts and intents of the heart."
Hebrews 4:12 MKJV

Additionally, your dominion is mighty. The word translated *'mighty'* in *2Corinthian 10:4* is a Greek word *'Dunatos.'* It has other translations like, something powerful, capable, able, mighty, possible, and strong.

The deduction from these renditions is that, to manifest your authority, you must realize that your weapons by God is powerful, mighty, and capable of overcoming any weapon that Satan and his hosts may possess. They also function in possibilities to prevail over any impossible situations that may be orchestrated against you by the host of darkness.

By your mighty weapon through God, the authority that reveals your dominion is an indomitable force against Satan and his demons. You are a man/woman operating in the realm of *'nothing is impossible'* because you are with God, and God is with you.

Therefore, be confident of this thing, you are a son of God in Christ Jesus, you cannot be conquered by any satanic host. You are the current possessor of dominion to reign in life in this world. Arise in your spiritual might and stamp down every foe that dares challenge God's purpose for your life. Tread them down until they are totally crushed under your feet.

Dominion Puts You in Your Rightful Position In God

Christian, nothing else can confirm your rightful position on earth as a child of God and make you reign over your world now except the authority that reveals your heritage dominion.

On the day, you confessed and received Jesus Christ as your Lord and Saviour, the whole heaven rejoiced, angels were glad, and God was pleased that you took such an important step. You are not redeemed to remain the same way you were. You are saved to occupy a rightful position in God through Jesus Christ.

Your new position is greater than any position any angel can occupy in the sight of God. The position is a highly exalted one, and the only way you can stand tall in your new office, here on earth is how you exert your authority in Jesus Christ, to reveal your dominion.

Heaven knows that you are not a usurper, but you have a legitimate right to be in your new position. You may be surprised to know this, even Satan too knows that you have every right to fill the position, but the world does not know, because they have been blind folded.

Repeatedly, you have permitted Satan to attack you with ignorance, to prevent you from comprehending that you are specially loved and favoured by God. Satan knows that you are an extension of God's rule on earth, and you exist to fulfill God's purpose as your primary assignment where you are.

Furthermore, the satanic hosts know that God has made available to you all authority you need in heaven and earth to fulfill these divine noble tasks. They know if they can keep you occupied with the pressures of this world, you would not be able to focus on your divine chores. They know, they know, and they know that you have been elevated to sit in Jesus Christ in heavenly places above all other creations. Paul emphasized on it:

"...and has raised us up together and made us sit together in the heavenlies in Christ Jesus..."

Ephesians 2:6 MKJV

What positions do you occupy by Jesus Christ? You are a king and lord, and you are to reign in life now, and with Christ for all eternity. These are the offices God has ordained for you to fill in Jesus Christ.

Remember in chapter one, we saw Satan then, as an arch angel had kingly and priestly rule on earth. His pride brought him down from the highly esteem position among the angels of God; he will rise no more.

Now, you are a king and lord, and you have been given authority to reveal your heritage dominion and display on earth the glory of Jesus Christ that comes with your reign. Until you reveal your dominion, the world will not know who you are.

Another office you occupy is a priestly office. If you do not exert your authority to display your kingly dominion, Satan and his demons may prevent you from standing in your priestly office.

You may ask how Satan could prevent you? He can prevent you in the same way he prevented Adam in the Garden of Eden. Adam was created a king, lord and priest created by God to perform similar function that Satan executed when he was in right standing with God.

Adam was to guard Eden with his glory and put forth his dominion to rule the earth from Eden. As he continued his reign, he would offer sacrifices of praise to God through a consecrated holy fellowship.

There was nothing like shedding of blood for sins when Adam was in right standing with God. It was after Adam sinned that God initiated the sacred doctrine of animal sacrifices, to manifest His eternal mercy and grace.

Adam really performed his priestly role whenever the presence of God came down during fellowship. As soon as he shifted his eyes from his main duties to embrace Satan's lies, then, he was unable to subdue Satan. Hence, he lost the opportunity to further offer the sacrifices of praise acceptable to God.

Likewise, if you refuse to exert your authority to manifest your heritage dominion, Satan will sidetrack you and prevent you from occupying your legitimate position of authority in God. By distracting you, he will preoccupy you with mundane matters that are inconsequential to God's purposes for you. Consequently, you might not be able to offer sacrifices to God as you ought.

Remember, God no longer require any blood sacrifice for sin from you, because Jesus Christ has offered His body of flesh as a perfect sacrifice, while He shed off His blood on the cross. God only anticipates your kingly, lordly and priestly sacrificial laudatory services, as you exert your authority to manifest your heritage dominion.

While you reign over your goodly heritage as God intends, you can offer sacrifices of praise to glorify His holy Name, to let people know Him. You have been called, chosen, and ordained to be a priest unto the LORD your God. Hence, arise and occupy your rightful position.

"But ye are a chosen generation, a royal priesthood, a holy nation, a peculiar people; that ye should show forth the praises of him who hath called you out of darkness into his marvelous light"
1 Peter 2:9 KJV

Your Dominion Possesses The Ultimate Power

There is nothing else that gives a Christian believer greater confidence to reign over his world, to reveal his heritage dominion than the authority in the Name of Jesus Christ. Authority in the Name of Jesus Christ possesses the ultimate power you can ever receive from God.

God may give you power to get wealth. He may give you some measures of grace above others. He may even give you a glorious vision to see things that are in heaven. Take note, Satan too has previously boasted that all the kingdoms of this world and their wealth and glory belonged to him.

By now you know Satan is a liar; the father of all lies. As Lucifer, he was in heaven before you were created and had seen God's glory manifested at different levels. He had ruled over the earth before mankind came into being, and he knew what possession of sovereign power all is about. The only thing he does not possess is the ultimate authority in the Name of Jesus Christ to have dominion over your heritage.

Jesus Christ is the only One that possesses the ultimate power among men and other creations that ever lived on earth or existed in heaven above. It pleases the Father to give His only Begotten Son, Jesus Christ the ultimate power over all things. Now, Jesus Christ has delegated His authority to whosoever receives and believes in Him.

Indeed, everyone that has received Jesus Christ as Lord and Savior has the most superior powerful authority heaven could afford humanity to reign in life, now and eternally. This power is what reveals and makes your dominion efficacious. There is no other power in heaven and on earth that is as effective as the authority that Jesus Christ has given you, to reveal your dominion.

While you exert your authority in the Name of Jesus Christ to demonstrate your heritage dominion, it makes the rulers of darkness deranged and quash, and changes impossibilities to possibilities. It is described in *Ephesians 1:19* as:

"...the surpassing greatness of His power toward us, the ones believing according to the working of His mighty strength."
Ephesians 1:19 MKJV

James, the Apostle also says the following about Elijah:

"Elijah was a man of like passion as we are. And he prayed earnestly that it might not rain, and it did not rain on the earth for the time of three years and six months. And he prayed again, and the heaven gave rain, and the earth caused its fruit to sprout."
James 5:17-18 MKJV

Elijah, in the above scripture, demonstrated an ultimate power to show forth the authority that revealed his dominion over the satanic 'powers' of his days. While he took charge of his God-given territory by dominion, the rulers of his days trembled at his utterances. Eventually, he reigned over his world, until he decided to quit.

Carefully consider this, Elijah, even though was a man of like passion as we are, he did not have the same privilege you have today as a Christian. The power of the Spirit could only descend on him whenever he had an assignment, but you have the power of God, the Holy Ghost resident in you all the time.

After he had finished his assignment by slaughtering the prophets of Baal and called down fire and prayed that rain should fall, he was threatened by Jezebel. What did he do? He ran away and asked God to take his life.

Why did Elijah run away? He ran away because of fear; he was afraid of what Jezebel could do to him. As he was frightened and did not know what next to do, he asked God to take his life. But you have the Holy Spirit, and His power is indwelling you 24/7; you should know what to do next. Fear must not be your option. Hallelujah!

Manifest Your Dominion Now!

Among many, one thing that can deprive you of staying in your heritage position in God is your immaturity in spiritual matters. Paul, the Apostle understood the danger of remaining a spiritual babe as he advises us by the Holy Spirit:

"But I say, Over so long a time the heir is an infant, he does not differ from a slave, though being lord of all; but he is under guardians and housemasters until the term appointed before by the father. Even so we, when we were infants, were in bondage under the elements of the world."

Galatians 4:1-3 MKJV

To understand better what Paul means in Galatians 4:1-3, let us look at the Greek word from which the word *'infant'* was derived. It was reded from the Greek word *'Nepios.'* It has other interpretations like a 'simple'-minded person, an immature Christian, untaught and unskilled.

Let us go further to look at the Greek word from which the word *'simple'* was translated in the Old Testament. It was derived from the Hebrew word *'Pethiy.'* Its other renditions are silly, seducible, foolish, open-minded, and simple.

The admonition from Apostle Paul was that, if you are a silly or seducible, or liberal Christian, you are still an infant spiritually and will not be able to exert your authority to display your heritage dominion as God intends. Because Eve was liberal, Satan was able to deceive her by serpent, and Adam, by Eve.

If you are still an immature Christian, it shows you are under the control of the rudiments of this world. To be spiritually matured, you must grow to become an adult-son of God and be heavenly minded. A spiritual infant does not always exert his authority over satanic hosts at the battle's front line. Even though he is a joint heir with Jesus Christ, he will be too timid to reveal his dominion.

I stated earlier that God did not create Adam a babe but a mature man to enable him handle spiritual things decisively and rule over his world. So, you too need to outgrow your Christian childishness and become a matured Christian-man and exert your authority, to reveal your dominion.

The dictionary meaning of 'man' is an adult person. Apostle Paul says further:

"When I was an infant, I spoke as an infant; I thought as an infant, I reasoned as an infant. But when I became a man, I did away with the things of an infant."
1 Corinthians 13:11 MKJV

"But when the fullness of the time came, God sent forth His Son, coming into being out of a woman, having come under Law, that He might redeem those under Law, so that we might receive the adoption of sons. And because you are sons, God has sent forth the Spirit of His Son into your hearts, crying, Abba, Father."
Galatians 4:4-6 MKJV

The word translated *'sons'* in Galatians 4:4-6 is from a Greek word *'Uihos.'* The Hebrew word for *'son'* is *'Bane.'* Its translations as 'a builder of the family' gives us a better understanding.

It will be unwise and an abomination to give responsibility of building a family to an infant; it is an adult man—a mature person's duty. Due to this, God did not create Adam an immature man, but an intelligence adult man with responsibilities to rare a holy family and replenish the earth.

Similarly, Christian, God has called and chosen you to be a builder of His family. Now is the time to get rid of your spiritual 'Nepios' (childhood) nature and put on your spiritual 'bane' (adult son) kingly garment. You are God's son, exert your authority, to manifest your heritage dominion over your heritage. Let the world see that, indeed, you are now in charge, and not Satan.

You must have an unwavering assurance that everything Bible says to you about the delegated authority that Jesus Christ has given you are true. Believe that you have authority, and the dominion the Last Adam, our Lord Jesus Christ, the Son of the Living God has retrieved from Satan is now yours.

Hence, by your authority, reveal your dominion and take charge of your relationship with God, marriage, family, finances, health, social life, etc. All these are your divine goodly heritage in God; they are the components of your world on earth. Do not be spiritually seducible and unskilled anymore. Do not let Satan and his hosts annex and have your divine goodly heritage again.

Beloved, it can never be too late, you can start right now. Satan has been defeated and lost his reign, and you have gained dominion now and forever. Do not be like the first Adam; exert your authority over the host of darkness straightaway and start reigning over your world.

Chapter 9

Satan Loses All Forever

The fact remains that Satan does not possess the dominion he stole from first Adam anymore. He lost it forever; he does not have any right to reign over the affairs of mankind again. Jesus Christ, the Second and Last Adam has retrieved the dominion from him. Today you have the delegated authority in the Name of Jesus Christ to reveal your dominion and reign over your world.

Now, apart from forfeiting the dominion he stole from the first Adam to Jesus Christ, what else did Satan lose when God's judgment came on him? Let us examine some of them below.

Satan Lost His Originality Forever

While God's judgment lasts on Satan, henceforward, he lost the most important expression of himself—his originality forever. Things have never been the same for him and his fallen angels. After they lost their originality, they also lost almost every other thing that came with it.

If you noticed Satan or any of his demons manifesting themselves anywhere, you must understand that they are no longer in their original state. They are totally corrupted and have lost their true luminousness and righteous nature. Satan never wanted anyone to know this fact, but God has revealed it to us in His Word. Paul, the Apostle informs us:

"Did not even Satan marvelously transform himself into an angel of light?"

2 Corinthians 11:14 MKJV

In order to understand better what Paul meant by the word *'transform'*, let us check the Greek word from which it was translated. It was derived from the Greek word *'Metaschematizo.'* It has other translation like to transfigure, disguise, to transfer, transform oneself.

From the other translations of the Greek word *'Metaschematizo'*, let us look at the dictionary meaning of the word *'disguise.'* It is 'camouflage'—an outward semblance that misrepresents the true nature of something.

So, if the word says Satan has disguised himself to be an angel of light, it shows he is no longer in his original state. He has become something else. The transformation referred to in the above scripture demonstrates that Satan, as at now has gone double. He is not an angel of light that he claims to be, everything about him changed when he became an enemy of God.

Pretense is now part of his nature. He always wants to be what God has not created him to be—to lure people into eternal damnation. Moreover, you now know, and I too know that, before his fall he was perfect among the creatures of God.

We know his archetype place was in Eden; he was the leading figure over other angels on earth. He was also on the holy mountain of God as a priest, offering sacrifices of praise to God. Now, he has lost both his leadership and priestly positions forever.

While Satan lost his original nature, the purpose of his creation and place in God, he forfeited other things as well. Let consider their lineations below.

Satan Lost His Rank Amongst God's Angels

According to the Old Testament of the Bible, angels also are often called the 'sons of God'. Some examples are listed in the scriptures below.

"...when the morning stars sang together and all the sons of God shouted for joy?"

Job 38:7 MKJV

"And a day came when the sons of God came to present themselves before Jehovah. And Satan also came among them."

Job 1:6 MKJV

"...that the sons of God..."

Genesis 6:1-2 MKJV

"...when the sons of God..."

Genesis 6:4 MKJV

The above scriptures tell us of a relationship that once existed between Satan and God and the angelic kinds. The word *'sons'*, as stated earlier in the last chapter was derived from the Hebrew word *'Bane.'* The meaning is 'a builder of a family.' From the English translation of *'Bane',* Satan and his fallen angels were part of God's family before their fall.

Today, holy angels are ministers to the saints of God in building God's kingdom and family. They are invisible helpers to God's children on earth, helping us fulfill His divine purpose.

"And of the angels He says, "Who makes His angels spirits and His ministers a flame of fire."

Hebrews 1:7 MKJV

"But to which of the angels, did He say at any time, 'Sit on My right hand until I make Your enemies Your footstool?' Are they not all ministering spirits, sent forth to minister for those who shall be heirs of salvation?"

Hebrews 1:13-14 MKJV

Straightaway, after Satan and his hosts left God's original purpose for their creations and sinned, equally, they fell from their ranks and files and forfeited their positions in the commonwealth of God's angelic 'sons.' Furthermore, the benefits that harmonized their offices were removed from them, to be earned no more, forever.

Satan Lost His Access To God

Before the advent of the Lord Jesus Christ, Satan could access heaven and stand in God's presence. Even though he has ceased to be a kingdom builder for God, he was still allowed access to heaven whenever other angels presented themselves to God.

Satan's principal job in heaven was to accuse the saints before God and cause confusion. He vehemently and repeatedly accused Job of feigned devotion until God removed His protection edge from Job's life, to test his sincerity.

"And a day came when the sons of God came to present themselves before Jehovah. And Satan also came among them. And Jehovah said to Satan, from where do you come? Then Satan answered Jehovah and said, from going to and fro in the earth, and from walking up and down in it. And Jehovah said to Satan, Have you set your heart against My servant Job, because there is none like him in the earth, a perfect and upright man, one who fears God and turns away from evil? And Satan answered Jehovah and said, does Job fear God for nothing?"

Job 1:6-9 MKJV

Satan had another access to God as noted in the book of *Zechariah 3:1-2*. While he stood before God, he fiercely accused Joshua, the high priest of sins, until the Lord intervened and rebuked him.

"And He showed me Joshua the high priest standing before the Angel of Jehovah, and Satan standing at his right hand to accuse him. And Jehovah said to Satan, May Jehovah rebuke you, Satan! May even Jehovah who has chosen Jerusalem rebuke you! Is this not a brand plucked out of the fire?"

Zechariah 3:1-2 MKJV

Moreover, Satan contended for the body of Moses, until Michael, the archangel rebuked him by the authority of the Lord.

"But Michael, the archangel, when contending with the Devil, he argued about the body of Moses, he dared not bring a judgment of blasphemy, but said, Let the Lord rebuke you!"

Jude 1:9 MKJV

Satan was able to accuse the saints before God prior to the death of Jesus Christ, at the time Jesus Christ paid the price to redeem mankind. Since Jesus Christ resurrected, Satan lost his access to heaven altogether. Nonetheless, for once he will attempt to enter heaven and accuse the saints and cause confusion, and war will break out in heaven. Finally, he will be chucked out and no longer gain access to heaven nor stand before God as before.

The Lord Jesus Christ foretold Satan's utter banishment from heaven. He will never be accommodated anymore.

"And He said to them, I saw Satan fall from Heaven like lightning."

Luke 10:18 MKJV

John the Beloved also saw what will happen to Satan and his host; he testifies.

"And there was war in Heaven. Michael and his angels warring against the dragon. And the dragon and his angels warred, but did not prevail. Nor was place found for them in Heaven any more. And the great dragon was cast out, the old serpent called Devil, and Satan, who deceives the whole world. He was cast out into the earth, and his angels were cast out with him. And I heard a great

voice saying in Heaven, Now has come the salvation and power and the kingdom of our God, and the authority of His Christ. For the accuser of our brothers is cast down, who accused them before our God day and night. And they overcame him because of the blood of the Lamb, and because of the word of their testimony. And they did not love their soul until death."

Revelation 12:7-11 MKJV

To correlate what Jesus Christ's declaration and John's testimonies, Peter says in *1Peter 5:8* that Satan can no longer access heaven. Now, he goes about the earth wanting to devour people.

"Be sensible and vigilant, because your adversary the Devil walks about like a roaring lion, seeking someone he may devour."

1 Peter 5:8 MKJV

In *Revelation 12:7-11*, John foretells that, **"there was war..."** in heaven; Satan and his hosts will fight the hosts of God. Satan and his fallen angels are no match for the hosts of God, therefore, at last, they will be cast down from heaven and no longer have any access to heaven, to stand before God. Jesus Christ prophesied the war incident that will take place in heaven before it was revealed to John.

Now, where is Satan and his hosts? Satan and his hosts are everywhere on earth—in the firmament, in the water, on the ground, under the earth, and in many other places they can be on earth, as stated in chapter four.

What is now their occupation on earth? Presently, they roam about with primary aim to devour as many people as possible.

The word translated *'devour'* in *1Peter5:8* is a Greek word *'Katapino.'* It has other renditions like 'to drink down, gulp entire, drown, swallow up.'

The English dictionary meaning of the word *'devour'* is, 'destroy completely' or 'eat up completely, as with great appetite.'

From these meanings, Satan's new occupation and title is 'Devourer of People.' Since he can no longer access heaven to accuse the saints before God, his only objective is to 'eat up the simple, open-minded, liberal, and seducible people wholly, as with great appetite. He and his hosts always desire to submerge the worldly people and unstable Christians in the river of sin, steal their heritage, until they are killed and destroyed.

"The thief does not come except to steal and to kill and to destroy. I have come so that they might have life, and that they might have it more abundantly."

John 10:10 MKJV

However, glory to God, Satan labours in futility since Jesus Christ came and destroyed his works. He has been exposed as a thief, while Jesus Christ reveals the facts about his primary objective on earth. His labour to steal and destroy the divine goodly heritage of any Christian that is in Christ Jesus is a bootless attempt.

Now, incidentally, even though Satan has lost his access to appear before God, he still finds a way to accuse Christians before God. How does he do it? He does it through unforgiving spirit that may possess a Christian. He knows that any sins a Christian forgives is forgiven by God, and any sins a Christian retains against anyone on earth is retained in heaven.

"Of whomever sins you remit, they are remitted to them. Of whomever sins you retain, they are retained."

John 20:23 MKJV

By unforgiving spirit, many in the Church have refused to forgive their fellow Christian brethren their offenses. Day and night, Christians accuse each other before God, while they refuse to forgive one another. May God have mercy.

Nevertheless, Christian, it is not too late to forgive your Christian brethren in order not to be used by Satan as an accuser. If you refuse, your prayer could be hindered, and you might become less effective in the battle of life, and not be able to reign over your world.

"And when you stand praying, if you have anything against anyone, forgive it so that also your Father in Heaven may forgive you your trespasses. But if you do not forgive, neither will your Father in Heaven forgive your trespasses."

Matthew 11:25-26 MKJV

"...Lord, how often shall my brother sin against me and I forgive him? Until seven times? Jesus said to him, I do not say to you, Until seven times; but, Until seventy times seven."

Matthew 18:21-22 MKJV

Satan Lost The Glory Of His Creation

What else did Satan lose because of his rebellion against God? He lost the glory of his creation; likewise, his hosts lost their glory too. It is a fact that every creation of God bears a weight of glory in their categories. Therefore, all sinless creation of God is a bearer of glory.

Satan had a weighty measure of glory and beamed dimension of resplendence rays of true light when he was in right standing with God. His endowed glory placed him in one of the foremost positions as an archangel and the 'anointed cherub that covers' among angels created by God.

Glory depicts supremacy among God's creations. Thus, Satan possessed the glory that came with the positions given to him by God, to depict his supremacy among his class. After his insurrection, he forfeited his glory and his true light, even though he could forge an angel of light.

"Did not even Satan marvelously transform himself into an angel of light?"

2 Corinthians 11:14 MKJV

From the above scripture, what Satan is currently displaying is counterfeit rays of glory, while he 'transforms' to an angel of God. As disclosed earlier, the word 'transform' means 'to disguise.' His original glory has been cursed with darkness as revealed in Genesis 1:2, and he has nothing left, except illusive glory.

Any light Satan manifests as glory is a sham and cannot withstand the rays of true angels of God. By his false transformation, he goes about today, deceiving the people of the world with conceited glory.

Nevertheless, you know, and the Body of Jesus Christ knows that the pursuit of worldly glory through Satan is an open door to unrighteousness. His deceptive glory lures people away from God, to worship 'creatures' rather than God, the Creator of all things. The acquisition and love for worldly glory does not give true gratification, and in the long run, it procures condemnation as a final heritage.

A True Life Story

As a teenager, as advised by my parent, straight off after I completed my secondary education, I got a temporary job with the Ogun State government, Nigeria. I worked as the finance cleric officer responsible for the revenue collection from Timber contractors and salary disbursements to junior officers at the Forestry Department.

One day, a young new colleague that was just transferred from another city to my office came to seek my advice on a crucial decision he was about to make. He said one of his colleagues at his former office and a contractor approached him and asked if he wanted to get rich quickly. He told them that wanted to be rich, and even become a millionaire."

So, they said there is a way he could become rich and be a millionaire within one year. He asked them how it could be. They said it would be through a direct initiation to Satan. They said, following the initiation, like a shot, people would rush to him to bless him with money.

Moreover, they promised that doors of business opportunities would suddenly open to him where he never expected. He would be encompassed with 'favour' and have 'power' to get riches. Within a year he would become so rich that his fame would travel across the nation and beyond.

He queried them further and asked how the initiation would go. They told him that he would buy certain things, and they would introduce him to a medium for sacrifices and initiation. However, the acquisition of the wealth would be limited a certain number of years, as determined by a demonic deity. Peradventure, a maximum of ten years or more, and afterwards, Satan had every right to claim his soul for all eternity. It will be a sacrosanct covenant.

He was so scared to the core of his being. He asked them to give him some time, while he discussed the matter with his parents. Instantly, they advised him not to tell his parents or anyone. As he considered the matter within himself, he said to himself, "If the matter is godly, why do they want it concealed? If it is genuine and virtuously alright, then everyone should benefit from it" In any case, that was the last time they discussed the matter with him.

Nevertheless, God intervened and delivered him from their further pressure. Within two weeks after their conversation, an unexpected transfer came for him, and he was moved from the office to my office. As a result, he lost total contacts with all the satanic agents, and they never cross path again.

At any rate, I advised him to reject the offer; it was ungodly. I told him it was Satan's scheme to rob him of God's good plan for him. Satan wanted to give him a delusory glory of this world at the expense of his soul and all the good things God has in stock for him.

Dear reader, I do not know where you have been and where you are right now. Perchance, Satan has sold you his deceptive glory through his agents and you think it is authentic. Perhaps, you have been initiated into a cult or about to be. I will advise you to flee the agents of darkness. The glory that Satan has been giving to the world is spiritually corrupt, fraudulent, and temporary. Surely, it will add eternal damnation to you at the end of your earthly sojourn.

On top of your fame, glamour, and the glory of your wealth in this world, Satan will claim your soul if you do not repent and receive Jesus Christ as your Lord and Savior, now. He has claimed the souls of many world-rich people and take them to hell, do not let him have yours.

True riches and glory belong God, and they could only be obtained through Jesus Christ, the Son of the Living God. He is the only One that gives life and blessings with no sorrow added to them. Surrender your heart to Him and be saved, now and for all eternity.

"The blessing of Jehovah itself makes rich, and He adds no sorrow with it."

Proverbs 10:22 MKJV

Satan Forfeits God's Anointing And Blessings

Every creature in their original state is endued by God with some peculiar blessings to fulfill the purpose of their existence through Him. With these blessings, they are positioned in their various classes and places to fulfill their divine purposes. By their nature, they tell of God's blessedness.

For instance, after God created the marine creatures and the fowls of air on earth. He unleashed His commanded blessings upon them that they might fulfill His purposes.

"And God blessed them, saying, Be fruitful and multiply, and fill the waters of the seas and let the fowl multiply in the earth."

Genesis 1:22 MKJV

Likewise, after He created Adam, He said to him:

"And God blessed them. And God said to them, Be fruitful, and multiply and fill the earth, and subdue it. And have dominion over

the fish of the sea and over the fowl of the heavens, and all animals that move upon the earth."

Genesis 1:28 MKJV

According to the English dictionary, the meaning of the word 'bless' is 'to confer prosperity or happiness on'. Also, the meaning of the word 'prosperity' is, condition of being successful, prosperous, and having good fortune. Therefore, God's blessings upon His creatures are empowerment to be successful, prosperous and have good fortune in accordance with His intentions.

At the time Satan was in right standing with God, he was endued with power to be successful, prosperous, and he had good fortunes, while he fulfilled God's intentions. The power manifested through the anointing that God conferred upon him.

"You were the anointed cherub that covers, and I had put you in the holy height of God where you were; you have walked up and down in the midst of the stones of fire. You were perfect in your ways from the day that you were created, until iniquity was found in you."

Ezekiel 28:14-15 MKJV

By the anointing and divine blessings, Satan was able to execute God's purposes perfectly. He did not possess his initial perfection without God. The initial perfection he exhibited as he fulfilled God's purposes was released upon him by the anointing and divine blessings. Emphatically, Satan was without blemish until sin was found in him.

Immediately after he sinned and God's judgment came upon him, the anointing was removed, and he ceased to be the 'anointed cherub that covers.' He was thrown out of Eden into utter darkness.

Since his rebellion, instead of being blessed, curses become the aura of his existence. He forever lost entirely his original anointing and blessings to function in perfection in whatever he does.

Satan Lost His Original Ministry

What matters to fulfill God's purposes are the endowments with divine blessings and anointing. Satan, having lost his original anointing goes about to dispense evilness all over the world. God's original purpose for him was not evilness as he displays today. His original ministry from God was to cover Eden and lead other angels to worship God.

"...The <u>workmanship</u> of your tambourines and of your flutes was prepared in you in the day that you were created."
Ezekiel 28:13 MKJV

From the above scripture, the word *'workmanship'* gives a good understanding of Satan's original occupation in God. However, since his fall, he ceases to be in the original business that God created him for. He lost it, forever.

Christian, you must stay within the perimeters of God's call on your life. Try not to be what He has not called you to be. If you want to retain your originality in His purposes, you must endeavour to know His call and plans for you and stay within their boundaries. Do not pursue another man's vision because it looks good and could help you to get on in life easily and faster.

A Christian's Confession

A Christian told me one day that God has called him into ministry. I asked what blueprint God has given him for his vision, ministry, and mission: particularly, what is God's objective for the ministry. To my surprise, he said what God had called him to do was just what another man of God he knew was already doing. He was not definite about it.

I advised him to go back to God and ask for the blueprints of what He wanted him to do. God is a God of clarity; a God of objectivity and plans, and every person and His assignment for them are unique in His sight. If he heeded my advice or not, I was not sure.

After a while, we met again and the issue about his ministry came up. I asked if he was able to receive any blueprints for the ministry from God. Again, he could not give any straightforward answers, as he stuttered. Since then, if he hears anyone talks about God's blueprints for their ministry, he will claim that is exactly what God had called him to do. Anyway, after a while, he left ministry work for a secular one.

Confusion is not of God; it all emanated from Satan. No matter the similarities in common goals of various ministries, yet there will be some uniqueness to differentiate their callings. God may call two Christians into the works of ministry at the same time, but His blueprints for them will not be the same, even though it is for a common goal, to win and prepare souls for heaven.

God would only give you anointing to fulfill the ministry He has given you, and signs, wonders, and miracles will follow. Anything outside His calling would result in operating by the flesh. Therefore, you could deviate into heresies and lead the flock of God astray.

You, your audience, and partners may look successful in the sight of people, regardless, there will be no reward for it. Please read *Matthew 25:18-30* and *2Samuel 7:1-13*.

From the account in *Matthew25:18-30*, the Lord of those servants rewarded each of them according to what He had called them to do. The servant that refused to fulfill his assignment was not rewarded with any good.

Similarly, in *2Samuel 7:1-13*, while David thought of building a temple to honour God. Prophet Nathan, one of his spiritual advisers had already given his approval for the project, however, God rejected David's intention, and He instructed him not to execute the project. It is someone else's assignment.

Hence, be careful. Do not copy another man's ministry's blueprint. If you abandon your original call and ministry and engage in an alternative one that God has not approved, you will not be rewarded for it in heaven. If you feel you have lost your original ministry, you can ask God for help, to search, and find and fulfill it. May God have mercy on us all in Jesus' Name. Amen.

Satan Ceases To Be Justified

To be acquainted and have a right standing with God require holy and righteous lifestyle. Holiness and righteousness are part of God's invariable attributes. He is holy and righteous; as a result, all His creatures were flawless in their original states.

Righteousness and holiness are the bedrock of the relationship between God, mankind, and angels. While they are holy and righteous, they are acceptable in His sight.

Likewise, Satan before his fall. He was perfect and flawless in his original state until iniquities were found in him. Subsequently, Satan's ways and deeds became blamable before God and could no longer stand justified. Hence, God threw him out of his original position and declared him profaned forever.

In the case of man, by the works of Jesus Christ on the cross, the sins of the world were atoned for by His blood. Now, every person's sin is pardoned; if they accept Jesus Christ as Lord and Saviour while they live, they are acceptable before God as righteous people.

However, as for Satan and his demonic hosts, no one could atone for their sins, therefore, they have been desecrated for all eternity. Thus, they remain unjustified and condemned forever. Amen. They have been charged with folly and fallen forever.

"Behold, He puts no trust in His servants, and His angels He charges with folly!"

Job 4:18 MKJV

"How you are fallen from the heavens, O shining star, son of the morning! How you are cut down to the ground, you who weakened the nations!... Yet you shall be brought down to hell, to the sides of the Pit..."

Isaiah 14:12-17 MKJV

Because of the magnitude of their sins, Satan and his angelic hosts were never pardoned. They will not be spared of their eternal punishment.

"For if God did not spare sinning angels, but thrust them down into Tartarus, and delivered them into chains of darkness, being reserved to judgment."

2 Pet. 2:4 MKJV

"And those angels not having kept their first place, but having deserted their dwelling-place, He has kept in everlasting chains under darkness for the judgment of a great Day"

Jude 1:6 MKJV

Therefore, Christian, if Satan comes your way to attack your privileges in God, remind him of his original position among the holy angels of God. He has become sacrilegious and removed from the commonwealth of God's righteous creations, never to gather with us anymore.

If he comes to question your access to God, let him know he does not have any access to God any longer. Henceforth, God does not listen to his accusations against you anymore. Thus, his attacks on you are not approved of God; they must be repelled. Now, God is willing to hear and answer your prayers. Now you can pray sincerely and call on God.

If he comes to ask you about your glorious hope in God, tell him that your living hope in Christ Jesus is guaranteed by God's oath. Declare that he has forfeited his original glory and his transformation into an angel of light is of counterfeit nature; very, very inconsequential when compared with the glory awaiting you in heaven.

Christian, rejoice today and forevermore. If you are a part of the Church of God, you are a possessor of all the glory of the Lord Jesus Christ had before He became man. He willingly transmitted it to you and the rest of His Church—*John 17:4-5, 22-23.*

Therefore, you have been glorified and exalted in Christ Jesus above all satanic hosts.

Furthermore, if Satan dares question God's anointing upon your life, unleash the real anointing against him to let him know that he does not possess the original anointing again. His anointing is fake and not a match to the one you possess now.

Christian, you are blessed of the Father and Satan and his hosts are cursed forever. Due to this, their weapons are also cursed, and none of them formed against you shall prosper and every tongue that they raise against you in judgment is condemned.

Satan, by any means may come against you in one way, regardless, he shall flee before you in seven ways. Fear not! Before now, God has given a command concerning you. He says:

"Touch not my anointed one and do My prophet no harm."
Psalm 105:15 MKJV

Satan and his hosts may impede you and cast doubt on your mind regarding God's call and ministry you have embarked on. Adjudge them by the fact that you have been chosen of God in Jesus Christ before the foundation of the world; nothing can change your election through Jesus Christ in God.

Now, Christian, you are God's workmanship already prepared in Jesus Christ for good works. You are God's ambassador to the nations of the world, set on the top of the mountains of nations, to defend God's interest. Let Satan knows he has lost his original ministry, and he cannot possess yours. It is your divine goodly heritage assignment in Christ Jesus.

Beloved, never fear what Satan and his hosts can do to you. Faithful is He who has called you; Jehovah Adonai is your Hiding Place; He will protect and see you through. God has begun His good work in you, He shall perform it until the day of Jesus Christ. Amen!

Additionally, Satan may accuse you of your sins. Announce to him that it is not by the works of righteousness that you have done, but by Jesus Christ; now, you stand justified before God. Jesus Christ has shed His blood and you have confessed your sins, and they have been forgiven, and you are justified and glorified.

Let Satan know that you are blessed; for, blessed is the man whose transgression is forgiven, whose sin is covered, and the Lord does not charge any iniquity against you. You are justified in Jesus Christ forever, and Satan remains condemned throughout eternity.

On the account of all that Jesus Christ did to restore things to what they were at the beginning of time, today, in Him, you have become God's original; you are not a counterfeit. Now, you can shout aloud: *I AM GOD'S ORIGINAL CREATION!* Amen.

Consequently, now, you are God's original 'new' creation. You are in the unequaled best position among God's creations. Enforce God's rule over your divine goodly heritage and the rest of the world, by your goodly heritage dominion. Forthwith, launch out in the greatness of God's power.

Chapter 10

Enforce God's Rule Over Your World

Dominion is for enforcement of the rule of law over a territory; it could be spiritual or physical enforcement. While spiritual laws are applied to spiritual territories, secular laws are applied within material regions. Although spiritual laws could be enforced on the material world, but material laws cannot be successfully enforced on the spiritual world.

What rule of law are you supposed to enforce? They are the spiritual laws set forth by God.

Before anyone can enforce the rule of law on any place or person, they must be authorized by the bona fide authority of the land. He or she may be or not be the citizen of the land.

In the United Kingdom for instance, no unauthorized person can just enforce the rule of law over the territory, whether he or she is a citizen or not. They must be authorized by the government, or else, it is a crime of impersonation.

Similarly, spiritually, you must be a member of the kingdom of God to qualify to enforce spiritual rules. You must have accepted

Jesus Christ as your Lord and Saviour. You must be a born-again Christian and absolutely abiding in Jesus Christ, and He in you; and you must know who you are in God.

It is not a matter of, if you are not a citizen of the kingdom of God, you could still enforce the rules of God's kingdom? The answer is No. You dare not. What operates here is a spiritual kingdom functioning under spiritual laws. It is a kingdom that you do not see with your physical eyes, but the rule of law is apparent, and its enforcement are done with spiritual might, through God.

The adversaries you want to enforce the rules on, to extinguish their reign are spiritual too, and they operate on legal principles. They know if you are a citizen of the kingdom of heaven or not. They know if you indeed belong to Jesus Christ or not.

In Acts *19:11-18* for instance, the seven sons of Sceva, the Jewish Chief Priest wanted to enforce the rule of God on a demon to set a captive free. Possibly, they had seen or heard of Apostle Paul, enforcing his dominion, and set the captive free by the authority in the Name of Jesus Christ. Without following due divine procedures, they wanted to enforce the rules. The result was not what they envisaged, while they were exposed as impostors.

"And God did works of power through the hands of Paul, so that even handkerchiefs or aprons from his skin being brought onto the sick, the diseases were released, and the evil spirits went out of them. And certain from the strolling Jews, exorcists, undertook to name the name of the Lord Jesus over those having evil spirits, saying, We adjure you by Jesus whom Paul preaches. And there were seven sons of Sceva, a Jewish chief priest, who did so. But answering the evil spirit said, Jesus I know, and I comprehend Paul, but who are you? And the man in whom the evil spirit resided leaped on them, and overcoming them he was strong against them, so that they fled out of the house naked and wounded. And this was known to all the Jews and Greeks who lived at Ephesus, and fear fell on all of them, and the name of the Lord Jesus was magnified. And many who believed came and confessed and showed their deeds."

Acts 19:11-18 MKJV

Clear Simple Steps To Becoming A Citizen Of Heaven

If you must be qualified to enforce the rule of God over the reign of satanic hosts, the procedures are clear and simple. You must be a bona fide citizen of the kingdom of heaven.

How can you become a citizen of heaven? The first step is to accept that you are a sinner and ask God for mercy and forgiveness of your sins. Then, give your heart to Jesus Christ and have faith in Him and everything He accomplished on the cross, as stated in the Bible. Ask Him to be your Lord and Saviour.

Additionally, having believed, and confessed with your mouth and accepted Jesus Christ, the Son of the Living God as your Lord and Savior, ask Him to baptize you with the Holy Spirit and give you His power to live a victorious Christian life. Many Christians that are demonstrating the power of the kingdom of God since the inception of the Church took similar steps and decisions at one time or other.

Jesus Christ did not come to die for a certain race, tribe, or nation, He came and died for the whole world, irrespective your status and the part of the globe you came from. He carried the sins of the world on Himself when He was crucified on the cross. Now, anyone that believes and accepts and abides in Him as his or her Lord and Saviour would no longer be judged by God again.

Jesus Christ has been judged in your place, in my place, and in the place of the whole world for sins. Everyone's sins, no matter the magnitude have been forgiven by God. Since Jesus Christ paid the price, everyone is supposedly justified in the sight of God.

Nonetheless, despite what Jesus Christ did, salvation is not automatically transferable; it must be arrogated to be activated. You must call on Jesus Christ as your Lord and Saviour to claim your justification and then, you will be saved.

"For God so loved the world that He gave His only begotten Son, that whoever believes in Him should not perish but have everlasting life. For God did not send His Son into the world to condemn the world, but so that the world might be saved through Him. He who believes on Him is not condemned, but he who does not believe is condemned already, because he has not believed in the name of the only-begotten Son of God."

John 3:16-18 MKJV

"But as many as received Him, He gave to them authority to become the children of God, to those who believe on His name, who were born, not of bloods, nor of the will of the flesh, nor of the will of man, but were born of God."

John 1:12-13 MKJV

As stated earlier in chapter one, I was born and reared up a Muslim. I prayed five times daily and obeyed the tenets of Islamic religion. I used to fast for thirty days during the Muslim's Ramadan festival period for many years, but all these could not connect me to the True and Living God. In 1975, I secretly invited Jesus Christ into my heart to be my Lord and Saviour after my Christian Religion Knowledge teacher told my class about Him. And in 1987 I publicly received Him as my Lord and Savior and became a citizen of the kingdom of God.

As a citizen of God's kingdom, I received power to enforce God's rule over demonic forces that were holding me, other people, and nations captive. Holy Spirit came mightily upon me, and He has since been residing within me. God empowered me with His anointing and authority to do exploits for His glory in the Name of Jesus Christ, His only begotten Son, since it has been exceptional.

So, now, you can see that God is no respecter of persons. God did not save me because I was a Muslim. He did not save me because of my race or national or tribe or complexion or status. He saved me because I was a sinner that called on the Name of His only begotten Son, Jesus Christ for salvation.

You may say to yourself, "But I was christened as a baby and given a Christian name, because I was born into a Christian family." That is not what eternal salvation is all about. You are not redeemed and saved based on your parental background or what you possess materially or who you socially are. Your eternal salvation is based on what Jesus Christ did on the cross.

The people that gathered on the day you were christened, including your family members, clergymen/women, and friends, unless they had taken their individual steps to receive God's eternal salvation, and truly accept Jesus Christ as Lord and Saviour, and remain in and live for Him, were not counted as part of the kingdom of heaven by God. Although they might be Church goers, performing some duties at Church; the activities are just religious exercises, taking them nowhere.

Every one of them will one day stand before God and account for their sins. They will not account for your sins; neither would you account for theirs. You too will stand alone before God on that day for accountability of your life on earth.

While the day of accountability will be a time of unspeakable joy for those that have unfeignedly accepted Jesus Christ as their Saviour, it will be a moment of disappointment for others that have feigned faith. However, you are an individual created in the image of God, you must decide for yourself today whom you will serve. God or Satan, the world or God's kingdom.

Salvation through Jesus Christ, the Son of God will give an individual a personal relationship with God, by the Holy Ghost; it is God's eternal design for the world. Because of this eternal design, Jesus Christ declares in John 14:6, *"I am the way, the truth, and the life: no man cometh unto the Father, but by me."* Indeed, Jesus Christ is the only 'Way' to heaven; He is the 'Truth heaven proclaims and the only eternal 'Life' that God can afford anyone. There is no other way in any form.

Hence, you must sincerely take the step of faith; believe and accept Jesus Christ, the Son of the Living God as your Lord and Savior, and you shall be saved. Then you shall be empowered by the Holy Ghost to enforce God's rules over your world, and send satanic hosts packing.

Jesus Came With A Kingdom

When Jesus Christ came into this world the first time, He announced that He came with a kingdom. He emphatically declares in *Luke 22:29*.

"And I appoint a kingdom to you, as My Father has appointed to Me."

Luke 22:29 MKJV

The word translated *'kingdom'* in *Luke 22:29* is the Greek word *'Basileia.'* It has other meanings like royalty, rule, a realm, kingdom, and reign.

From the same scripture above, let us also examine the word *'appointed.'* It was reded from the Greek word *'Diatithemai.'* Other renditions are, appoint, make, testator, disposed by assignment, compact or bequest.

By these two Greek words, Jesus Christ was stressing a message to His disciples and the Church. The message is that He came as a Testator of the reign of God; and as His Father has appointed Him, hence, every Christian believer is an assignee of the rule of the same kingdom, by Him.

A testator is someone who makes a lawful valid will, statement or testimony. So, Jesus Christ came to bear a legal valid testimony that the reign of God has come into the world of man once again as it was before the fall of Adam and Eve. It is binding on Him and God.

Therefore, everyone who believes in Jesus Christ as Saviour, is an assignee, and must testify to the truth of God's rule and enforce it. The meaning of *'testify'* is to 'provide evidence for something.' The evidence of your dominion begins at the point of your testifying in words and deeds to everything Bible says about Jesus Christ.

In all generations before now, all true believers in the Lord Jesus Christ lived to provide evidence, in words and deeds that the kingdom of God has come to stay. And based on the assured promise that Jesus Christ gave in *Luke 12:32*, they proclaimed by authority that, Satan's reign has been judged and defeated by the Lord Jesus Christ. Therefore, the Father has given His Church a goodly heritage kingdom.

"Do not fear, little flock, for it is your Father's good pleasure to give you the kingdom."

Luke 12:32 MKJV

God's rules cannot be enforced over any place and anything without your divine authority to showcase your kingdom. The truth remains that, Jesus Christ came into this world with a kingdom. You have been assigned the kingdom as a heritage by Him, to rule and reign.

Your kingdom begins with you, while it extends to other facet of your life, including your family, finances, ministry, social life, etc. Henceforward, begin to enforce God's rule on them now.

Chapter 11

Nature Of God's Kingdom

To rightly enforce God's rule on earth, you must know the quintessence of His kingdom. Jesus Christ gave some clues into the mysteries of His kingdom. He announces:

*"You are from beneath; I am from above. You are of **this world**; I am not of **this world**."*

John 8:23 MKJV

*"...**My kingdom is not of this world**. If My kingdom were of this world, then My servants would fight so that I might not be delivered to the Jews. But now **My kingdom is not from here**."*

John 18:36 MKJV

Indeed, Jesus Christ is not of this world, ditto the kingdom He receives of the Father and the kingdom He gives to His Church.

Now, let us look at the word translated *'world'* in the above scriptures. It came from the Greek word *'Kosmos.'* The other construes from *'Kosmos'* are orderly arrangement, decoration, order, constitution, government, etc.; this includes people that are in it.

From the above renditions, the attributes of God's kingdom that Jesus Christ announced are revealed. They are analyzed as the following.

God's Kingdom Is Invisible

There are two principal kingdoms on earth; they are the Spiritual and Man's substantial kingdoms. The Spiritual kingdom can be divided into two categories: God's kingdom and Satan's. Both Spiritual kingdoms are the invisible forces operating in the world, and they have overbearing influences over Man's kingdoms to direct their affairs. Since Adam relinquished his dominion to Satan, the latter has been having greater control over the affairs of mankind in this world.

When Jesus Christ said that His kingdom is not of this world, he implies the invisibility of God's kingdom. It is a kingdom that cannot be visualized or be comprehended by natural senses.

The world's view on things is by logical proofs, which does not comply with the nature of God's kingdom. So, to fully grasp what God's kingdom is all about, you must renew your mind from world's orientation and quit reasoning like mere people.

Mostly, your thought determines your actions, and your actions reveal your intentions. Oftentimes, your intentions reveal your ways of life to show where you belong, either in God's kingdom or Satan's roguery worldly kingdom.

The Jews asked Jesus Christ when God's kingdom would come, and He responded in *Luke 17:20-21.*

*"And being asked by the Pharisees when the kingdom of God would come, He answered and said, The kingdom of God does not come with observation. Nor shall they say, Lo here! or, behold, there! For behold, **the kingdom of God is in your midst.**"*
Luke 17:20-21 MKJV

Jesus Christ explained that God's kingdom was already within the Jews, yet they could not perceive it. Why could they not discover God's kingdom? They could not discover the kingdom because of spiritual blindness and their mindset. They had boxed God in their minds and limited spiritual matters to logical proofs. Like most people in the world, they were looking for a physical kingdom with material proofs. Therefore, they asked Jesus Christ,

"...By what authority do you do these things? And who gave you this authority to do these things?"
                                                          Mark 11:28 MKJV

However, as a Christian, the proofs you can show to people about God's kingdom is by evidencing the spiritual power and authority that is within you with signs and wonders. God's kingdom that the Church represents is habitually revealing its heritage-dominion through its citizens by signs, wonders, and miracles, to exert heaven's rule over the satanic kingdom on earth.

The key to the manifestation of God's kingdom is the recognition of the spiritual power you have within and living in the consciousness of it, to reveal its authority, to put any situation under subjection. This is how Jesus Christ manifested signs, wonders and miracles that followed Him while He sojourned on earth.

The word *'midst'* was derived from the Greek word, *'Entos.'* It has other interpretations like "within" (your soul) and inside. In other words, it means the manifestation of God's kingdom depends on your perception of the spiritual power that is within you, and your willingness to utilize its power to show forth its works in the material realm, through your authority.

In the world, kingdoms manifest their powers in tangible forms. However, in God's kingdom, power manifests through Holy Spirit that is within. Although Holy Ghost's power is invisible, but He manifests its works physically for people to see. Holy Ghost's power is spiritual, and it only manifests by faith to reveal the kingdom's power that is residence within a Christian believer.

God's kingdom and its power are at present within you; hence, manifest them, now.

God's Kingdom Is Heavenly And Supernatural

As stated earlier, Jesus Christ announced to the Jews that His kingdom was not of this world. What was He referring to? He only wanted people to know that He came from God and His divine heritage kingdom from the Father was heavenly and supernatural; nothing in this world can be compared with it. It is beyond the realm of humanity.

What is heavenly? In summary, it is anyone or anything that originates from and is of God or belonging to Him.

What is supernatural? It is a phenomenal that is above what nature can explain. It is also something that is not subject to explanation according to natural laws.

This takes us back to the time of creation. God is a Spirit; everything about His works is first heavenly and spiritual before their physical manifestations. The foundation and order of things in His kingdom are first heavenly and spiritual too. In other words, God's kingdom is emphatically heavenly supernatural, beyond natural origins.

Adam for instance, was created a supernatural being to reign over a spiritual kingdom on earth. God did not make him a weakling man void of capabilities to understand spiritual things until he was influenced by Eve to sin, and he instantly lost his true spirituality and intelligence. Since then, every man has gradually lost their true spirituality and its awareness; they are unable to genuinely comprehend spiritual matters as they should.

As Jesus Christ emphasized on the difference between His kingdom and the world's, it takes a great depth of cognizance of true spirituality to understand the affairs of God's kingdom, because,

"...the natural man does not receive the things of the Spirit of God, for they are foolishness to him; neither can he know them, because they are spiritually discerned."

1 Corinthians 2:14 MKJV

"And I say this, brothers, that flesh and blood cannot inherit the kingdom of God, nor does corruption inherit incorruption."

1 Corinthians 15:50 MKJV

God's kingdom is heavenly and if you are a Christian, God's supernatural force is already within you. Therefore, assume your true spiritual position in Jesus Christ, to conduct and showcase the supernatural ability of God's kingdom from within you. You are not limited to the natural realm; stop living like a mere man.

God's Kingdom Has A Distinct Orderliness

Another feature of God's kingdom is its distinct orderliness. Orderliness is evidenced in the manner its affairs are conducted, totally different from the world under satanic influence. The world's systems are full of unrighteousness, chaos, and disorderliness, whereas the kingdom of God is exact opposite.

In God's kingdom, the serenity of its nature is exhibited in orderliness to all to imitate. The rules are clearly outlined in righteousness for all its citizens to comprehend, and grace is given for compliance. So, as a citizen of God's kingdom, if you want to enforce your dominion, you must align with its divine systems. Paul, the Apostle, counsels in *Ephesians 4:17-18*:

"This I say therefore, and testify in the Lord, that ye henceforth <u>walk not</u> as other Gentiles walk, in the vanity of their mind, Having the understanding darkened, being alienated from the life of God through the ignorance that is in them, because of the blindness of their heart."

Ephesians 4:17-18 MKJV

From the above scripture, the words translated *'walk not'* were derived from the Greek words *'Meketi'* and *'Peripateo.'* The first of the two has other renditions like: no further and not anymore. The latter also has other interpretations like, to tread all around, to live, be occupied with.

The message from the above interpretations is, as a citizen of God's kingdom you must not, anymore and in any way be occupied with vanity mindset or live or order your affairs like the people of the world. Again, Paul reiterates:

"See then that you walk circumspectly, not as fools, but as wise."
Ephesians 5:15 MKJV

The word translated *'circumspectly'* is from the Greek word *'Akribos.'* It has other translations like, exactly, diligently, and perfectly. The impression is that a citizen of God's kingdom should be perfect and diligently live exactly as stated in God's rules, and not as defined by the world.

Furthermore, Apostle Paul counsels:

"...let us walk in the same rule; let us mind the same thing."
Philippians 3:16 MKJV

The word translated *'rule'* in *Philippians 3:16* is the Greek word *'Kanon.'* It was also rendered as, a standard of faith and practice, boundary, and sphere.

Likewise, the word translated *'mind'* is from the Greek word *'Phroneo.'* Other translations from it are entertain, have a sentiment or opinion, be wise, to be mentally disposed, set the affection on, savour and think.

The notion is that, in God's kingdom, there are standards of practice, and every citizen's mental disposition must be towards them; having all their affections set on them. A citizen's opinions, thoughts and sentiments must be entertained within the spheres and boundaries of the standards, to demonstrate orderliness.

The standards are divine; they are not set according to the rules of this world that put people under burdens and keep them in bondage for destruction. If the Church allows world's system to infiltrate divine standards, from that moment she will start losing her kingdom power.

The moment the Church leaders permit worldliness, the Church will start losing their distinctions. Where there is compromise with the world, divine standards would be lowered, and erosion of its orderliness is inevitable.

God never wills that the world system would replace His standards and direction for His Church. God sets His standards by His words and gives directions by the Holy Ghost; however, they have been ignored for so many reasons by those that love compromise more than obedience.

In the early Church, to show the distinctions of orderliness, Apostles and the rest of disciples resisted the infiltration of world's standards with spiritual violence. They waged spiritual wars where and when necessary. They put their lives on the line and paid the price to establish the sacrosanctity of divine orderliness for the posterity of the Church. Their stand was:

"...We ought to obey God rather than men."

Acts 5:29 KJV

However, today, profane people are continuously occupying spiritual positions in the Church, leading undiscerning Christians astray. Subsequently, the Church is progressively becoming worldly, as she accommodates worldly sentiments in her affairs. And the world is more and more becoming churchy, exhibiting feigned relationship with God.

Moreover, the Church gatherings in many places have become the clubs of hypocrites, clowns, entertainers, and money brokers. While they mock the sacredness of divine presence that brings orderliness, they gratify the appetites of their sensual souls.

Nowadays, Holy Spirit has since left many Church congregations, as sensual people take over leadership positions, while the world gives directions and dictates the pace for them. True messages that proffer solutions for disorderliness are censored by the world, to further weaken the Church kingdom today. May God have mercy, and intervene quickly, and build His Church.

Nevertheless, in these last days, the true Church will emerge stronger in divine orderliness than before. Her distinct divine orderliness shall astonish the world and showcases the divergence between God's kingdom and the kingdom of this world. The zeal of the Lord shall accomplish it, in Jesus Name. Amen.

God's Kingdom Is Free Of Satan's Dominance

Freedom from satanic dominance is the reality of things in God's kingdom; it is one of its principal attributes. It is not that the hosts of darkness will not rise against the Church, but they will never prevail. Church's victory was determined before the battle was set in motion. The victory was accomplished two thousand years ago.

As stated earlier, *'dominance'* is the power or right to give orders or make decisions. Also, it denotes supremacy over others.

Therefore, while Jesus Christ says His kingdom is not of this world, He is referring to a kingdom that the satanic systems will not overcome. Satan is the 'prince of the power of the air', and by his hosts, he influences the ways of life of the people of the kingdoms of this world. Because of his supremacy over the world, his decisions prevail over their affairs, by scheming.

"...you once walked according to the course of this world, according to the prince of the power of the air, the spirit that now works in the children of disobedience; among whom we also had our way of life in times past, in the lusts of our flesh, fulfilling the desires of the flesh and of the thoughts, and were by nature the children of wrath, even as others."
Ephesians 2:2-3 MKJV

In *1 Samuel 8:5-6*, the children of Israel asked for a king to govern them according to the systems of this world:

"And they said to him, Behold, you are old, and your sons do not walk in your ways. Now make us a king to judge us like all the nations. But the thing was evil in the eyes of Samuel, when they said, Give us a king to judge us. And Samuel prayed to Jehovah."

1 Samuel 8:5-6 MKJV

The children of Israel did not realize the consequences of their demands to be like other nations. By their posture, they sent a clear message to God, saying, "God, we don't want Your rule over our lives and nation. We don't want to receive orders from You anymore." In their ignorance, they preferred to be under the dominance of' the prince of the power of the air' that rules over nations of the world. Consequently, God said to Samuel:

"...For they have not rejected you, but they have rejected Me, that I should not reign over them."

1 Samuel 8:7 MKJV

And wherever and whenever God is rejected, it is demonic spirits that take over.

Now, when Jesus Christ announced His kingdom, He drew a line between His kingdom and the kingdoms of this world and presented sundry variations. He said, His kingdom is not of this world. Moreover, He declared the battles of dominance would often occur between His Church (His ambassadors) and the satanic kingdom; however, Satan's kingdom shall not prevail. He said:

"...I will build My church, and the gates of hell shall not prevail against it."

Matthew 16:18 MKJV

Gates in the Bible signify a place in a city or nation where stakeholders gather to take decisions on issues. They plan and determine what the outcome of things would be from the gate-place.

Jesus Christ's message was that no decisions reached by the satanic kingdom would dominate His Church and kingdom. God's kingdom that He came to establish on earth would never experience any form of control or defeat from the forces of darkness.

The word translated *'prevail'* was derived from a Greek word *'Katischuo.'* It also construed as, to overpower.

The notion here is that it does not matter what the satanic schemes and attacks are, God's kingdom has greater invincible prowess and shall never retreat or be overpowered by the hosts of darkness. Because of her greater invincibility, satanic hosts have never been able to stop the advancement of God's kingdom by the Church at any time on earth.

Has God's kingdom been confronted by the satanic hosts from the spirit realm? Yes! Many times. Has God's kingdom been in conflicts with satanic human hosts on earth? Yes! Here and there. Yet, Satan's kingdom has never had dominance over God's kingdom, both at the spiritual and material levels.

Instead, the kingdom of God has been on the move, spreading increasingly across the globe. Indeed, the Church has been moving on from glory to glory, victory to victory and triumph to triumph in the face of many battles. Hallelujah!

Christian, now, be convinced that you are an integral part of God's kingdom; you cannot be stopped by any satanic host. You can only be stopped by yourself if you give way to the flesh to dominate you.

Hence, in order not to be stopped, resist the works of the flesh, and gird up your strength by the Holy Ghost, and move the kingdom of God forward. The gates of hell shall not prevail against you, in Jesus' Name. Amen!

Chapter 12

Heavenly Essence Of God's Kingdom

God's kingdom has a distinctive orderliness from the systems of this world, as enumerated before now. Indeed, God's kingdom is heavenly, supernatural, invisible, and free from satanic dominance, because of its all-encompassing overwhelming invincibility. If God's kingdom has all these aforesaid attributes and more, then the deduction is that its nature is peculiar; it is like no other anywhere, at any time.

If God's kingdom's nature is peculiar, then the implementation of its rules must be in line with its heavenly features. Anything outside the framework of its attributes would be the opposite of God's original intention.

The Lord Jesus Christ, Prophet Haggai and Apostle Paul gave us some clues into these distinctive features as stated below.

"For the kingdom of God is not eating and drinking, <u>but righteousness and peace and joy</u> in the Holy Spirit."
Romans 14:17 MKJV

"For the kingdom of God is not in word, but <u>in power</u>."

1 Corinthians 4:20 MKJV

"But God, who is rich in mercy, for His great love with which He loved us."

Ephesians 2:4 MKJV

"that you should walk worthy of God, who has called you to His kingdom and glory."

1Thessalonians 2:12 MKJV

"Jesus said to him, I am the Way, the Truth, and the Life; no one comes to the Father but by Me."

John 14:6 MKJV

From the above scriptures, there are some words that describe the heavenly essence of God's kingdom. Some of them showcase God's attributes to reveal the heavenly features of His kingdom on earth. These features are outlined below.

➤ Righteousness
➤ Peace And Prosperity
➤ Joy Everlasting
➤ Power And Authority
➤ Love And Sanctified Brotherhood
➤ Glory And Life
➤ Truth And Faithfulness
➤ Kings And Priests
➤ Grace And Mercy
➤ Immovable

Essentially, as we consider these attributes, we will have a better understanding of how God wants His Church to enforce the rules of His kingdom on earth.

The Kingdom Of Righteousness

Since the fall of Adam and before the advent of Jesus Christ, righteousness before God could only be obtained in two ways. The first one is by trust in God for what He says He is and what He could do. Next, God views on a person's obedience to His commandments as righteousness.

To be a righteous person before God goes beyond having mere trust in Him. It requires full obedience to His instructions and complete compliance to His standards. If He finds trust, obedience, and compliant postures in a person, then He would impute righteousness.

Things were not that way when Adam was created. He was not created to have a prerequisite of righteousness to be accepted before God. He was righteousness personified; very perfect and blameless before God until he was influenced by Eve to sin, after she failed to comply with God's standard and instruction; subsequently, they both fell.

Before his fall, whatever steps Adam took were in righteousness. Whatever word he spoke was amplified in righteousness. He did not have to work out any righteousness before his person was accepted by God. Righteousness was part of his inherent nature, and he was accepted by God.

Attaining Righteousness In The Old Testament

In *Genesis 7:1* God said to Noah,

"And Jehovah said to Noah, You and all your house come into the ark, for I have seen you righteous before Me in this generation."
Genesis 7:1 MKJV

Before Noah was declared as the only righteous person in his generation by God, he possessed some elements of trust in Him; he amply obeyed and thoroughly complied with God's standards. Noah exemplified the traits of righteousness prior to, and in Genesis 6 when God instructed him to build an ark. Noah believed in the Person of God, complied with His standards, and carried out His instructions as specified, even though he could not see any tangible proofs to hold on to.

While the rest of the people in Noah's generation were disobedient, evil and noncompliance to God's standards, Noah prepared his heart to follow God wholly. Noah trusted God and complied with His standards and executed the details of His instructions.

The word translated *'righteous'* in Genesis 7:1 was a Hebrew word *'Tsaddeek.'* The other interpretations are 'just, lawful and correct.'

From these translations, it is assumed that Noah believed God and carried out His instructions to show his conformity to God's standards. Therefore, God declared he was righteous.

Genesis 6:22 and Genesis 7:5 confirm Noah's righteousness.

"Noah did so, according to all that God commanded him, so he did."
Genesis 6:22 MKJV

"And Noah did according to all that Jehovah commanded him."
Genesis 7:5 MKJV

"By faith Noah, having been warned by God of things not yet seen, moved with fear, prepared an ark to the saving of his house, by which he condemned the world and became heir of the righteousness which is according to faith."
Hebrews 11:7 MKJV

Furthermore, Abraham's righteousness was confirmed by his trust in God.

"And he believed in Jehovah. And He counted it to him for righteousness."
Genesis 15:6 MKJV

How did Abraham demonstrate his believe? He did by his believe in the Person of God and His promises, and he obeyed His instructions. Abraham's obedience manifested by his believes in God, and his believes made him obeyed whatever God commanded him. The instructions were carried out without any gainsaid. Thus, his obedience was counted as righteousness.

Likewise, other Old Testament saints too. By their works of trusting God and obedience and compliance to divine standards were counted righteous.

"And what more shall I say? For the time would fail me to tell of Gideon and Barak and Samson and Jephthah; also David, and Samuel and the prophets, <u>who through faith</u> subdued kingdoms, <u>wrought righteousness</u>, obtained promises, stopped the mouths of lions,"

Hebrews 11:32-33 MKJV

Abraham, Noah, Sarah, Gideon, Barak, Samson, Jephthah, David, Samuel, the true prophets in the Old Testament and many others are examples of people that believed God, obeyed His instructions, and complied with His divine standards. Hence, they were accepted by God as righteous people. All these people obtained righteousness by their works.

Prerequisites Of Righteousness In The Old Testament

There are two ways into righteousness in the Old Testament. The first is by works; the second is by faith. While the first reveals obedience, the other unveils relationship of trust with God. The latter must be in place before the former could be accepted by God. If a person had both, God would impute righteousness to him or her.

In other words, a person must have a relationship of trust with God first before his works of obedience. By these two he or she is accepted by God. The impression is that a person must first know God and understand His way by a relationship before He could accept his righteous obedience.

The works of righteousness that bring rewards from God begin with a relationship of trust with Him and then followed by obedience. It would amount to foolishness to obey a person you do not trust or know or meet or have a relationship with such, except you are under duress or hypnotism. Today, because many people, including many that professed to be Christians do not know God, they do not obey His instructions.

If you are a Christian, you should, by relationship of trust, know the person of God and His attributes, including His integrity and standards. From the point of knowing Him, then you can follow His voice and Words, to obey His instructions.

"That I may know Him..."

Philippians 3:10 MKJV

"Then we shall know, if we follow on to know Jehovah..."

Hosea 3:2 MKJV

Cain and Abel exemplified the variations in their relationships with God as they sought His acceptance. By his righteous obedience, Abel offered sacrifices acceptable to God, and due to Cain's carnal gesticulation, he and his offering were rejected. How did Abel know what could be acceptable to God or not? He knew it by following God through a heart-to-heart relationship of trust first; then he complied and obeyed.

"And in the end of days, it happened, Cain brought to Jehovah an offering of the fruit of the ground. And Abel also brought of the firstlings of his flock and of the fat of it. And Jehovah had respect to Abel and to his offering, but He did not have respect to Cain and to his offering. And Cain glowed with anger, and his face fell."

Genesis 4:3-5 MKJV

The above incident in Genesis 4:3-5 reveals the first-time the blood of an animal was shed by man as a sacrificial offering to God, after the fall of Adam. Before now, the ground was already cursed because of sin, and anything coming out of it was cursed.

After the fall of man, God started relating with people majorly by His Spirit. For Abel to offer the firstlings of his flock and their fat, it must have been by the leading of the Holy Spirit. Or how would he have known God's mind and what would be acceptable to Him, except by the Holy Spirit? How could he know the presence of the Holy Spirit, except by communion, as he forged an intimate relationship?

Abel would have known God's standards, and how to comply and obey His instructions by the Holy Spirit. But Cain did not have such a relationship with the Holy Spirit. For God to be justified when He speaks, Holy Spit would have attempted to bring Cain into fellowship, however, he rejected Him.

Afterwards, during Noah's generation, God confirmed the relationship between Holy Spirit and man to crystallize what happened between Holy Spirit and Cain. People in the generation of Noah rejected Holy Spirit's relationship gestures while they followed the way of Cain, even though He was pleading with them. Like Abel, only Noah followed the presence of the Holy Spirit. Thus, God said:

"And Jehovah said, My spirit shall not always strive with man, in his erring; he is flesh..."

Genesis 6:3 MKJV

"And Jehovah repented that He had made man on the earth, and He was angry to His heart."

Genesis 6:6 MKJV

The word translated *'strive'* in Genesis 6:3 is a Hebrew word *'Deen.'* Its other renditions are, to rule, judge, contend and plead.

In other words, since the fall of Adam and Eve, the Spirit of God has been in the world convicting, contending, ruling, judging, and pleading with an average man to reconcile with God. He always contends and pleads to show all mankind the right path to God in their conscience. However, they reject Him.

After God accepted Abel's offering, the 'strange spirit' at work in Cain manifested, and Cain was wrath. It was an evil spirit. Therefore, God said to him:

"If you do well, shall you not be accepted? And if you do not do well, sin crouches at the door; and its desire is for you, and you shall rule over it."

Genesis 4:7 MKJV

The impression in Genesis 4:7 was that Cain, by his works did not do well before God. Why didn't he do well? Cain did not do well because he did not have a heart-to-heart relationship of trust with God, by the Holy Spirit, even though He had several opportunities. Cain continued to strive with the Holy Spirit. Subsequently, he and his works were regarded as evil and not accepted.

"not as Cain who was of the evil one, and killed his brother. And for what did he kill him? Because his own works were evil, and his brother's things were righteous."

1John 3:12 MKJV

Many people in the Old Testament were counted unrighteous and incurred God's wrath because they did not believe Him and did not comply with His standards and obey His commandments. When God speaks, and His words are believed and taken as His infallible statement, your belief must be followed by compliance and obedience. Then your works of faith, compliance and obedience would be counted as righteousness. Nevertheless, every unrighteousness shall be judged by Him.

As stated earlier, there are two major forces that are contending to rule the world of man. God's force is one and Satan's is the other. The first force works by righteousness and the latter works out evil. Regardless, today, God is looking for people that would have a heart-to-heart relationship of trust with Him, and comply with His standards and obey His commands, despite Satan's schemes and temptations.

The only way a person can take sides with either God or Satan is by their relationship of submission. So, anyone that takes sides with God by a relationship of trust, and complies with His standards, and obeys His commands will be deemed righteous.

Disobedience to God's commandment is an emblem of noncompliance; an act of unrighteousness that would incur His wrath instantly or later. Any unrighteousness would burn down the bridge that connects a soul to God and the relationship will breakdown, and eternal separation will result. Hence, if you are not on God's side, the only other side you could be is Satan's.

Some people claim they do not believe in anything, and some say they do not believe in the existence of either God or Satan. By satanic weapon of ignorance, they have been deceived to believe the lies of demons that neither God nor Satan exist. Both do exist and there are apparent signs everywhere today to prove their operations, as they contend for mastery in the world of man. One for good and the other for evil.

"For the unseen things of Him from the creation of the world are clearly seen, being realized by the things that are made, even His eternal power and Godhead, for them to be without excuse. Because, knowing God, they did not glorify Him as God, neither were thankful. But they became vain in their imaginations, and their foolish heart was darkened. Professing to be wise, they became fools."

Romans 1:20-22 MKJV

Immediately God's existence is denied by anyone, it is an act of unrighteousness that puts them on the side of the Devil, to work evilness against God, knowingly or unknowingly.

Attaining Righteousness In The New Testament

Corroboratively, the Old and New Testaments bear striking similarities, as evidenced today.

The word translated *'righteousness'* in the New Testament is the Greek word *'Dikaiosune'*. It was also translated as 'equity, justification, virtue, purity of life, integrity, rightness and correctness of thinking, feeling, and acting.

God executed His redemption plan by sending His only Begotten Son Jesus Christ into the world; Jesus Christ is the perfection of righteousness for all mankind. Now, there is no justification in any form that anyone on earth can attain to before God without first believing in Jesus Christ and accepting the redemptive works that

He did on the cross. Jesus Christ is the only way to God.

However, today, many people still believe that some religious observations that bring people into bondage would give them peace with God without Jesus Christ. As a result, they observe and worship river, stones, trees, sun, moon, and other earthly elements.

Ofttimes, prayers are offered to some demonic angels, and incenses are burnt by observers of mundane religions, while they claim to worship God. Hence, Apostle Paul condemned the Athenians for idol worshipping in *Acts 17:22-23* and counselled the Colossians against such practices in *Colossians 2:16-19*.

The relationship God desires is a momently heart-to-heart intimacy with Him by Jesus Christ, through the fellowship of the Holy Spirit. In other words, you must first accept Jesus Christ and His redemptive works as being done on your behalf, and you must continuously abide in Him as He abides in you to the end of your earthly sojourn.

Immediately you take the above steps, it is seen by God as your works of righteousness, and you are automatically declared righteous by Him.

"For He has made Him who knew no sin, to be sin for us, that we might become the righteousness of God in Him."
2 Corinthians 5:21 MKJV

Therefore, your eternal salvation does not depend on your personal works but on the works of Christ, as you entirely abide in Him. In Jesus Christ, all your sins are forgiven. So, while God sees the faith towards Him, through Jesus Christ in your heart, He declares you righteous by Christ; and you also have eternal life.

Any God's commandments you must obey to show forth righteousness must be through Jesus Christ. Christ' words are God's commands. Even though as a Christian you are not justified by works; regardless, your deeds on earth will determine your rewards in the eternal kingdom of Jesus Christ. Jesus Christ says:

"And this is the will of Him who sent Me, that everyone who sees the Son and believes on Him should have everlasting life. And I will raise him up at the last day."

John 6:40 MKJV

"And why do you call Me Lord, Lord, and do not do what I say?"

Luke 6:46 MKJV

"Not everyone who says to Me, Lord! Lord! shall enter the kingdom of Heaven, but he who <u>does the will of My Father in Heaven.</u>"

Matthew 7:21 MKJV

God's Will In A Nutshell

Now, what is God's will? God's perfect will for anyone that wants to attain righteousness in the New Testament is to believe in His Son, Jesus Christ, and they shall be saved. And anyone that believes in Jesus Christ will love Him and obey His commandments.

Obeying Christ's commandments is not a matter of partial compliance, it is complete submission to God's will and counsel, despite any perceived weakness. Regardless, it does not depend on human ability, but wholly rests on the grace of Jesus Christ, just as God said to Apostle Paul:

"...My grace is sufficient for you, for My power is made perfect in weakness..."

2 Corinthians 12:9 MKJV

Accordingly, if you believe in Jesus Christ and love Him, His grace is always available to you to obey His commandments. Then, in all situations, no matter the challenges, you can boldly say, *"I can do all things through Christ who strengthens me." Philippians 4:13 MKJV*

Acknowledge this fact, God is not trusting your natural abilities to please Him, but He looks forward to what He can accomplish by through you by His grace. Hence, the manifestation of your righteousness lies in your total conformity to God's will, by grace.

At all times, the righteous intent of your heart must be God's will, which can only be discovered in Jesus Christ. Within God's will is stocked up the purpose of your creation. Through the manifestations of the purpose of your creation is where the demonstration of your heritage dominion lies.

If you do anything outside God's will, you would not be able to enforce His rules precisely and maximally, as He ordains. Therefore, knowing what the will of God is for your life, and preparing your heart to perfectly submit will put you in a better position to exert your dominion over Satan and his hosts.

"...and having readiness to avenge all disobedience, when your obedience is fulfilled."

2 Corinthians 10:6 MKJV

"And if we are careful to do all this commandment before Jehovah our God, as He has commanded us, it shall be our righteousness."

Deuteronomy 6:25 MKJV

Now let us consider other features of God's kingdom.

The Kingdom Of Eternal Peace And Prosperity

God's kingdom is the kingdom of peace and prosperity; unremittingly, it grants peace and prosperity to its citizens. In the Old Testament of the Bible, there are different Hebrew words translated 'peace.' Let us consider one that is exactly related to the 'peace' in discussion.

*"Mercy and truth have met together; righteousness and **peace** have kissed each other."*

Psalm 85:10 MKJV

*"Jehovah will give strength to His people; Jehovah will bless His people with **peace**."*

Psalm 29:11 MKJV

The word *'peace'* in the above scriptures was translated from the Hebrew word is called *'Shalom.'* The other words translated from the word are 'completeness, soundness, welfare and peace.'

In addition, in the New Testament, the word *'peace'* that is closely related to this subject was derived from the Greek word *'Eirene.'* It has other meanings as 'peace, prosperity, security, safety, quietness and rest.'

*"**Peace** I leave with you, My **peace** I give to you. Not as the world gives do I give to you. Let not your heart be troubled, neither let it be afraid."*

John 14:27 MKJV

*"For the kingdom of God is not eating and drinking, **but** righteousness and **peace** and joy in the Holy Spirit. For he who serves Christ in these things is well-pleasing to God, and approved by men."*

Romans 14:17-18 MKJV

*"And the God of **peace** shall bruise Satan under your feet shortly...."*

Romans 16:20 MKJV

One of the words from the above translations of *'Eirene'* is *'completeness.'* The word completeness means 'a state of being complete and entire; having everything that is needed.'

Another interpretation from *'Eirene'* is *'Soundness.'* It means 'a state or condition free from damage or decay.'

Also, stemmed out of the word *'Eirene'* is the word *'Prosperity.'* Prosperity means 'an economic state of growth with rising profits and full employment; a state of having fortune.'

Likewise, the word *'security'* was construed from the Greek word *'Eirene.'* Security is a state of being free from danger and injury. It is freedom from anxiety or fear. In other words, whatever that is secure could be regarded as being in safety.

All the above renderings from the Old and New Testaments characterize the *'Peace and Prosperity'* essences of the kingdom of God. It is the realm where you have everything that is needed for your well being. Concurrently, you are free from damage or decay in your spirit, soul, and body.

It is the kingdom whereby nothing good is lacking. As a citizen of the kingdom of peace and prosperity, it also means that you should be enjoying increase of goodness, and always be in complete rest and tranquility without any form of pain, fear, and anxiety. All the above translations are what should be the features of true prosperity in any life and nation.

Many people have used worldly standards in terms of the material wealth gained at a point in time, to measure true prosperity. The amount of wealth possession without peace do not reflect true prosperity.

Possession of material wealth without true peace and prosperity of the spirit, soul and body is an indirect curse on anyone. While it is of God to bless with power to get wealth, to showcase prosperity, also, He always gives true peace to enjoy the blessings of prosperity. But He does not give material wealth to His people at the detriment of the prosperity of their souls.

"But thou shalt remember the LORD thy God: for it is he that giveth thee power to get wealth..."

Deuteronomy 8:18 KJV

"The blessing of Jehovah itself makes rich, and He adds no sorrow with it."

Proverbs 10:22 MKJV

"Beloved, in regard to all things I pray that you prosper and be in health, even as your soul prospers."

3John 1:2 MKJV

What is true peace? True peace is having Jesus Christ enthroned at the pinnacle of your heart. It is Jesus Christ in you and you in Him.

He is the Prince of Peace that calms the soul, no matter the storms of life. When this is the case, there will be peace within and without, no matter what.

Pains and sorrows are components of a natural life. Regardless, if you are a child of God, they should never complement your existence. Thus, if you are a citizen of the kingdom of God and sorrows and pains are following your blessings, you need to do some spiritual checks on yourself. It could be there is an opened door to the hosts of darkness, knowingly or unknowingly.

Ask the Lord to reveal the door to you and teach you how to overcome the attacks of the enemies. Have the assurance that you are a child of God's kingdom; true prosperity and peace are yours, already guaranteed.

True riches are from God; however, it is majorly for kingdom expansion on earth; it is not to amass the mundane things of this world that have no eternal rewards. It must be used to lay treasures in heaven for your eternal rewards.

The Kingdom Of Everlasting Joy

As a citizen of God's kingdom, you must understand that the kingdom you are part of is the kingdom of Joy; always bubbling with overplus joy, everlastingly. The kingdom of God is not a kingdom of sorrow and grief. No matter the level of sorrow you might come in with, it would eventually turn into exceeding great joy as you become a citizen.

On the day you received Jesus Christ as your Lord and Savior, despite your remorsefulness and the tears you shed for your past mistakes and sins, the joy that overwhelmed your heart could not be quenched by the burdens of the baggage of sins and sorrows that accompanied you.

Possibly, while tears were rolling down your cheeks, simultaneously, you had joy overflowing your heart. It is the joy of salvation. It is the type of joy whose origin cannot be explained or articulated by human senses. It always bubbles from within and manifest without.

King David, the Psalmist of Israel pleaded with God and said:

"Restore unto me the joy of thy salvation..."

Psalms 51:12 KJV

And the Lord Jesus Christ says:

"I have spoken these things to you so that My joy might remain in you and your joy might be full."

John 15:11 MKJV

The joy of God's kingdom is the joy of the Lord. It infuses strength to a fainting spirit and gives hope to all weak souls. The material world around you may collapse, and its understructures may give way, but the joy of the kingdom will guarantee your confidence today, and forever. Thus, you are sure that, no matter what, your tomorrow is in good hands, favourably secured.

Moreover, our God is a joyful God. His kingdom is a place where He rejoices with great singing over His people, while He rests in His love for us with great affection.

Zephaniah says:

"The LORD thy God in the midst of thee is mighty; he will save, he will rejoice over thee with joy; he will rest in his love, he will joy over thee with singing."

Zephaniah 3:17 KJV

Are you longing for real joy? Stop searching and let me introduce you to the Kingdom of Joy. True Joy can only be discovered in no other place than God's kingdom.

Many people cannot differentiate between joy and happiness. Joy is the manifestation of something that occurs within, while happiness is a result of something that happens on the exterior. Happiness is always sparked by the state of situations as seen, heard, and read. Joy comes because of a force that is permanently residing in you.

Jesus Christ says, *"...My joy might remain in you and your joy might be full."* Holy Spirit is the power at work in you, greater than any external force. Thus, the joy of God's kingdom is powered by Him. No inferno of hell can quench it.

Holy Spirit Is The Spirit Of Everlasting Joy

What more, Holy Spirit is the Spirit of everlasting joy. His joy cannot be extinguished by any circumstances of life; it endures forever. During unfavorable conditions, He will be the anchor of your strength. Conditions vary as phases of life unfold; yet, Holy Spirit remains constant, and by His joy, He is the Stabilizer of your life in whatever situation.

David knew if Holy Spirit is gone, then the true joy of his life would cease. Therefore, in *Psalm 51:11-12*, he pleaded that God should not take Holy Spirit from him, and He should restore the joy of his salvation.

Joy Can Only Be Expressed By You

The world is a place of many sorrows, where joy fluctuates and diminishes gradually and fades away. Because the world does not have the Holy Spirit, unbelieving mankind is afflicted and impaired with hopelessness; and people are stricken by legions of troubles of this life.

As there are sorrows in the world, there is outstanding and greater joy in the kingdom of God. The joy of God's kingdom surmounts the sorrows of world's calamities, and it dries up many rivers of griefs.

Joy can only be expressed by you because you have Holy Spirit and belong to God's kingdom. If you are weighed down with sorrows of this life, by the Holy Spirit, you can gather your strength and lift your soul from where it is laid down. Let the joy of the Lord spring up and begin to flow from your inner most being.

Joy of God's kingdom is one of the life's spiritual essentials that distinguishes you from the rest of world, at the time of pain or difficult situations. The world cannot understand why you are always cheerful, despite what you have gone through in life.

As people come around, they expect to see in you a depressed soul, for them to have a pity party with you. Instead, they see somebody that is full of life, with ripples of greater vigor of joy. They see a dynamic person always overflowing with joy, and they marveled. They might not be able to unfold the mysteries of your joyful postures; however, you know that your Source is the river of God that produces joy, and it flows ceaselessly. Holy Spirit is the River of Living Waters in you because you are a city set upon the hill of God.

"There is a river, the streams whereof shall make glad the city of God..."

Psalms 46:4 KJV

A True Testimony From A Christian Brother

A Christian brother called me a while ago for counseling and prayers concerning his job. He was going through persecution and racial discrimination at his place of work in the Great Britain.

As a medical doctor, he is a born again Christian and a leader of a Christian fellowship at his workplace. Apart from this, he occupies a senior position, which his colleagues, because of the colour of skin thought one of them should have.

In addition, his immediate boss always finds faults in whatsoever he does. The necessary work supports he needs from his boss are never given to him. To humiliate him before his junior colleagues, whenever he wants to contribute to discussions during team meetings his boss always addresses him with utter disrespect and hush him down like a little child. Openly, his boss has threatened to sack him, unless he complies with his bidding.

The Christian man was not moved at all. He knew he was not being persecuted on his job for any incompetence, but rather he was, because of his relationship with Christ. Also, he felt he was being discriminated against because of his race. However, despite all the negativity meted at him, his countenance neither changed nor was his spirit cast down.

One day, his boss had a one-to-one appraisal and action-plan meeting with him. During the meeting, his boss' burst forth to show his resentment for him. He sounded out on him and said: despite all his threats to the Christian brother, he observed that the Christian brother is always full of joy. He said he was expecting to see a man that is full of sadness, instead, he saw a man that is full of joy.

Then, the Christian brother answered his boss and said to him, he would not be able understand the source of his joy and strength. He said the Source is invincibly invisible, and it is beyond man's comprehension; it is Jesus Christ in him, the hope of glory. With his confession, his boss abruptly ended the meeting.

Indeed, the Christian brother's joy emanated from an invisible place. The secret of his joy and strength during persecution and threats meted at him is the Lord Jesus Christ; He is the Source.

The dear Christian brother belongs to the kingdom of joyous people; a kingdom that is always in joy. It is indeed a kingdom where the river of the Holy Spirit is flowing continuously from within God's people and manifest His works outwardly.

Anytime his boss threatens him, instead of being filled with fear and sorrow, Holy Spirit always releases the river of joy from within him; and the joy of his salvation manifests without for the people around to see an inexplicable joy.

His joy does not depend on the external situations to show forth. It depends on Who is inside of him—Jesus Christ, the Hope of

Glory.

Likewise, in any situations, a testimony like this can be yours.

The Kingdom Of Power And Authority

God's kingdom is the kingdom of absolute sovereign power; its citizens are vested with its divine authority. By His sovereign power, God controls and rules in the affairs of heaven and earth, all the time. God's children on earth possess the delegated authority to exercise dominion to reign in life.

"Absolute power corrupts absolutely"; it is only people that keep their conscience free from evil that can sense when absolute power has corrupted absolutely. Indeed, absolute power in the hands of a depraved mankind will utterly corrupt them. However, the delegated authority in the custody of a child of God is divinely vested, to be exerted in righteousness over the forces of darkness unlimitedly, by the leading of the Holy Spirit.

In the world of man, many leaders cannot comprehend the mystery of the kingdom power that God's children possess. Certainly, on earth, God's children possess the authentic power with delegated authority to exert their sovereignty.

Authentic power belongs to God and it is infinitely invincible, higher than any other in all degrees and manifestations, spiritual or material, or in whatsoever other forms. It is unlimited as it rules over the spheres of all things, both in heavens and on earth, all the time.

True unvanquishable power is known for its divine genesis and consistence dependability. It functions in righteousness to exhibit truthfulness, to honour God and bless humanity and other creations on earth. The Church of Jesus Christ as an extension of God's kingdom on earth, is the possessor of the power, vested authority to root out Satan and his hosts at any time.

Often, kingdoms have come and vanished into history as their powers and influence are reduced to rubbles. Nevertheless, only

God's kingdom has withstood the test of time unendingly, despite the forces that are against it. On earth, its enduring power is in the custody of the true Church, to teach principalities and powers God's manifold wisdom.

For a kingdom to be everlasting, it must be in constant possession of the ultimate heterogeneity power from generation to generation, whether spiritual, political, economic, military powers; God's kingdom displays all aspects.

Kingdoms of this world are known for their power variations. Their degrees are up and down, today, and tomorrow; they fluctuate like a yo-yo; they are never constant.

However, incessantly, God's kingdom power has supremacy over all other powers, in the heavenlies, on earth and under the earth. It has endured throughout all generations of man.

The Psalmist says:

"Thy kingdom is an everlasting kingdom, and thy dominion endureth throughout all generations."

Psalms 145:13KJV

And Daniel confirms,

"How great are His signs! And how mighty are His wonders! His kingdom is an everlasting kingdom, and His rule is from generation to generation."

Daniel 4:3 MKJV

On earth, since the creation of Adam, God always uses mankind as an extension of His kingdom. Even though in sundry ways, man has failed and missed the mark of righteousness extremely, yet God in His infinite love, mercy and grace has never stopped choosing and using mankind as His principal agents to accomplish His purpose on earth. Irrespective of horrendous wickedness of mankind, God can still use whosoever He wants for His purpose on earth. May He continuously use us for His righteous intentions.

Like the wicked religious leaders that influenced the crucifixion of the Lord Jesus Christ. They thought they were getting rid of a 'blasphemer of God and a deceiver', as they vilified Jesus Christ, but little did they know they were fulfilling God's purpose. Nevertheless, by His humility, and obedience in death, and by His resurrection, the Lord Jesus Christ gives salvation to all humanity.

The fact that we live in a generation that is so perverse does not mean that God's kingdom does not exist in righteousness. For the fact that many Christians have compromised their faith does not mean that God's kingdom power has ceased to exist in the Church.

God has some remnants in such a time as this; He has set them apart to show the world that indeed, the Church is an extension of His righteous kingdom on earth, to reveal the power and authority of His kingdom. Are you among the righteous in God's kingdom?

Jesus Christ, before His death said to His disciples.

"And I appoint a kingdom to you, as My Father has appointed to Me,"

Luke 22:29MKJV

"...the kingdom of God come with power."

Mark 9:1 KJV

"And he said unto them, I beheld Satan as lightning fall from heaven. Behold, I give unto you power to tread on serpents and scorpions, and over all the power of the enemy: and nothing shall by any means hurt you..."

Luke 10:18-20 KJV

"But you shall receive power, the Holy Spirit coming upon you. And you shall be witnesses to Me both in Jerusalem and in all Judea, and in Samaria, and to the end of the earth."

Acts 1:8 MKJV

Similarly, Jesus Christ is saying to you today, He has appointed you the kingdom Of God, and the kingdom has come to you with power, and the power is within you, by the Holy Spirit.

The Most Powerful And Effectual Kingdom

God's kingdom is not a weakly wussy kingdom, as some in the Church have presented themselves to the world. It is the most effectual and powerful spiritual kingdom anywhere, at any time.

In all realms of heavens and earth, God's kingdom is the most all powerful, placing decisive limits over all satanic worlds, powers, and schemes. Hastily, you must acknowledge you are an integral part of it and manifest its power and authority to reign over your world.

If a kingdom operates without adequate security power, sooner or later it will become a bedlam of adversity to its citizens. But the kingdom of our God has never lacked adequate power in any ramifications, for its citizens to exert their authority at any time. The power is perpetual and always advancing in greatness.

The Greek words translated power and authority are *'Dunamis'* and *'Exousia'* respectively.

Other words translated from *'Dunamis'* are ' force, strength, ability, miraculous power, mighty wonderful work, etc.

From *'Exousia',* other words derived are privilege, force, capacity, competency, freedom, mastery, power ' power of rule or government that must be submitted to by others ' worldwide, explicitly, metonymical, etc.

What knowledge should we gain from these meanings? The above meanings denote that God's kingdom possesses all the above attributes, and more. Its citizens have privileges and power to enforce the kingdom rules universally, and righteously dictate the pace for the world. Whatever commands they give must be obeyed by all, Satan and his hosts are not exempted.

Even though the kingdoms of this world are often controlled and manipulated via their leaders by the power of the prince of the air, however, by the authority and power invested in the Church, satanic hosts' dominance on any earthly kingdom can be checkmated.

God is the Controller-General of the earth, and He has not lost control of the universe to Satan. Satan may control the hearts that are delivered to him, to rule the world's kingdoms by them, yet he can only go as far as God allows him. God has the ultimate rule.

"The king's heart is in the hand of Jehovah as the rivers of water; He turns it wherever He will."
Proverbs 21:1 MKJV

Daniel buttressed on the above scripture in Daniel chapter 4. He says:

"This matter is by the decree of the watchers, and the demand by the word of the holy ones, so that the living may know that the Most High rules in the kingdom of men, and gives it to whomever He will, and sets up over it the lowest of men."
Daniel 4:17 MKJV

Jesus Christ says to you, you have been appointed a kingdom, and the kingdom comes with authority and power of privileges. So, if God's kingdom comes to you with authority and power, then, where is the authority and power?

Every appointed representative of a constituted establishment is invested with power to act on behalf of the represented department. When you are an appointed representative of an organization, you are directly or indirectly a part of it; to some extent, you are vested with power of the organization.

In the same vein, every born-again Christian is an appointed earthly representative of the kingdom of heaven. They possess divine authority and power as invested by Jesus Christ, to rule on behalf of God, as an extension of His kingdom on earth.

As indicated above in Luke 22:29 and Acts 1:8, today, Jesus Christ still says to all Christian believers that are members of His kingdom, *"I give unto you authority... and you shall receive power.*" The power and authority are not offered to everybody in the world, it is peculiar to His Church, and you are an integral part of the Church. Hence, power and authority belong to you.

Christian, the authority and power unleashed to you for possession have some qualities that must be understood, or else, you may not know their worth, and how to use them effectively. These qualities are analyzed below:

- ➢ **Immunity** – They can protect you fully against any enemy and their weapons.

- ➢ **Operations** – They have capabilities to produce effective results, as desired.

- ➢ **Influence** – They have prestigious potentials and positive or negative effects on anyone and anything.

- ➢ **Universality** – They have worldwide applicability and impact.

- ➢ **Guaranteeability** – They are responsible for guaranteed excellent achievements.

- ➢ **Royal Dominance** – They evidence distinguished and supreme royal rankings among Christians and other God's created beings, including satanic hosts.

- ➢ **Hyper-Strengths** – They have supernatural enormousness, speed and durability.

- ➢ **Decisiveness** – They are prompt to determine what happens in heaven and earth according God's will.

- ➢ **Constantness** – They are known for their unvarying nature; they are steadfast in purpose and uninterruptible by time.

Now You Have The Kingdom's Authority And Power

Now, you know that God's kingdom power and authority are

available to you. How can you claim them?

The authority and power of God's kingdom are from the all-powerful, all-mighty and all-encompassing Living God. Jesus Christ is the ultimate main Holder, and Holy Spirit is the main Distributor. They do not come by the government of this world. They do not come through any religion. They do not come by traditions of men.

As a child of God, you may find yourself in the corridors of powers of governments of this world, just like Joseph, Daniel, Esther and Mordecai, and many others. Regardless, you are not in the position because of your connections, but God who rules in the affairs of men has allowed you to be in the position in such a time, to accomplish His purpose.

So, see the position as your current territory, given to you by God to execute His intentions. Stand shoulder-high for the things that pertain to God's, while in the service of man. Extend the rules of God over the place and watch as God touches lives and saves souls through you.

Since the authority and power at work in you are always sovereign, they are supposed to make the rulers of this world tremble and submissive to you instantly, and not otherwise. Unleash your power and authority and take charge with God today.

The Kingdom Of Love And Sanctified Brotherhood

God is love as Christians know, even though the world may seldom agree with us. God's love is the type that the world cannot express or fathom. It is supernaturally unconditional, and sacrificial. Thus, God's kingdom is established on love and advances on the wings of love.

More so, God's kingdom is a place of sanctified brotherhood, where unfeigned love exists among its citizens. The citizens are spiritual offspring that are born of God; and they are purified by the blood of Jesus Christ. Therefore, they possess God's nature, and love one another unconditionally.

"Beloved, let us love one another, for love is of God, and everyone who loves has been born of God, and knows God. The one who does not love has not known God. For God is love."
1John 4:7-8 MKJV

On this side of eternity, no one can comprehend God's love, or totally grasp the motives of His love towards mankind. It is beyond what any human minds can understand; however, when we, Christians get to heaven, we will appreciate God more than we have ever done, as we further know His intentions of love for us.

God's expression of love is not by quantitative righteous works of man; instead, it is the impulsive factor that caused Him to become a man and died in our place. God is love and the expressions of genuine and unfeigned love always emanates from Him.

Love is of God, and God always relates to mankind in love. It would be difficult for anyone to give what they do not have. Satan does not have love, so he cannot give it. He possesses hatred and wickedness; as can be seen in the world today, he displays auras of evilness everywhere.

God is love; therefore, He expresses it as an integral part of His attributes. Whenever you show God's love towards someone, it is because God is at work in your life. Through your expressions of love, you evidence that you have God's nature, and you are part of His kingdom.

Love should be reciprocal. Love expressed and not reciprocated with love is love unappreciated, and it expresses a wasted opportunity to do good. It is like drivers on dual carriage ways as they come across each other in the traffic. At times, they beep the horn and flash the head lights of their cars to give compliments and appreciate each other along the way. If you are driving and a driver on the opposite lane beeps the horn and flashes the headlights of his car to give you compliments, and you do not reciprocate, you will miss the opportunity of the good moment.

When love is demonstrated, there must be a complimentary response from the receiver to express goodness and appreciation. However, some respond to love with warmth and others with coldness, some firmly and others negatively. Though, your warmth and positive responses to God's love have brought and establishes you, as part of His kingdom.

Unfortunately, not many people in the world today appreciate or understand God's love; hence they do not respond warmly and emphatically. The God of love has proved His love to the world by becoming a man, in the person of Jesus Christ. He went to the cross and died for the sins of the world. He was buried and He resurrected on the third day.

Forty days after His resurrection, He ascended on high, and He is seated at right hand of glory in heaven, making intercessions for us. Moreover, He is coming very soon for His Church, and afterwards He will return to establish His Millennium Kingdom.

If not because of His unfeigned love for mankind, God could have created another being to replace human beings, while He allows everyone to perish in their sins forever. Love made Him reconcile mankind to Himself through His cross while humanity was yet in their sins. Without fail, God and His love are endlessly amazing.

"And without controversy great is the mystery of godliness: God was manifest in the flesh, justified in the Spirit, seen of angels, preached unto the Gentiles, believed on in the world, received up into glory."

1 Timothy 3:16 KJV

*"For **God so loved** the world, that he gave his only begotten Son, that whosoever believeth in him should not perish, but have everlasting life."*

John 3:16 KJV

"And through Him having made peace through the blood of His cross, it pleased the Father to reconcile all things to Himself through Him, whether the things on earth or the things in Heaven."

Colossians 1:20 MKJV

The words *'so loved'* make God's love go beyond any human comprehension. It is too much for unregenerated souls to work out.

Dear reader, now that you are saved, you are a part of the kingdom of Sanctified Brotherhood. In God's kingdom, love is a command; it is a doctrine; it is God's will, especially for a healthier Christian brotherhood. How often do you teach and respond to God's love? How far do you go to express love to all humanity? How frequently do you reciprocate God's love from your Christian brethren? Do you express genuine love as required by God?

"This is my commandment, That ye love one another, as I have loved you."

John 15:12 KJV

"...Love the brotherhood..."

1Peter 2:17 KJV

Complete submission to God's will and ways is not easily achieved; it requires momentary sacrificial gestures, by grace's power. Genuine love granted during life's hard conditions is categorically, a sacrificial one. It is love that goes extra miles to reveal righteousness. Jesus Christ demonstrated His love for us, and now, correspondingly, we are commanded to love the brotherhood sacrificially.

Types of Love

There are many words translated into love in the Bible. Let us consider a few of them from the New Testament to buttress this subject.

Phileo

'Phileo' is affection or kindness towards someone. It is used to show some signs of love, or to be fond of someone. This is the type of love demonstrated in marriage between a man and a woman — *Matthew 23:6; Revelation 3:19*

Agape
'Agape' is an affection or benevolence or good will. It is a selfless and sacrificial love of one person for another without sexual motivation — *Matthew 24:12; 2 Corinthians 13:14*

Philadelphia
'Philadelphia' is fraternal affection, in other words, brotherly love. It is love that is displayed by brothers and sisters towards one another as members of the same family — *Matthew 23:6; Revelation 3:19*

Agapao
'Agapao' is love (Agape) in action. A love at work through selfless and sacrificial benevolence service. It is demonstrated without inordinate or immoral ulterior motives — *Matthew 5:43; Galatians 5:14; Ephesians 2:4*

Philanthropia
'Philanthropia' is love, kindness and benevolence for all mankind — *Titus 3:4*

Philandros
'Philandros' is a kind of love expressed by a wife towards her husband — *Titus 2:4*

Philoteknos
'Philoteknos' is love and expressions of maternal love for a child – – *Titus 2:4*

Ethelo
'Ethelo' is a desire or wish or delight to do something — *Mark 12:38*

Philaguria
'Philaguria' is love of money. It is an inordinate desire of gain or greed for wealth — *1 Timothy 6:10*

The greatest of all the above types of love is 'Agape' and it must become 'Agapao' in its expression.

Whatever love you think you have, whether it is *'Phileo'* as in your marriage, or *'Philadelphia'* for your Christian brethren or *'Philanthropia'* for the generality of mankind, let the bedrock of it be *'Agape'* and its diffusion be by 'Agapao.'

When *'Agape'* becomes *'Agapao'* through you, it becomes the greatest expression of love above all.

'Philaguria' is avarice, which is the root of all evil. Never let it take hold of you. Any Christian that exhibited it will make a shipwreck of their Christian faith.

Paul, the Apostle gives us the attributes of *'Agape';* He says:

"Love is patient and kind; love does not envy or boast; it is not arrogant or rude. It does not insist on its own way; it is not irritable or resentful; it does not rejoice at wrongdoing but rejoices with the truth. Love bears all things, believes all things, hopes all things, endures all things. Love never ends..."
1 Corinthians 13:4-8 ESV

'Agape' is God's love; it is so supernatural. It is love demonstrated by God while He displayed His eternal attributes through Jesus Christ, towards mankind. No angel, including Satan and his fallen angels has ever experienced this type of love from God; and they can never.

In collaboration with *1 Corinthians 13:4-8*, while you were a sinner, God was patient and expressed His kindness towards you, to show His love attribute. Now that you are a believer, His love for you always intensifies greatly, and it will never fail.

Thus, as a citizen of God's kingdom, as you go in to conquer and dominate your territory, remember, you are of God, and God is love. Express God's love to everyone you meet along the way, except Satan and his hosts. Among Christian brotherhood, evince love with patient and be kind to all, ditto to unbelievers.

Relate with people in humility and conduct your endeavors with godly manners to manifest genuine love. Bear all things, believe all things that are of God; hope in God and endure all things for His sake to prove your love; however, be ruthless to all satanic hosts.

God is the only One that can give you Agape; so, covet it. Ask Him to pour it sufficiently into your heart. You will be transformed by it, and its overflow from your life will graciously impact the Christian brotherhood and great multitudes of people around the world.

"...the love of God is shed abroad in our hearts by the Holy Ghost which is given unto us."

Roman 5:5 KJV

The Kingdom Of Life And Glory

God is life and glory, ditto His kingdom. Successively, He emits life gloriously unendingly, and He establishes and arrays His kingdom in life and glory. His dwelling place is glorious and at His presence is perpetual life. His Names and ways are glorious; they diffuse life momentarily.

God's creations are gloriously made to have life to show forth His praise. There is nothing that comes out of God and retains its originality in Him that does not possess life and glory.

At first, Adam was created to possess a glorious life that distinguished him from other creations. In God's kingdom, nothing dies while they remain in their original state. What shows superiority amongst creations is the weight of glory that each one carries. Hence, David, the king of Israel says in *Psalm 8:3-8*:

"When I look at Your heavens, the work of Your fingers, the moon and the stars which You have established; what is man that You are mindful of him, and the son of man, that You visit him? For You have made him lack a little from God, and have crowned him with glory and honor. You made him rule over the works of Your hands; You have put all things under his feet: all sheep and oxen,

yes, and the beasts of the field; the birds of the heavens, and the
fish of the sea, and all that pass through the paths of the seas."

Psalm. 8:3-8 MKJV

Paul collaborates that glory differentiate superiority among God's creations and says:

"...But the glory of the heavenly is truly different, and that of the
earthly different; one glory of the sun, and another glory of the
moon, and another glory of the stars; for one star differs from
another star in glory."

1 Corinthians 15:40-41 MKJV

In *Psalm 8:3-8* above, David related to us how God created man, Adam a little lower than Himself and advantageously lifted him with honour above other creations, including angels. Even though Bible tells that angels excel in strength more than man today, and one angel bears a weight of glory more than another, however, man was not created to be subjected to them.

Man is created to be subjected only to God and to receive directives from Him; oftentimes, He may use His holy angels to give such instructions.

Adam became weaker in his glorious essence after he allowed sin into his life, and his glory diminished. Regardless, infinite thanks be to God for Jesus Christ, our Lord; He has paid for our redemption. Now, our restoration to glory is in place and the consummation of our redemption is nearer than we can ever imagine.

While first Adam falls, his fall does not only affect the generations of mankind, but also, it affects all God's creations under man on earth. Although, as man's restoration is consummated, the glorious manifestation of the sons of God with Jesus Christ will also unconditionally impact the restoration of other creations to their original state.

"For the earnest expectation of the creature waiteth for the
manifestation of the sons of God. For the creature was made

subject to vanity, not willingly, but by reason of him who hath subjected the same in hope, because the creature itself also shall be delivered from the bondage of corruption into the glorious liberty of the children of God."

Romans 8:19-21 KJV

Dear reader, if you are a Christian, consciously bear in mind that now, you are a creation of glory through our Lord Jesus Christ. Your glory, through Jesus Christ surmounts all other creations' glory.

If the above is the case, what is glory? For a better understanding let us look at some words translated glory in the Bible.

Glory In The Old Testament

In the Old Testament, the first and most common Hebrew word from which glory was translated was *'Kabod' Exodus 16:7, 2Chronicles 7:2; Genesis 45:13; Genesis 31:1; Exodus 28:2.*

Other words translated from *'Kabod'* are weight, splendor, honour, abundance, and reverence. Now let us examine the meaning of 'Kabod' by its translations.

➢ *Glory*
Great beauty or splendour that is overwhelming. The quality in a person or thing which secures general praise or honour.

➢ *Weight*
The relative importance granted to something.

➢ *Splendor*
A quality that outshines the usual.

➢ *Honour*
A tangible symbol signifying approval or distinction

➢ *Abundance*
An overflowing fullness or ample sufficiency in terms of wealth, money, treasure, etc.

➢ *Reverence*
An act of showing respect

Glory In The New Testament

In the New Testament, the word *'glory'* was stemmed from the Greek words *'Doxa'* and *'Doxazo.'* While 'Doxa' is the noun, *'Doxazo'* is the verb.

The word *'Doxa'* has other translations like opinion, judgment, view, estimate, dignity, honour, praise, worship etc.

Now, let us have the English meanings of some of these translations as listed below.

➢ *Opinion*
A belief that a person has formed about a topic or issue. The judgment or sentiment which the mind forms of persons or things.

➢ *Judgment*
An opinion formed in judging something. The final award; the last sentence.

➢ *View*
A way of regarding or understanding something, an opinion, a theory, situations, or topics.

➢ *Estimate*
A rough calculation or assessment of the value, size, or cost of something. A judgment of the quality of something or somebody. The respect with which a person is held.

➢ *Dignity*
The quality of being worthy of esteem: elevation of mind or

character.

➤ *Honour*
Recognition of importance or value; respect; veneration. The state of being morally upright, honest, noble, virtuous, and magnanimous.

➤ *Praise*
An expression of approval and commendation.

Kabod And Doxa's Commonalities

Now, from the meanings of the words derived from *'Kabod'* and *'Doxa'*, the Old and New Testament words for glory, it can be deduced that God's kingdom is adorned with weights of splendor, abundance, and honor, far greater than any other.

It is the kingdom decked with dignity and righteousness.

It is the glorious kingdom where its citizens voluntarily offer reverence, praise, and worship to God, and reverence one another.

Before He created man, God had a kingdom of glory in mind; it would be like no other on earth. Today, the world's kingdoms are feeble and decorated with artificial ornaments of glory, and they are often compromised with evil in all facets, and none measures to God's required standard.

However, God's glorious kingdom is the kingdom where He is the ultimate Head and Law Giver, and His glorious nature abides in His citizens. It is also the kingdom where the power of His glory subdues all satanic hosts, to taper them off forever.

God wants the resplendence presence of His person, by the Holy Spirit in every mankind while the nimbus of His kingdom fills the world. His position in mankind and their world would be the rallying point that no other should surmount in heaven and earth.

Nevertheless, Satan and his host terribly misestimated how far God could go to defend His position among His creations as they rose in insurrection against His will, while they wanted to take over the sacred sovereign position only reserved for God over His creations.

'Doxa', the New Testament Greek word for glory gives a better understanding of God's glory. It somehow reveals the depth of God's position concerning Him and His creations. It unveils the mind of God concerning His kingdom and creations.

As creations align with God's opinion, judgment and view at any time, His way will be revealed, and His works will be seen, and voluntary praise and worship will be ascribed to Him. As God is placed in His highest place of all by praise, worship and adoration, His glory will fall on the earth.

God's glory, opinion, judgment, and view concerning anything are the unquestionable forces that reveal His sovereignty and will, which every creation must accept. Satan and his hosts drew the battle line the moment they oppose His sovereignty and will on earth. Even though satanic hosts have always been opposing God's sovereignty and will, regardless, in God's kingdom, His sovereignty and will in all things must remain intact.

'Opinion' is the belief that a person forms about a topic or issue. It is the judgment or sentiment which the mind forms of persons or things.

'Judgment' is the final award or final sentence concerning a thing.

'View' is a way of regarding or understanding something, an opinion, a theory, situations, or topics.

'Estimate' is the quality of something or somebody or the respect with which a person is held.

Therefore, as a member of God's kingdom, your judgment, opinion, estimate and views must coordinate with God's view, estimate, opinion, and judgment, or else you will suddenly find yourself in insubordination to God's authority.

So, permitting God's opinion, estimate, judgment, and view to prevail over every other opinion, judgment, view and estimate you may hold, is the emblem of your submission to His sovereignty, will and the glory you ascribe to Him. As a result, this stance will manifest the blessings of His glory in your life as a citizen of His glorious kingdom.

Thus, in all your daily endeavors and walk on earth, God's opinion, view, judgment, and estimate must be held in high esteem and should be displayed for the world to know that you are a member of His glorious kingdom. While you do this, you will momentarily disseminate the same glory everywhere and the world will see God in the highest place of all and bless Him through you.

The Kingdom Of Truth And Faithfulness

Truth may be lacking in the world and infidelity may characterize many relationships, however, in God's kingdom, it is not. Truth and faithfulness are part of its foundations They are part of the forces that unveil the nature of God in its citizens, to exhibit righteousness for the world to be integrous.

In the face of misrepresentations and disappointments in the world, godly attributes of truthfulness and faithfulness reveal uprightness and draw the line between God's integrity and Satan's deceit. They reveal the great gulf between God's holiness and Satan's untrustworthiness, and show the world that God is invariable, no matter the situation. God remains constant, and He can deliver whatever He has promised.

"God is not a man that He should lie, neither the son of man that He should repent. Has He said, and shall He not do it? Or has He spoken, and shall He not make it good?"
Numbers 23:19 MKJV

"For I am Jehovah, I change not. Because of this you sons of Jacob are not destroyed."
Malachi 3:6 MKJV

In God's kingdom, God's words never return to Him void because of His truthfulness and faithfulness. They are infinite; they testify that He is veracious.

Likewise, in the 'true Church' of Jesus Christ, truth and faithfulness are changeless; they are some divine entities of God's sons. While they conduct their enterprises among the children of the world, truthfulness and faithfulness are part of the factors that attest to the nature of God in them, to prove they are indeed citizens of the heavenly kingdom.

Hence, dear reader, are you a citizen of heaven? If you are, let truth and faithfulness characterize your life. Let the leaven of deceitfulness be purged from you and put on the whole nature of the New Man in Christ Jesus. The world would see the difference between you and them and emulate godliness they observe in you.

The Kingdom Of Kings And Priests

Assuredly, God's kingdom is a kingdom of priests and kings. If you are a Christian, already you are a king and priest with our Lord Jesus Christ in God's glorious kingdom.

John the beloved says:

"Beloved, now are we the sons of God, and it doth not yet appear what we shall be: but we know that, when he shall appear, we shall be like him; for we shall see him as he is."

1 John 3:2 KJV

Consider the phrase *'we shall be like Him'* as it appears in the above scripture. It is more than just a mere statement. Jesus Christ is the eternal King and High Priest in God's kingdom in heaven and earth. Therefore, His Church will not only be arrayed with His glory, but also will serve as subordinate kings and priests, under His kingship and lordship, forevermore.

John the beloved narrated his experience of what shall happen in heaven after rapture. He says:

"And from Jesus Christ, who is the faithful witness, and the first begotten of the dead, and the prince of the kings of the earth. Unto him that loved us, and washed us from our sins in his own blood, <u>And hath made us kings and priests unto God and his Father;</u> to him be glory and dominion forever and ever. Amen."

Revelation 1:5-6 KJV

"And they sung a new song, saying, Thou art worthy to take the book, and to open the seals thereof: for thou wast slain, and hast redeemed us to God by thy blood out of every kindred, and tongue, and people, and nation; <u>And hast made us unto our God kings and priests: and we shall reign on the earth."</u>

Revelation 5:9-10 KJV

Why is God's Church a kingdom of priest and king? Firstly, it is a restoration to how things were when Adam lived in Eden before sin. So, the Church is a kingdom of holy people that God has set apart for Himself on earth.

Secondly, the Church is an essence of the Body of Jesus Christ on earth. Jesus Christ is the Head, and the Church is the rest of His Body. Jesus Christ is the High Priest to God, while His Church is His Body-of-Priests, serving God under Him.

If you are genuinely a Christian, you are a part of the New Jerusalem that is the bride of Jesus Christ. You are a core member of His Body, the bone of His bone and the flesh of His flesh. As a result, you have been made an eternal king and priest with Him. Christ is the King of kings, and the Lord of lords, and the High Priest to the priests of God.

Referentially, Satan occupied the two positions of a king and priest in Eden, when he was in right standing with God. This was treated extensively in the early chapters. You can read it all over again. Satan lost these glorious positions and man by Adam gained them forever. Amen!

What are the roles of a king and priest in God's kingdom? On earth, it is part of a king's patrimony to rule, reign and oversee the affairs of a given territory, particularly in the fear Of God. He has an obligation to exercise his dominance over the land of his territory as a lawgiver and judge.

Where there is a supreme king among many kings within a kingdom, the lesser kings and lords always rule over smaller territories. They are supposed to be loyal subordinates to the supreme king and take orders from him.

As things are with earthly kings in their kingdoms, somehow, they are in God's kingdom. Jesus Christ is our Sovereign King and Lord and His Church as lesser kings, shall rule with Him in His kingdom all over the nations of the earth.

In the nearest future, God's kingdom shall be the only government on earth and His Church shall execute His will in righteousness as He intends; the people of the world shall see His glory and righteousness. Thus, Christian, you are a citizen of God's kingdom and a king and lord in Christ.

"And the seventh angel sounded; and there were great voices in heaven, saying, The kingdoms of this world are become the kingdoms of our Lord, and of his Christ; and he shall reign forever and ever."

Revelation 11:15 KJV

As priests in God's kingdom, the Church will continually offer sacrifices of praise to God and Jesus Christ, our King forever. God always inhabits the praises of His people. We belong to God eternally and we shall praise and worship Him forever.

Apostle John says again:

"After this I beheld, and, lo, a great multitude, which no man could number, of all nations, and kindreds, and people, and tongues, stood before the throne, and before the Lamb, clothed with white robes, and palms in their hands; And cried with a loud voice, saying, Salvation to our God which sitteth upon the throne, and unto the Lamb. And all the angels stood round about the throne, and about the elders and the four beasts, and fell before the throne on their faces, and <u>worshiped</u> God, Saying, Amen: Blessing, and

glory, and wisdom, and thanksgiving, and honor, and power, and might, be unto our God forever and ever. Amen."

Revelation 7:9-12 KJV

The word translated *'worshiped'* is the Greek word *'Proskooneho.'* It has other meaning like 'kiss, like a dog licking his master's hand, prostrate oneself in homage and reverence'.

In other words, we shall forever kiss, prostrate to pay homage and give reverence to our King and Lord Jesus Christ forever and ever. Adam held this position before his fall; He was the King and Lord over all the earth. Therefore, as the Church of God's kingdom, we have been restored in Christ Jesus to offer praise and worship to Him and God forever.

Your Service Begins Now

Christian, your kingly and priestly services do not begin when you get to heaven, they start now, here on earth. Indeed, they must begin from here; in a world where so many people are against God and His agendas, you must be loyal and dedicated to Him.

Your Heavenly Father, the Almighty God knows you belong to Him now, and you have Him as yours forever. So, distinguish yourself from the worldly crowds and worship Him as Daniel did in Babylon.

Let the world worship whosoever and whatsoever they choose, but you are a priest of God in Christ Jesus. Offer to God your sacrifices of praise; adore and magnify His holy Name now and endlessly.

The Kingdom Of Grace And Mercy

Grace is favor dispensed at the expense of Christ. Grace is bestowal of restoration of forfeited blessings to an accused and guilty person after pardon, instead of condemnation.

Due to the degree of his offense, under a certain law, a confirmed guilty offender that is supposed to lose all the benefits accorded to his status suddenly receives pardon and restoration. During trial procedures, he was found guilty, however, the force of clemency intervened on his behalf. He was exonerated of all offenses and discharged despite his guiltiness, and then restored to his original position and given blessings beyond his imaginations. This is mercy overlaid with grace.

Mercy first came to his rescue, and the accused was pardoned, despite being guilty. Then grace was revealed after he was pardoned, and he was restored to his original position with blessings more than he previously forfeited.

This divine benignity is not found in the world, but only in the God's kingdom. The world always cries vengeance, vengeance. Vengeance when offended. Vengeance when hurting. Vengeance when incriminated. Vengeance, vengeance. People use vengeance as a weapon to correct wrong doings. Oppositely, in God's kingdom mercy and grace are always available to give a second chance, to pick up the broken pieces and make them whole again.

Jesus Christ did it and brought us under His grace. All humanity stood condemned before God until Jesus Christ came and took on our condemnation, paid the price and reconciled us to God through His blood and cross. He restored and magnanimously blessed us beyond our dreams. Now and forever, we live to enjoy God's favour at His expense, everlastingly.

"And the Word was made flesh, and dwelt among us, (and we beheld his glory, the glory as of the only begotten of the Father,) full of grace and truth...And of his fullness have all we received, and grace for grace. For the law was given by Moses, but grace and truth came by Jesus Christ."
John 1:14-17 KJV

Even though Jesus did it for all humanity, salvation and grace are not spontaneously applied to any life. Salvation must be intentionally and genuinely received from God, and grace must be accessed through Jesus Christ. So, if Jesus Christ is rejected by anyone, forfeiture of God's eternal salvation and grace is inevitable.

Grace is what makes anyone stands in God's kingdom to please Him and be everything He has been created and called them to be. If grace is let go, what is left of their efforts, are works of the flesh that can never please God.

In the world, people believe in luck. Luck is a hope that, by chance something good may happen to somebody. It only happens in the world and not in God's kingdom. It is the reasons many people engage in gambling to become rich. They believe that one day luck will come their way.

Ominously, many Christians too, have stopped living under God's favour today. They have become gamblers, living under the unguaranteed spell of luck like the people of the world, instead of possessing the benefits of grace. Therefore, their disappointments never end.

Grace is God's disposition of kindness and compassion towards His people. It is a special privilege that no one in the world can enjoy without Jesus Christ.

Child of God be aware that you possess grace in God by Christ Jesus. You are a part of the kingdom of grace and God always looks at you through the eyes of His graciousness.

While you work under grace, you have the supernatural capability to accomplish things that a natural person cannot. The grace of God is the spiritual supplement that gives power that surmounts your weakness; it will invigorate you to live above all weaknesses of a natural man. Access grace today, and divine strength shall be unleashed on you to forge ahead until you reach the end of God's purpose for your life.

"...My grace is sufficient for thee: for my strength is made perfect in weakness. Most gladly therefore will I rather glory in my infirmities, that the power of Christ may rest upon me."
2 Corinthians 12:9 KJV

Challenges Are Overcome Through Grace

The kingdom of grace is where all challenges of life are overcome, and excellence is attained. Grace does not retreat in the face of challenges; it always presses on to the end of its goal and overcomes all impediments.

The kingdom of God is always on the move; it has never been stagnant for a moment. Grace does not manifest in idleness, but it steadily works through diligence. If because of your challenges, you want to remain inactive in your divine assignments, you will never discover grace that has been made available to advance.

In God's kingdom, grace is discovered and then accessed when you are determined to obey God and press on to accomplish His purpose. Grace upon grace from the fullness of the Lord Jesus Christ is unleashed as you advance with God's intentions.

"But by the grace of God I am what I am: and his grace which was bestowed upon me was not in vain; but I labored more abundantly than they all: yet not I, but the grace of God which was with me."
1 Corinthians 15:10 KJV

Additionally, grace is given to complement the measure of the gifts of Christ invested in you. The gifts are given to you to subdue every opposition in your territory to keep your divine goodly heritage. There is no way you can operate any gift of God without grace.

God's kingdom is distinguished from the kingdoms of the world as divine gifts are displayed by its citizens. Demonstrations of the gifts of Christ cannot be perfected without grace; it is the bedrock on which they are bestowed and revealed by Christians. Hence, *"...unto every one of us is given grace according to the measure of the gift of Christ." Ephesians 4:7 KJV.*

Do not Frustrate The Grace Of God

Despite the above facts on grace, if care is not taken, God's grace can be frustrated through hardness of heart and insensitivity to the

Holy Spirit. Things of the kingdom of God are not stereotyped, their activities and occurrences are always spontaneous as Holy Spirit moves. No one can determine the extent of His operations.

Oftentimes, the move of the Spirit could override your personal agendas or some traditions you have put in place. No matter your plans, Holy Spirit can overturn them and introduce new ones. Your refusal to embrace His instructions will prevent you from accessing more grace. Consequently, your Christian life could slip into a mere religious practice that might keep you in bondage.

In fact, as a Christian, challenges of life always surface to test your resiliency and the strength of the measure of grace you possess. In the face of challenges, if more grace is accessed, challenges will be easily conquered, while you scale over to the next level.

Therefore, dear Christian, determine to keep pressing forward, enforcing the rule of God over your territory, by grace. May God bestow more grace on you in Jesus' Name. Amen.

The Immovable And Indestructible Kingdom

Many kingdoms have come and gone on earth, as they were shaken out of their foundations. The only kingdom that has ever remained since its inception and continues to persist unshakably is the kingdom of God.

Do not get me wrong, the Church has had one persecution too many. Yes, she is progressively troubled on every side, and trials and temptations have buffeted her very often. However, amid all these things the Kingdom Church that Jesus Christ purchased with His blood has remained immovable and indestructible. She has been growing stronger and stronger every day, covering the face of the earth, and acquiring more territories.

What kingdom in the world has gone through what the church has gone through since her inception that is not shaken? There is none. They have all been shaken to their foundations, rendered desolate, and they are no more.

The Church of Christ is the materialization of God's kingdom on earth, and Jesus appoints His Church the kingdom. The true Kingdom Church, as an integral part and extension of God's heavenly kingdom on earth is the attestation of God's kingdom power today; it is still rugged and invincible.

The True Church Is Invisible

The true Church in her current form is invisible, hidden within mixed multitudes of people that claim to be Christians. Nonetheless, God knows those that are really His Church. As things were in the days of the Lord Jesus Christ on earth, they are in the Church today. Great multitudes of people flocked after Jesus Christ, but a few were His true disciples.

It is the few Christians that are sincerely the Church of Jesus Christ that have claimed the kingdom appointed to them. They are the true members of the Kingdom Church on earth. In Christ's eternal kingdom, they shall sit and reign with Him.

"And I appoint unto you a kingdom, as my Father hath appointed unto me; That ye may eat and drink at my table in my kingdom, and sit on thrones judging the twelve tribes of Israel."
Luke 22:29-30 KJV

"And Jesus said unto them, Verily I say unto you, That ye which have followed me, in the regeneration when the Son of man shall sit in the throne of his glory, ye also shall sit upon twelve thrones, judging the twelve tribes of Israel."
Matthew 19:28 KJV

As a result, the world is yet to grasp the mystery of the Kingdom Church. They will not understand the mystery of her citizenship until the day of rapture, and we shall be separated to be with the Lord Jesus Christ forever. The wheat shall be separated from the shaft into the heavenly barns.

After the great event of rapture, the true Church shall return with the Lord Jesus Christ to establish His kingdom and millennium reign. Therefore, in the book of Hebrews, Apostle Paul counsels and says to the true Kingdom Church:

"Wherefore we receiving a kingdom which cannot be moved, let us have grace, whereby we may serve God acceptably with reverence and godly fear:"

Hebrews 12:28 KJV

The words translated *'cannot be moved'* in the above scripture is the Greek word *'Asaleutos'*. It has other renditions like 'unshaken and immovable.'

In other words, God's Kingdom Church is too great to be destroyed, too outstanding to be perpetually trodden down and too powerful to be overthrown by any force, whatever they may be. You and I are citizens of the kingdom; we are unshaken and immovable people. Jesus Christ has already declared to us that satanic hosts shall never prevail over His Church.

"... I will build My church, and the gates of hell shall not prevail against it."

Matthew 16:18 MKJV

Gates in the Bible signifies a place of decision. The persecutions, trials, and temptations that the Church may face as a result of the decisions of the kingdom of hell can never surmount the Church.

The Kingdom Church is active, always advancing God's intentions on earth. Holy Ghost is our Leader; we are supercharged, marching on, and exerting the victory of Jesus Christ, stamping down Satan and his hosts in all ramifications. They dare not stand in way of the Holy Spirit as He works with, and in, and through the Church.

You Are Not Forsaken

So, Christian, are you facing persecutions? Be strong, you are not forsaken; God is on your side, you shall surely be delivered. Do you have any troubles or engaged in certain life's battles? Never despair, your victory is already guaranteed, you shall never be conquered; the Lord shall fight for you and you shall hold your peace.

Are you under a siege by unbearable life's conditions? Do not be frightened, the Lord will make a way where there seems to be no way; you will overcome and escape. Are you perplexed or down cast? Never be deterred; arise, let the Lord be your strength; do not give up, just look up; divine Help is nearer to you than you can imagine.

Child of God, it does not matter what you are passing through right now and how challenging they may be, they shall soon come to an end. It is not because of what you are materially in this life; it is because of who you are now in Christ. You are a child of the King of kings and Lord of lords. You are a citizen of the kingdom that cannot be shaken. Therefore, be never moved or shaken by any situations.

When a kingdom is not shaken by whatsoever means, it signifies the stability of its foundation, the might of its armoury, the weight of glory of wealth at its disposal and the essential qualities of its leaderships and citizens. All these cogent features and more are what makes a kingdom strong and outstanding.

God Almighty is the foundation of His kingdom and His resources are indiminishable; they are far greater than the resources of all the nations of the earth put together countlessly. They are sourced from heaven above and are within your reach.

"For every beast of the forest is mine, and the cattle upon a thousand hills. I know all the fowls of the mountains: and the wild beasts of the field are mine...for the world is mine, and the fullness thereof."

Psalms. 50:10-12 KJV

"The silver is mine, and the gold is mine, saith the LORD of hosts."

Haggai 2:8 KJV

"Blessed be the God and Father of our Lord Jesus Christ, who hath blessed us with all spiritual blessings in heavenly places in Christ:"

Ephesians 1:3 KJV

"According as his divine power hath given unto us all things that pertain unto life and godliness, through the knowledge of him that hath called us to glory and virtue:"

2Peter 1:3 KJV

Thus, David believed and declared:

"God is in the midst of her; she shall not be moved: God shall help her, and that right early. The heathen raged, the kingdoms were moved: he uttered his voice, the earth melted. <u>The LORD of hosts is with us</u>; the God of Jacob is our refuge. Selah."

Psalms 46:5-7 KJV

What did you notice from the above scriptures? Did you see that the 'LORD of host' is among His Church as her Help and Refuge that never fails? The Lord of Hosts is the King of the Kingdom Church. He is amid His people.

All the hosts of heaven and arsenals of war are at the LORD's disposal and you equally have access to them; they are on standby for you. At your call, the LORD of Hosts shall direct them into action in your favour. You are too dangerous for Satan and his hosts to come against. You are a powerful force to be reckoned with; you are an integral part of the Kingdom Church.

Do you know the reasons why powerful nations of the world display their weapons publicly? It is to show their strength and warn and scare away their enemies. The powers at work on your side are so enormous and mighty, and as satanic hosts notice them, they always tremble and flee.

So, arise in your divine might and take back the goodly heritage you have allowed the enemy to take from you; dominate your territory and enforce the rule of God over all. Now is the time to root out Satan and his hosts wherever you are.

"...my beloved brethren, be ye steadfast, unmovable, always abounding in the work of the Lord, forasmuch as ye know that your labor is not in vain in the Lord."

1 Corinthians 15:58 KJV

Chapter 13

Root Out Satan And His Hosts

As stated earlier, the authority that manifests your dominion in Jesus Christ is legitimate, invisible, and mighty weapon through God. It is an arsenal of warfare against the common unrepentant enemies of God and mankind. By now, you know that Satan and his fallen angels are the enemies.

Everywhere satanic hosts are they oppose God's purpose for any of His creation, including you. They may execute their activities directly or indirectly in any part of the world, using human beings as mask to unleash their wickedness.

Unless you have made up your mind to engage them in spiritual warfare, using the authority in the Name of Jesus Christ and the power of the Holy Ghost to exercise your dominion over them, you might not be able to reign as God intends.

God, or Jesus Christ would not come down again to do certain things for you and me, because He has delegated the authority to us, backed by the Holy Spirit to get the work done. While you stand in your authority, the whole heaven stands with you to put the host of darkness to flight.

It is therefore now your responsibility to rise in the power of the Holy Ghost, use your authority, rule over and root out Satan and his demonic forces from your territory in the Name of Jesus Christ. In God's kingdom, your authority always reveals your dominion, while your dominion manifests your rule over your divine goodly heritage in Christ Jesus. God gave Jeremiah dominion over nations and said to him:

"Behold! I have this day set you over the nations and over the kingdoms, to root out, and to pull down, and to destroy, and to throw down, to build, and to plant."

Jeremiah 1:10 MKJV

In line with the sequences in this book, let us once again examine two words from the above scripture. They are 'nations' and 'kingdom.'

The word *'nations'* was derived from the Hebrew word *'Goy.'* It has other translations like gentile, heathen, and people.

The word *'kingdom'* was translated from another Hebrew word *'Mamlakah.'* Other interpretations inferred from it are 'kingdom, dominion, realm, reign and sovereignty.'

In other words, God's instruction to Jeremiah was, he has been chosen by Him to have sovereignty and dominion over all realms of the heathen nations, to annex and possess them as his kingdom territories for God.

Who are heathens? They are unbelieving people, totally separated from God. Their lifestyles do not comply with God's ways. They are people under the control of the god of this world, in bondage under the satanic hosts. God sent Jeremiah to root out satanic influences over their affairs, whatever they may be.

Similarly, today, God's directive to Jeremiah is still relevant to His children in the Church, particularly you. His message is, He has 'now' set you over kingdoms and governments that do not align with His purposes and plans in this world as it was in the days of Jeremiah.

Satan and his hosts have influences over the leaders of the nations of the world to execute evilness; however, you have the mandate from God, the Creator of heaven and earth to conquer.

When were you given the mandate? You received the mandate on the day you received Jesus Christ as your Lord and Saviour; you became a citizen of God's kingdom. Today you have been set over any satanic system that once enslaved you. Hallelujah!

For what purpose have you been chosen? Firstly, you have been chosen to root out, pull down, destroy, and throw down everything satanic hosts stand for in your world. Secondly, God wants you build and plant His intentions within your domain.

The words translated 'root out' came from the Hebrew word 'Nathash.' They have other renditions like 'to pull up, expel, root out and pluck up.'

Also, the words translated 'pull down' were derived from another Hebrew word, 'Nathats.' Other interpretations derived from them are to break down, cast down, throw down, beat down, destroy, overthrow and break out'.

Additionally, the words 'to destroy' were construed from the Hebrew word 'Abad.' It has other translations like 'perish, vanish, go astray and be destroyed'.

Lastly, the words 'to throw down' were also translated from the Hebrew word 'Haras'. It is also reded as 'to tear down, break down, overthrow, beat down, break, break through, destroy, pluck down, pull down, throws down, ruined, destroyer, utterly'.

Now, let give some new meanings to the above interpretations to get a better understanding. They mean that God has assigned you to expel and fully destroy every satanic reign over your world and other people's life across the globe.

There is no kingdom without people, and there are no people without a kingdom. So, the kingdoms and nations in Jeremiah 1:10 were not referring to an empty geographical space but to the inhabitants.

God has not only assigned you to expel and destroy utterly Satan's works over all the nations of the world, but you are also called to build and plant. What should you build and plant? Before we look at the answer to this question let us see other renditions from the words, 'to build' and 'to plant'.

The words *'to build'* were derived from the Hebrew word *'Banah.'* They were also reded as to build, rebuild, establish, and cause to continue.

The words *'to plant'* came from the Hebrew word *'Nata'*. Also, they have other interpretations like 'to plant, fasten, fix and establish'.

From here, you can see that as you expel and destroy completely satanic works over the nations of the world, God wants you to replace what you have destroyed with His will and righteousness and securely fastened, fixed, and established them.

In this context, what are God's will and righteousness? They are the benefits of the good news of God's kingdom. Give people the good news. Let them know that God wants to reconcile with them through His Son Jesus Christ, the Redeemer, and let their sorrows be replaced with the joy of the Lord. Where there has been despair and death, let there be an exchange with the hope and life of God in Christ Jesus. Where a curse exists in the land, supplant it with blessings.

Afterwards, fasten what you have reconstructed in the lives of people through reorientation in line with God's purpose for them. Carefully note, this was the same assignment God gave to Adam. He was instructed to **REPLENISH**; that is, refill and bring back to original position. Today, God wants you to bring people back to the place of sound knowledge of His will and purpose in Christ.

Do you realise that after Jesus Christ triumphantly dealt with Satan and his demons and finished His works, He gave to every believer the authority of His Name and instructed them to go and teach nations all He has commanded? You are a commissioned member of His Church; He says to you:

"... All authority is given to Me in Heaven and in earth. Therefore, go and teach all nations, baptizing them in the name of the Father and of the Son and of the Holy Spirit, teaching them to observe all things, whatever I commanded you. And behold, I am with you all the days until the end of the world. Amen."

Matthew 28:18-20 MKJV

God has called, chosen, and given you a lifetime primary assignment. Arise, obey His commandment, and make a triumphant warrior's move; build and plant His kingdom by the authority of Jesus' Name in the very place you are right now.

Do not delay anymore; now, spread your dominion over your entire neighbourhood, city, nation, and continent and manifest your reign. Rule and root out all satanic hosts. Plant and build God's righteousness in the Name of Jesus Christ.

Now, you have been nominated as God's ambassador on earth, to rule and reign over the very particular place you are presently. Hence, occupy your position.

Chapter 14

You Are An Ambassador Of God's Kingdom

Every government on earth has representatives in other nations of the world. These representatives are called ambassadors and diplomats. The pattern is the same in the kingdom of God.

An ambassador is a person, a minister of the highest rank in the designated foreign country. He is the senior representative of a government in the country,; he is chosen and sent forth by a sovereign ruler and commissioned with a legal authority to transact business on behalf of his country with the government of his assigned foreign country.

He is supposed to be faithful to the leader that has sent him on assignment and should not become entangled with the customs of the nation of his assignment, even though he may be familiar with their cultures.

His work base in the foreign country is called embassy. At an appointed time, by the discretion of his nation's leader, he could be recalled from the nation of his assignment to his home country to give account of his stewardship.

Christian, you are an ambassador of everything God's kingdom stands for in the world of man. You are a minister of the highest ranking and the senior representative of the kingdom of God on earth.

You are not in this world by accident or just to exist. God has sent you forth on a legal divine mission; you possess the authority of heaven to transact God's business on earth.

You became God's ambassador the very day you received Jesus Christ as your Lord and Saviour. Consequently, you are supposed to be faithful to the Person that has chosen and sent you. You should not be entangled with the affairs and customs of this world.

On the day you were commissioned by Jesus Christ, He said to you:

"...as my Father hath sent me, even so send I you."
John 20:21 KJV

Where are you sent? You are sent to the nations of the world as an emissary of Jesus Christ and His kingdom; He is the supreme Leader of the kingdom. You have been sent on a mission to where you are right now.

Apostle Paul realized this fact and said: *"...I am an ambassador..."*
Ephesians 6:20 KJV

Then again, he said to the Christians in Corinth that:

"...we are ambassadors on behalf of Christ..."
2 Corinthians 5:20 MKJV

You are God's kingdom ambassador and your time is limited in the place of your assignment on earth. Because your time is short here on earth, you shall soon be called back to heaven, your home country to give a full account of your stewardship. So how you spend your time in the place where you are now, which is the place of your assignment, is very crucial.

Time moves on momentarily without waiting for anyone. Hence, you should always be watchful to catch up with it and be prompt when it is now. Seize the opportunity and do the works you have been assigned to do as a representative of God's kingdom on earth.

Types Of Ambassadorial Rankings

> *Ambassador Extraordinary*
> He/she is a diplomat of the highest rank sent on a special mission and accredited as a permanent representative to another country or sovereign.

> *Ambassador Plenipotentiary*
> He/she is a diplomat of the first rank with treaty-signing powers.

> *Ambassador At Large*
> He/she is an ambassador with special duties who may be sent to more than one government during the term of his assignment.

> *Envoy*
> He/she is an accredited representative or agent. He/she is a person sent on a mission to represent the interests of someone else, or an organization.

The above are special ambassadorial rankings representing the interest of their home nations in another nation or in an organization as special representatives. These distinguished ambassadorial positions are like the fivefold ministry that Paul described in *Ephesians 4:11*. These ministries are special gifts to the Body of Christ and God's kingdom.

Dear reader, all these are what you are for Christ Jesus in this world. Are you called to be an apostle, or a prophet, or an evangelist, or a pastor, or a teacher? Are you in help ministry's works within the Body of Christ? Maybe you are just a lay member of the Body of Christ? Whatever your role may be in the Church, you are an ambassador for God.

Primary Duties Of An Ambassador

Every ambassador representing a nation, or an organization has some specific duties that must be executed at their places of assignments. The duties are to:

- ➢ Protects Their Country's Interests And Policies Against Any Other

- ➢ Sustains Diplomatic Relationship Between Their Nation And The Host Country

- ➢ Engages In Public Relations Between The Two Nations

- ➢ Educates To Uphold Their Country's Policies In The Host Nation

- ➢ Engages In Consultatory Role For Their Country

- ➢ Governs On Behalf Of Their Nation's Leader

- ➢ Protects The Rights And Welfare Of The Citizens Of Their Home Country In The Host Nation

- ➢ Preserves The Heritage And Culture Of Their Home Nation

Protects His Country's Interests And Policies Against Any Other

An ambassador, with rightness should protect the interest of his nation, according to the policies of the ruler and the constitution of his land in the nation of his assignment. He is supposed to have a clear separation between his nation's interest and personal ones, to avoid a clash of interest.

As a Christian, your home nation is in heaven above, where God dwells, and the place of your assignments are the nations of the earth; particularly where you are right now.

One of the cogent assignments of an ambassador is to protect the interest of his nation and the policies of the ruler that sent him on assignment with rightness. Likewise, it is your duty as a citizen of God's kingdom to protect the interest of Jesus Christ who is your ultimate Ruler in righteousness.

What are the policies of the Lord Jesus Christ? The summary of His policies is, 'SALVATION' to all mankind by the preaching of the 'GOSPEL', and win SOULS! SOULS! SOULS!

God's interest and policies lie in His plans for all humanity across the globe to be 'SAVED.' He does not discriminate based on the colour of their skin, status or languages in order to save them. He wants all mankind saved within the dispensation of grace before it is too late. The scripture says in Proverbs and 2Peter:

"...my delights were with the sons of men."

Proverbs 8:31 KJV

"The Lord is not slack concerning his promise, as some men count slackness; but is longsuffering to us-ward, not willing that any should perish, but that all should come to repentance."

2 Peter 3:9 KJV

Because God is delighted in you, He sent His Christian labourers to preach the gospel to you. While you heard the gospel and repented of your sin and surrendered your life to Him, He forgave all your sins and saved your soul. Today you are His child; an ambassador of His kingdom, to the world.

Similarly, He takes pleasure in the people where you are right now and wants to save their souls. It does not matter what the world has called them, He is interested in them.

They could have been named murderers, yet He is interested in them. Possibly, they are coloured evil; He is interested in them. Perhaps, they have been rejected and cast away by their communities; He is interested in them. They may be rich or poor; He is interested in them. They may be white or black, green or yellow, orange or purple; He is interested in them all.

God is not a respecter of persons. He loves and delights in every single soul on earth, whether they are Christians or non-Christians. He wants them to hear the good news of His redemption plan in Jesus Christ. According to *2 Peter 3:9,* God is *"not willing that any should perish, but that all should come to repentance." KJV*

God's interest and policies should be your delight to protect at all times. His interest and policies should be your primary interest and policies, to reach out to the people in your territory, and preach the gospel of His kingdom to them, and win their souls.

Many kingdoms of the world are governed by oppression to exhibit evilness. A lot of people in this world groan under the burdens of the repressive rule of many leaders in their nations. They are subjugated under great burdens of difficulties, too much for their souls to bear. Jesus Christ wants you to let them see the difference between their current kingdom and God's kingdom that you represent. If they spot the difference, they can reconcile with God and cross over into His domain.

Therefore, Holy Spirit says through Apostle Paul:

"...God exhorting through us, we beseech you on behalf of Christ, be reconciled to God."
2 Corinthians 5:20 MKJV

"For our conversation is in heaven; from whence also we look for the Savior, the Lord Jesus Christ:"
Philippians 3:20 KJV

The word translated *'conversation'* in *Philippians 3:20* above is a Greek word *'Politeuma.'* It also reded as, a community and commonwealth of citizenship.

They indicate that even though you are locally resident in your neighbourhood, however, you belong to a community that is larger than your vicinity. This community is not earthly, it is heavenly based. It is beyond what the human mind can comprehend. It is spiritual; it is glorious.

Hence, see your current vicinity as your assigned territory. Engage yourself with the interest and policies of your Sovereign King, Jesus Christ. Increase His domain all over your acquired territory and spread the gospel of His kingdom all over, to accomplish your ambassadorial duties.

Sustains Diplomatic Relationship Between His Nation And The Host Country

Another primary duty of an ambassador is to maintain diplomacy between his home country and the nation of his assignment. What is diplomacy? It is the method and pattern of conducting relations between one state and another, by engaging tactful and subtle skill, in order to resolve or altogether avert enmity by peaceful means. In other words, it is negotiating alliances, agreements, treaties between nations peacefully.

If you look at the world today, there is turmoil everywhere; confusion is here and there. The world is in a state of perplexity and all leaders do not have the right answers. They do not understand why the world is always in a state of shock and horror everywhere, all the time.

You should know better than many leaders of this world. You are aware of the origin of the issues, and you know where the solutions can be found.

The issues did not begin with man. It has its origin with Satan when he rebelled against God ever before man was created. Subtly he deceived Adam by Eve and robbed him of his godly heritage, including his dominion over the earth; consistently, he succeeded in setting all generations of man against God, their Maker. Since then, ignorance, confusion, turmoil and perplexity have been in the world.

God has now provided a solution by Jesus Christ's ultimate sacrifice on the cross. His suffering, His battered flesh, His shed off blood and His agonizing cry of *"IT IS FINISHED"* have paid the price to reconcile man to God.

Sickness, diseases and infirmities are consequences of sin. Jesus' body was lacerated so that diseases, infirmities and sicknesses would no longer have dominion over your body.

Stripes of wounds were laid on Jesus Christ's body so that everyone that believes in Him would be healed. Diseases, infirmities and sicknesses were initially strangers to man, they were not part of him at the beginning. Today they are venomous intruders, and whenever they manifest in the body of any man, the result is always painful and devastating, and sometimes fatal.

Jesus Christ shed His blood to atone for the sins of the world once and for all; therefore, the world can have peace with God. His agonizing cry of "It is finished" has put an end to whatever enmity that may be between humanity and God. Sins are forgiven and their consequences are removed in Him, and reconciliation is heretofore in place today.

"For it pleased the Father that in him should all fullness dwell; And, having made peace through the blood of his cross, by him to reconcile all things unto himself; by him, I say, whether they be things in earth, or things in heaven. And you, that were sometime alienated and enemies in your mind by wicked works, yet now hath he reconciled."
Colossians 1:19-21 KJV

"And that he might reconcile both unto God in one body by the cross, having slain the enmity thereby: And came and preached peace to you which were afar off, and to them that were nigh."
Ephesians 2:16-17 KJV

In the above scriptures, the word translated *'reconcile'* is from the Greek word *'Apokatallasso.'* It has other translations like a 'full reconciliation or to bring back to a former state of harmony.' This is what God and His Son Jesus Christ have done for all mankind.

God's intention through His Son, Jesus Christ is to bring back every man to the former state of harmony with Him. God wants to have a relationship with an average man in the world today, by peaceful means. Therefore, God has appointed you, Christian as His diplomat to take His message of reconciliation to an average person you come across in life.

Jesus Christ is the Intermediary of peace between God and man. He negotiated the peace treaty and signed it with His precious sacred blood. You have been chosen to let the people of the world know that the peace treaty has been put in place and God wants reconciliation, now.

So, as God's diplomat, extend God's diplomacy to whosoever comes across your path in life. Let them know that God wants to be at peace with them and not at war. The time of enmity is past, and the era of peace and harmony is here. Would you indeed be God's ambassador?

Engages In Public Relations Between The Two Nations

Public Relation is another primary duty of an ambassador. It is one of the cogent duties of his office.

Now, what is public relation? Public relation is the practice of creating, promoting, or maintaining goodwill and a favourable image of an institution, public body, etc. among the public. It can also be between two nations or a nation and many nations.

A public relation officer is the plain window glass through which the public see into the world of his organization. He could be said to be an image appearing in the mirror to people. The image in the mirror is not the original, however, it is a picture of what the real thing looks like.

If you want to have a first impression of what an organization is all about, you can get it through its public relation officer. He is the billboard through which anyone can gather some information about his organization.

He is like a beam of light that wants to penetrate through the darkness in people's minds, to give information on the objectives of his organization. Until now, people may be ignorant of what his organization does. Public relation officer is the one that sells his organization to the public. Summarily, the public relation officer is image the launderer for his organization.

Likewise, an ambassador is an image launderer for his country in the nation of his assignment. He is the number one public figure that foreign nations can gather information about his country from, and then form their opinions.

So, Christian, you are an ambassador for Jesus Christ; you are an image launderer for the kingdom of heaven in the nation where you are now and where you may be in the world in the future.

You are the glass through which unbelievers can see Jesus Christ. You are the sign board where they can find out some information about God's kingdom and what Jesus Christ has done for them on the cross, to form their opinions. For sure, you are the light through which the world of darkness can see the light of God's glory.

Until now, millions of people across the world are ignorant of who God is and what His plans are for their lives. Some have tried to see God through the glass of Islam that Muhammad and the Qur'an have given them. As a result, they have presented a god of hatred by their religion; they have spattered abroad unforgiveness and bitterness on the hearts of many, while death reigns over them instead of life; whereas, the only true God is love, forgiving, and compassionate.

Many have tried to know the plans of God for their lives through the glass of Buddhism, Hinduism and Rosicrucianism. The results have been emptiness upon emptiness for their souls.

Some have also tried to understand God through the glass of paganism and other religious movements, thinking they could find Him. The experiments have not led them to the Living God but into satanism and eternal damnation.

Countless numbers of people are dying daily, thinking they would pass from death to life through their religion and self-righteousness. They have not known or embraced Jesus Christ as the Lord and Saviour of their souls. Hence, the outcome has been eternal disappointments for their souls and eternal separation from the only True God.

Therefore, as an ambassador for Christ, and a member of God's kingdom, let people see the rays of the light of Jesus Christ that is beaming through you and glorify God. Jesus Christ said,

"You are the light of the world. A city that is set on a hill cannot be hidden. Nor do men light a lamp and put it under the grain-measure, but on a lampstand. And it gives light to all who are in the house. Let your light so shine before men that they may see your good works and glorify your Father who is in Heaven."
Matthew 5:14-16 KJV

Another duty of a public relation officer is to collect people's opinions about his organization and present them to his organization for deliberations.

By now you know that people have different opinions about the God of Christians and what He did through Jesus Christ. As God's ambassador, you are not incommunicado with heaven. You always have access to God's throne room momentarily. Present their opinions to God in prayer and ask Him to open their eyes of understanding and spectacularly reveal Himself to them, and turn their situations around.

Opinions are things of the mind. Many times, opinions express what strongholds Satan is using to hold people captive. Wage spiritual war against the satanic hosts and shatter the strongholds; cast down any contrary knowledge and imaginations about God.

Then, people will come to know the only True and Living God; they will understand His plans and purposes for their lives, and receive His Son, Jesus Christ as their Lord and Saviour, and glorify

His Name. In consequence, you will easily conquer and dominate the territory for God.

Educates People To Uphold His Country's Policies In The Host Nation

An ambassador's role would not complete if he does not rightly educate his host nation on the objectives of his nation, in order to uphold his country's policies. People in the nation of his assignment are ignorant of what his nation's policies are and might have formed wrong opinions about his country. Their opinions may not be based on an authentic first-hand account of how things function daily—socially, economically and politically.

It is the duty of an ambassador to furnish the people of the nation where he is assigned with accurate knowledge of things in his home country. Therefore, people, by him need to be educated.

Education is a method of refinement. The ambassador must refine people's minds for them to know and have better understanding what his home country is all about.

Alongside, people of the world must be well-educated on what goes on in God's kingdom you represent as an ambassador. Some people would come to you to get some information for them to make up their minds. As soon as their minds are made up to join you, let them be properly educated. In the process, you must uphold God's standard.

The Queen of Sheba heard some information about the kingdom of Solomon. Instead of depending on some second-hand information she had received from people, she went directly to Solomon to get first-hand information and acquire more knowledge.

"And when the queen of Sheba heard of the fame of Solomon concerning the name of the LORD, she came to prove him with hard questions. And she came to Jerusalem with a very great train, with camels that bore spices, and very much gold, and precious stones: and when she was come to Solomon, she communed with

him of all that was in her heart. And Solomon told her all her questions: there was not any thing hid from the king, which he told her not. And when the queen of Sheba had seen all Solomon's wisdom, and the house that he had built, And the meat of his table, and the sitting of his servants, and the attendance of his ministers, and their apparel, and his cupbearers, and his ascent by which he went up unto the house of the LORD; there was no more spirit in her."

1 Kings 10:1-5 KJV

After her visit to Solomon and received actual information about Solomon and his kingdom, she said,

"And she said to the king, It was a true report that I heard in mine own land of thy acts and of thy wisdom. Howbeit I believed not the words, until I came, and mine eyes had seen it: and, behold, the half was not told me: thy wisdom and prosperity exceedeth the fame which I heard."

1 Kings 10:6-7 KJV

As seen in the above scriptures, the Queen of Sheba came to learn wisdom at Solomon's feet, and she learned more than what she was told previously.

Education is a process of learning, and it has many gradual stages in order to achieve intended results. As Christ's ambassador your intention and desired result should be for the people of the nation where you reside to receive Jesus Christ and become members of the kingdom of God. Knowing and receiving Jesus Christ as Saviour is the major policy of God's kingdom; it must be upheld by you and other Christians.

Education on God's kingdom should be offered to people without any prequalification. Everyone is qualified to come just the way they are. Is he a murderer? Let him come, just the way he is. Is he a reject of the society? Let him come. Is he poor or rich? Let him come. Is he black, yellow, orange, green, white complexioned? Let him come. Is he a great sinner like Apostle Paul? Let him come, just the way he is. He will not be rejected; he will not be cast out.

Educate and impart the knowledge of God's kingdom to them and uphold His righteous policies. They will serve Jesus Christ in the fear of God, by grace and be blessed.

The Lord Jesus Christ says to such:

"Come unto me, all ye that labor and are heavy laden, and I will give you rest. Take my yoke upon you, and <u>learn</u> of me; for I am meek and lowly in heart: and ye shall find rest unto your souls. For my yoke is easy, and my burden is light."

Matthew 11:28-30 KJV

Isaiah also prophesied:

"Ho, everyone who thirsts, come to the waters; and he who has no money, come, buy and eat. Yea, come, buy wine and milk without money and without price."

Isaiah 55:1 MKJV

Jesus Christ's message to all mankind in *Matthew 11:28-30* is, *"Everyone come."* It is all-inclusive; no one is left out. He said they should come and learn.

The word *'learn'* was translated from the Greek word *'Manthano.'* It has other words translation like, to increase knowledge, understand, be informed and get accustomed to.

Prophet Isaiah also said *"come."* Also, education is a process whereby knowledge is increased.

The kingdom of God is the only kingdom that everyone is free to come without fear of being turned back. Let them come, just the way they are.

Like the Queen of Sheba went to Solomon and was not turned back, and she learned of Solomon's wisdom and kingdom, let people come and learn of Jesus Christ at your feet. As you educate them and uphold God's standard, you are gradually removing satanic blindness and influences from their life, and conquering your territory for Jesus Christ.

Engages In Consultatory Role For His Country

Consultation is another role an ambassador must engage in if he is to succeed in his assignment.

What is consultation? It is a conference between two or more people to consider a question or seek advice or exchange information. It could be with anyone.

Because an ambassador is the highest representative of his country, the question that may be asked could revolve around the state or policies of his nation. The advice or the answer he gives could make the people in his host country take the next step, either positive or negative towards his country.

All the nations of the world are a Christian's places of assignments. Nations have questions that are not yet answered. They have problems that are yet to be resolved. They have wounds that are yet to be healed. They have pains that are yet to be relieved. They are engaged in wars yet to be overcome.

As an ambassador for Christ Jesus, you should always be ready to give answers to their hearts' probing and minds' searching questions by Holy Ghost. The answer you give must always lead them to the cross of Jesus Christ and point them towards the kingdom of God.

The prophet Isaiah said this:

"Arise, shine; for your light has come, and the glory of Jehovah has risen on you. For behold, the darkness shall cover the earth, and gross darkness the peoples; but Jehovah shall rise on you, and His glory shall be seen on you. And the nations shall come to your light, and kings to the brightness of your dawning."
Isaiah 60:1-3 MKJV

In the above scripture, God is saying you should rise and shine because His glory is upon you and nations and kings are coming to you. Why are they coming? Just like Queen of Sheba when she came to Solomon for advice and answers, people will come to you with their troubles and confusion.

Remember the whole world today is in gross darkness, reeling back and forth in perplexity. Nations and kings of the world are looking for solutions at all cost. The leaders are confused and do not have lasting right answers. Unfortunately, answers are not where they are searching. The answers are in the kingdom of God; the true Church of Jesus Christ holds the answers.

Surely, You and I, Christians across the globe have the solutions. Look at what happened to Joseph in Egypt. The leaders of Egypt and their magicians did not have answers to the heart-searching and mind probing dreams of Pharaoh. Only Joseph did.

Christian, today, you are a type of Joseph. As he was God's ambassador to the world in his generation, you should be. God gave him Egypt as his nation of assignment. He had answers to their perplexed situations; while he gave solutions, people sought him out, and he became a force to be reckoned with.

"Then Pharaoh sent and called Joseph. And they hurried him out of the dungeon. And he shaved and changed his clothing, and came in to Pharaoh...And Joseph said to Pharaoh... And the thing was good in the eyes of Pharaoh, and in the eyes of all his servants. "
Genesis 41:37 MKJV

Likewise, Daniel while in Babylon.

"...And the decree went forth that the wise men should be slain; and they sought Daniel and his fellows to be slain. Then Daniel answered with counsel and wisdom to Arioch the captain of the king's guard, which was gone forth to slay the wise men of Babylon:...Then Daniel went to his house, and made the thing known to Hananiah, Mishael, and Azariah, his companions: That they would desire mercies of the God of heaven concerning this secret; that Daniel and his fellows should not perish with the rest of the wise men of Babylon. Then was the secret revealed unto Daniel in a night vision. Then Daniel blessed the God of

heaven...The king answered and said to Daniel, whose name was Belteshazzar, Art thou able to make known unto me the dream which I have seen, and the interpretation thereof? Daniel answered in the presence of the king, and said, The secret which the king hath demanded cannot the wise men, the astrologers, the magicians, the soothsayers, show unto the king; But there is a God in heaven that revealeth secrets, and maketh known to the king Nebuchadnezzar what shall be in the latter days. Thy dream, and the visions of thy head upon thy bed, Are these;"

Daniel 2:1-28 KJV

After Daniel had revealed the dream and gave answers to the King of Babylon's heart-probing questions, how did the king response?

"The king answered unto Daniel, and said, Of a truth it is, that your God is a God of gods, and a Lord of kings, and a revealer of secrets, seeing thou couldest reveal this secret."

Daniel 2:47 KJV

And Daniel's answers pointed Nebuchadnezzar to the God of Israel, and the king worshipped the Almighty God.

So, fellow Christian, arise, take charge and conquer your territory. Put yourself in the position God has ordained for you and start using the gifts of the Holy Spirit you have been gifted. Let your mouth bring forth wisdom and your lips righteousness. People will come and seek knowledge of God's kingdom from you.

Like Joseph and Daniel, who knew that they were God's highest representatives in Egypt and Babylon respectively, and they conquered their nations of assignment, you are also God's ambassador where you are now. Let your mouth bring forth wisdom as the people of the world come to you for consultation.

"The mouth of the just brings forth wisdom; but the perverse tongue shall be cut out."

Proverb 10:31 MKJV

Governs On Behalf Of His Nation's Leader

An ambassador has a governing power that the nation of his assignment recognizes on behalf of his country. Because of the executive powers vested in him from his home country, he becomes a respected authority and a force in his nation of assignment.

He is accorded the title of and addressed as "His Highness" and act on behalf of his leader and nation with dignity. He is free to use his ambassadorial powers within his jurisdiction, according to the stated rules allowed by his home country and his nation.

When his ambassadorial office privileges are not respected by the host nation, it could result in a diplomatic collision. The query of violation of rights could be raised by his home country against his country of assignment.

Likewise, as God's ambassador, you are a *"Highness"* where you are, and you should be respected. You have been endued with power and authority from heaven above to act on behalf of Jesus Christ on earth.

You possess God's Kingdom authority and power to govern on behalf of Christ within your territory. You are in the position to execute God's judgment and command on any part of the earth.

Wherever you are now, the power and authority of God is with you. You do not need permission from anyone on earth to execute these powers. You have been endowed with the most powerful power on earth and your office must be respected everywhere you go. You are an institution that must be highly esteemed.

As Jesus Christ said, any principality and power that does not obey your decree would be judged spiritually and ruthlessly dealt with.

"...I beheld Satan as lightning fall from heaven. Behold, I give unto you power to tread on serpents and scorpions, and over all the power of the enemy: and nothing shall by any means hurt you."

Luke 10:18-19 KJV

"And these signs shall follow them that believe; In my name shall they cast out devils; they shall speak with new tongues; They shall take up serpents; and if they drink any deadly thing, it shall not hurt them; they shall lay hands on the sick, and they shall recover."

Mark 16:17-18 KJV

Your Majesty, dear Heavenly Ambassador, the powers you possess make the rulers of this age tremble and flee at your order. Due to this, you are unstoppable by any demonic principalities and powers. At your utterance, they must obey your authority in Christ Jesus.

Your divine authority and power are for you to govern and dominate your territory. Put Satan and his hosts where they belong under your feet, and then reign in life over your territory and preserve your divine goodly heritage for God.

Protects The Rights And Welfare Of The Citizens Of His Home Country In The Host Nation

Furthermore, an ambassador, in his obligation towards his home country must ensure that fellow citizens of his home country are well treated in the country of his assignment.

It would amount to inhumanness and negligence of duty for an ambassador to learn about his fellow home nation's citizen mistreatment in the country of his assignment and look the other way. If such mistreatment to any of his fellow home nation's citizens occurs, it is the duty of the ambassador to take up the matter with the authority of his country of assignment for diplomatic redress .

When a citizen of his home country is in trouble, it is the duty of an ambassador and his staff members to provide adequate help as much as possible for them. His fellow citizen is not supposed to be abandoned in his plight in the foreign country.

Besides, as God's ambassador all the above obligations apply to you. You have spiritual responsibilities to know the welfare of your fellow Christian brethren in all facets of life. As a citizen of heaven, you, including other Christians are foreigners on earth. Heaven is our home and the nations of the world are our places of assignments.

Have you seen your fellow Christian brethren under a heavy burden of life in this world? It is your responsibility to lift his burden through prayers and other benevolence acts.

Have you seen a Christian under afflictions of sickness, diseases and infirmities? It is your duty, as God's ambassador to elevate them by prayers; rebuke the demonic spirits of affliction and set your brethren free.

Have you seen or heard that Christians within your reach are in challenging circumstances? Reach out to them and show them godly care.

You are God's ambassador in this world, firstly to your family and home; and secondarily to your Christian brethren, and then to the rest of the world. Make yourself available and let heaven minister relief through you.

Our Lord Jesus Christ narrated a story to confirm this message. It is the story of a good Samaritan.

"And answering, Jesus said, A certain man went down from Jerusalem to Jericho and fell among robbers, who stripped him of his clothing and wounded him, and departed, leaving him half dead. And by coincidence a certain priest came down that way and seeing him, he passed by on the opposite side. And in the same way a Levite, also being at the place, coming and seeing him, he passed on the opposite side. But a certain traveling Samaritan came upon him, and seeing him, he was filled with pity. And coming near, he bound up his wounds, pouring on oil and wine, and set him on his own animal and brought him to an inn, and took care of him. And going on the next day, he took out two denarii and gave them to the innkeeper, and said to him, Take care of him. And whatever more

you spend, when I come again I will repay you. Then which of these three, do you think, was neighbor to him who fell among the robbers? And he said, The one doing the deed of mercy to him. And Jesus said to him, Go and do likewise."

Luke 10:30-37 MKJV

The priest and Levite in the above scripture saw their fellow countryman lying helplessly after the enemies' attacks. As they came down the route at different times, they turned their blind eyes and refused to have pity on the man. They recognized his helpless situation, however, they passed on the opposite side.

Sadly, every person that was supposed to offer help in the above story failed in their primary duty as ambassadors of their country, while they refused to attend to their fellow country's man's desperate needs.

Alike, many Christians today are going through many satanic attacks, and they groan under pains. Supposedly by coincidence, have you come across any of them within your territory? Some of them could be people you see frequently or total strangers. What righteous works have done to minister to their needs?

Beloved Christian ambassador, let your eyes be opened to their plights; make a move to attend to their needs, either through prayers or deeds of love. Do not pass by on the opposite side. God has appointed you His ambassador and positioned you where they are right now to see their needs.

Jesus Christ, the Leader of your heavenly home country, according to the above scripture is saying to you, ***"Go and do likewise."*** Rebuke the devils from their lives and set them free; thereby fulfill your ministry.

Preserves The Culture And Heritage Of His Home Nation

One of the components of what makes up a nation and distinguishes her from other nations is their ethnic heritages. These manifest in their beliefs, ideas, religions, values, social and knowledge; ergo they are the common foundations of their social life.

Oftentimes, these ethnic heritages manifest in all areas of their life. A man may be residence in a nation, even though his ethnic heritage differs, however, his residency does not make him a citizen of the nation. He could only become a citizen either by birth, claiming the nation as a place of birth if the law allows him, or by parentage links to the country, or by naturalization.

Due to common ethnic heritages, people from the same country may like to establish a living community in another nation in order to keep the ethnic heritages of their home nation. They do this in order to preserve their ethnic heritages for posterity and for other beneficial reasons.

This makes Asians, in particular stand out of many races that may be in any foreign nation. Many people of Asian origins, even though may integrate into a foreign nation of residence's lifestyles, nonetheless, still prefer community living in order to preserve their ethnic heritages for posterity.

Jews are another typical example of ethnic community living. While many races in a foreign nation are losing their ethnic heritages fast, Jews have been able to keep theirs intact, despite their integration into a foreign society.

It will be very wrong for an ambassador not to maintain the ethnic heritages of his home country in his host nation. Even though he lives in a foreign land, far away from his home nation, it is part of his obligation to maintain and preserve the ethnic heritages of his nation in the foreign land.

In the same sense, as God's ambassador part of your duty is to maintain and preserve the heritages of God's kingdom on earth. The heritages of God's kingdom are different from the ethnic heritages of the nations of this world. In many ways, they clash with world's ethnic heritages.

God's Kingdom heritages, as outlined in the Bible must manifest in your beliefs, ideas, social, values and knowledge. Accordingly, the heritages will form your actions and manifest in your conduct among the people of the world.

In order to preserve His kingdom heritages, in Leviticus 18:24, God gave a strict warning to the children of Israel not to mingle with the people in the promised land they were about to conquer.

"Do not defile yourselves in any of these things. For in all these the nations are defiled, which I cast out before you."

Leviticus 18:24 MKJV

God said through Moses, *"Do not defile yourselves in any of these things."* 'These things' includes the cultural heritages of the initial people in the promised land. Why did God say so? It is because the cultural heritages of these nations were abomination to God. And God was raising up Israel as His people and nation to impact the whole world with His kingdom heritages.

On the same note, Paul, the apostle says:

"And be not <u>conformed</u> to this world: but be ye transformed by the renewing of your mind, that ye may prove what is that good, and acceptable, and perfect, will of God."

Romans 12:2 KJV

"This I say therefore, and testify in the Lord, that ye henceforth <u>walk</u> not as other Gentiles walk, in the vanity of their mind, Having the understanding darkened, being alienated from the life of God through the ignorance that is in them, because of the blindness of their heart:"

Ephesians 4:17-18 KJV

From *Romans 12:2*, the word *'conformed'* was translated from the Greek word *'Suschematizo'*. It has another translation like, fashion alike.

Likewise, the word *'walk'* in *Ephesians 4:17* was translated from the Greek word *'Peripateo.'* It has other translations like to live, to follow, to be occupied with, tread all around, etc.

God's impression in the above scriptures was that as an ambassador of His kingdom, the world is a foreign land to you, no matter where you are. You must not compromise nor fashion your life after worldly lifestyles. You must live to follow and imbibe the heritage and culture of God's kingdom.

As soon as all ramifications of your life truly exhibits the heritages and culture of God's kingdom, the difference will be clearer to the people around, and they will be magnetized to the kingdom. Although ethnic heritages and culture are the cornerstone for social integration and relationship among nations, howbeit, let your life reflect the heritages and culture of God's kingdom. People will be blessed, and God will be glorified.

Benefits Of The Office Of An Ambassador

An ambassador enjoys certain prerogative benefits in the nation of his assignment. The benefits are outlined as follows:

- ➤ Diplomatic Immunity From The Law Of The Host Country
- ➤ Consistence Sustenance By His Home Country
- ➤ Legally Protected While He Resides In The Host Country
- ➤ Principal Link Between His Country And The Host Nation
- ➤ Prerogative Powers To Act On Behalf Of His Country
- ➤ Dominion Over A Specific Territory Within Another Nation

Diplomatic Immunity From The Law Of The Host Country

Full diplomatic immunity from the laws of the host country of an ambassador is one of the greatest benefits he enjoys. It is a legitimate immunity that allows him safe passages at all times. If he remains a senior ranking representative of his home country, even though he lives in his host country, he is not under their rule, but under the rule of his home country.

Supposing he commits any crime in his country of assignment; whatever it may be, he is immune from prosecution by his host nation. He cannot be arrested or forced to testify in the court of law. He can only be expelled to his home country for necessary discipline. However, it is of a moral duty that he should be a worthy representative of his home country. His immunity should not be a license to crime.

Christian, this is one of your privileges on earth. As God's ambassador in this world, you are immune from the law of sin and death, and quite free from the rules unleashed by satanic hosts. Satan is the god of this world, and he and his hosts always operate under the laws of sin and death to wreak havoc on human souls. However, you are immune unreservedly from all.

The above reference is not to the government laws put in place to maintain orderliness in your society, please take note. Even though satanic hosts may manipulate people in authority to invoke evilness, nevertheless, God still allows human government for the good of all. If there is any evilness in laws, you can overturn it by prayers and intercessions and other righteous moves.

"Let every soul be subject to the higher authorities. For there is no authority but of God; the authorities that exist are ordained by God. So that the one resisting the authority resists the ordinance of God; and the ones who resist will receive judgment to themselves. For the rulers are not a terror to good works, but to the bad. And do you desire to be not afraid of the authority? Do the good, and you shall have praise from it. For it is a servant of God to you for good. For if you practice evil, be afraid, for it does not bear the sword in vain; for it is a servant of God, a revenger for wrath on him who does evil. Therefore you must be subject, not only for wrath, but also for conscience' sake. For because of this you also pay taxes. For they are God's servants, always giving attention to this very thing. Therefore give to all their dues; to the one due tax, the tax; tribute to whom tribute is due, fear to whom fear is due, and honor to whom honor is due."
Romans 13:1-7 MKJV

Satanic hosts diffuse all sorts of evilness all over the world wherever people live as they take decisions over territories on earth. Regardless, you are immuned from their vileness because you are a citizen of heaven and an ambassador of God.

Diplomatic immunity is a matter of security for an ambassador while he goes about his obligations in the host nation. In the same degree, you have divine securities as you execute God's assignment on earth. You are not restricted by the satanic kingdom's laws that may be operating anywhere in the world.

What are the components of the satanic laws? The summarized elements are confusion, ignorance, death, misery, destruction, sorrow, and wickedness. All problems in the world are summed up within these elements.

As stated earlier in chapter two, Satan and his fallen angels received these punishments from God as judgment for their insurrection. Inevitably, they bear and diffuse the aura of their punishments anywhere they are. While you are God's ambassador, your life and territory should be free from laws of confusion, ignorance, death, misery, destruction, sorrow, and wickedness.

The decisive point for the laws that operates in the kingdom of God is mercy and grace, and then peace and love. You have obtained mercy and supposed to be living under grace. Peace and love belong to you.

Have you noticed any confusion in your life? God is not the Author. Reject confusion and obtain clarity from the Holy Spirit.

Are you ignorant of God's plan for your life? Hitherto, you have Holy Spirit within you to understand the mystery of God's kingdom. Ask Him to help you understand God's plan for you.

Ignorance is a satanic weapon unleashed on the world by Satan. Due to this, many nations in the world grope in darkness today. Nevertheless, by the Holy Spirit, you can know those things that have been designedly given to you of God. Reject ignorance and receive the Spirit of understanding and spiritual eyesight.

Do you feel surrounded by the spirit of death? Jesus Christ came that you might have life in abundance. Death has been swallowed up in victory. You shall not die but live and declare the works of the Lord. Reject death and claim life from the Holy Spirit by Jesus Christ.

Are miseries of this world: sickness, diseases, and misfortunes all upon you? Jesus Christ has conquered them all on the cross. They are not supposed to hold you bound. Arise and reject the miseries and break yourself free from all their components.

Are destruction, sorrow, and wickedness targeted at you? You have an assurance that negates the laws of hell that are operating in the world. Do not let them control you, you are not under their rule anymore.

"And you, being dead in your sins and the uncircumcision of your flesh, He has made alive together with Him, having forgiven you all trespasses, blotting out the handwriting of ordinances that was against us, which was contrary to us, and has taken it out of the way, nailing it to the cross. Having stripped rulers and authorities, He made a show of them publicly, triumphing over them in it."
Colossians 2:13-15 MKJV

What is ordinance as used in the above scripture? Ordinance is law; an edict or decree or authoritative order. Thus, Jesus Christ has blotted out all ordinances of the law of sin and death by His blood; they have been nailed to His cross forever. They are not supposed to govern your life in any way; you have been immuned from them all. You are God's ambassador on earth.

Consistence Sustenance By His Home Country

Another benefit that an ambassador enjoys is his sustenance by his home country; his essential needs are supplied from his home country. He does not depend on his host country's government for his wages nor relies on their economy for his sustenance.

He sees his home government as his source. While need arises, supplies are abundantly released by his home country. So, always, he looks forward to the government of his home country to provide and take care of him categorically and satisfactorily.

Likewise, as God's eminent ambassador, God is your Source. There is an economy that heaven operates, it does not depend on man's efforts for growth. It is always supernaturally flourishing and more than enough.

An embassy and ambassador that do not tap into the resources of his home country will soon run bankrupt. You need to have this revelation and understand its principles before you can tap into it. Therefore, Paul said to God's ambassadors in Ephesus:

"Blessed be the God and Father of our Lord Jesus Christ, who hath blessed us with all spiritual blessings in heavenly places in Christ:"

Ephesians 1:3 KJV

Did you catch the revelation in *Ephesians 1:3*? *'All spiritual blessings in heavenly places in Christ'* are available for the Church. Because you are a Christian, you can claim them.

Now let us consider two words from the above scripture. They are 'blessings' and 'heavenly.'

The Greek word from which the word *'Blessings'* was interpreted was *'Eulogia.'* It is also rendered as, fine speaking, commendation, adoration, benefit, largeness, bounty, etc.

The word translated *'heavenly'* is the Greek word *'Epouranios.'* Other words interpreted from it are, beyond the sky, heavenly regions, celestial, or the place of abode of God.

The words rendered above reveal that, as God's ambassador, you have certain benefits and bounties available to you in heaven's treasury, your home country. They are beyond Satan's grab.

Furthermore, one of the words translated from the Greek word *'Eulogia'* is *'commendation.'* Among the meanings of commendation are 'an award given for very good performance' and praise or 'thanks.'

In other words, as God's ambassador, here on earth, He wants to first reward you for your very good performance on your divine assignment with those heavenly benefits. God has been waiting for you to claim them through thanksgiving. Therefore, release your praise and thanksgiving to Him for every one of them.

"Do not be anxious about anything, but in everything by prayer and supplication, with thanksgiving, let your requests be made known to God."
Philippians 4:6 MKJV

If they are not claimed, they remain where they are in the heavenly places, even though they are yours. Now is the time to begin to claim them.

I am not referring to the general providence that God showers on everyone; on both wicked and just or believer and unbeliever alike. The blessings referred to in *Ephesians 1:3* are special blessings that God has prepared for those that love Him.

"But as it is written, 'Eye has not seen, nor ear heard," nor has it entered into the heart of man, "the things which God has prepared for those who love Him.'"
1 Corinthians 2:9 MKJV

They are spiritual blessings and you cannot see them physically; your material ears have not heard about them and your heart cannot imagine them. They are mysteries that must be unfolded and understood through Holy Ghost.

"But God has revealed them to us by His Spirit; for the Spirit searches all things, yea, the deep things of God."
1 Corinthians 2:10 MKJV

Now, you have understood that they must be claimed as they are revealed to you by the Holy Ghost, because they are spiritual benefits located in your heavenly home country.

How can you make spiritual blessings manifest in the physical? It is by faith, hope, patience and leading of the Holy Ghost.

Let me use this analogy. In this modern day of technology innovations, people do not go about carrying large sum of money in bags anymore. Whenever there is any transaction, it is done by bank money transfer.

Also, when an ambassador wants to claim some supplies that are parts of his benefits, especially for his financial needs, he places a demand on his home country as stipulated in the law of his home country. In response, his home country would not go about carrying cash in bags and send to him, except in rare cases. It is done through a bank money transfer technology, or else it could be termed as money laundering, which is an offense.

Money is wired from his home country into the embassy's bank account in the host nation for disbursal. The equivalent of what was sent would be received in the currency of the country of his assignment by conversion, before it could be useful and spent.

Because he needs a confirmation from his home that the money has been sent, he would wait for it to manifests in his embassy's bank account, or in his personal bank account for withdrawal. Because he knows the sincerity of his leader and nation, he is at rest and believes all things would come through as assured.

Faith in God is very, very essential in converting spiritual blessings into the material. One of the ways you can please God is by your faith. It is the 'spiritual wire' by which heavenly blessings are transferred and converted into the material world.

"But without faith it is impossible to please Him, for he who comes to God must believe that He is and that He is a rewarder of those who diligently seek Him."

Hebrews 11:6 MKJV

Faith is the expression of conviction and confidence in God. The first thing you must have before you ask God for anything is to know His sincerity. Can God lie? Can He renege on His promises? No, He will never, God is truthful and faithful to the end.

Inclusively, you must be convinced and have confidence that He would grant your request; no matter how large or little. Now is the appropriate time; go ahead and ask. He is the God of all flesh and nothing is too hard for Him to do, especially for you.

And just as the ambassador needs to wait for the money to reflect in his embassy's account for disbursal, you must also wait in hope and have patience for answers to manifest. Never tolerate fear or anxiety, because they negate faith.

"Therefore do not cast away your confidence, which has great recompense of reward. For you have need of patience, so that after you have done the will of God you might receive the promise..."
Hebrews 10:35-38 MKJV

David caught the revelation that, as God's ambassador on earth, he is sustained by God. Thus, he said:

"I will lift up my eyes to the hills. Where shall my help come from? My help comes from Jehovah, who made Heaven and earth. He will not allow your foot to be moved; He who keeps you will not slumber. Behold, He who keeps Israel shall neither slumber nor sleep. Jehovah is your keeper; Jehovah is your shade on your right hand. The sun shall not strike you by day, nor the moon by night. Jehovah shall keep you from all evil; He shall keep your soul. Jehovah shall keep your going out and your coming in from this time forth, and even forevermore."
Psalms 121:1-8 MKJV

David knew that even though he was on earth, his sustenance did not depend on any nation's economy or man's limited resources. He was perfectly persuaded that the God of heaven was his Source. He would not allow him to be moved at any time of needs. God is sincere, He would deliver.

In case there are some delays in manifestations of answers, just continue to hold on to God with thanksgiving, without wavering, knowing that answers are on the way; definitely, they will come through.

Bible tells of Elijah, the prophet in *1Kings 18:41-45*. As God's ambassador, he wanted to dominate his territory, the nation of Israel for God, hence he decreed that there would be rain. He expected to see some signs in the sky afterwards, but nothing showed up. What did he do? He went on his knees and prayed seven times until there was a manifestation. He did not give up on God or on what he had decreed earlier.

"And Elijah said to Ahab, Go up, eat and drink, because of the sound of plenty of rain. So Ahab went up to eat and to drink. And Elijah went up to the top of Carmel. And he threw himself down on the earth and put his face between his knees. And he said to his servant, Go up now, look toward the sea. And he went up and looked and said, Nothing. And he said, Go again seven times. And it happened at the seventh time, he said, Behold, there arises a little cloud out of the sea, like a man's hand. And he said, Go up and say to Ahab, Bind up and go down, so that the rain does not stop you. And it happened in the meantime the heaven was black with clouds and wind, and there was a great rain..."
1 Kings 18:41-45 MKJV

There is nothing wrong in your continual standing in prayer when manifestations seem delayed. The only wrong thing is if you are standing in anxiety, fear, and doubt. Anxiety is the open door to fear and doubt to come in, to nullify your faith. Therefore, stand firm with thanksgiving, believing God.

In these last days, the world's economy is going through divine judgment and uncertainty is everywhere. But as God's ambassador, you are not supposed to partake in God's wrath, you have been saved from it.

The economy of heaven, your home country does not depend on the resources of this world to flourish. It is eternal and constantly replenished. It is built on heavenly resources and functions on God's eternal ordinances. The Lord Jesus Christ that put them in place says:

"Therefore do not be anxious, saying, What shall we eat? or, What shall we drink? or, With what shall we be clothed? For the nations seek after all these things. For your heavenly Father knows that

you have need of all these things. But seek first the kingdom of God and His righteousness; and all these things shall be added to you."
Matthew 6:31-33 MKJV

And Paul also emphasizes in Philippians 4:6-7 and 4:19

"Do not be anxious about anything, but in everything by prayer and supplication, with thanksgiving, let your requests be made known to God. And the peace of God which passes all understanding shall keep your hearts and minds through Christ Jesus."
Philippians 4:6-7 MKJV

"But my God shall supply all your need according to His riches in glory by Christ Jesus."
Philippians 4:19 MKJV

In the days of Elijah, the economy of Israel was going through some divine judgments. But because he was God's ambassador, God competently provided for him. He was fed in famine and was satisfied. Please read 1 King 17.

Dear Christian, you are God's ambassador. God is your Source and not to the world's leaders; thus, look up to Him. World's economic shortages and confusions cannot stop the supply of heavenly resources to you; no matter what happens, supplies will come through and you shall be satisfied in famine.

You are God's righteousness in Christ, and He shall never suffer the righteous to be moved. He shall keep your going out and coming in throughout your time in this world. He will give you peace that passes all understanding.

God has earthly strongholds, full of abundant silver and gold. They are located here and there, beyond Satan's knowledge and grips. Turn into God's strongholds now, by faith, and withdraw silver and gold to satisfy your godly desires.

Note, Satan may have the world's economy in his holds, but he does not have heaven's economy in his hands, neither does he have

God's earthly strongholds of gold and silver under his control, God has it for you to spend. Hence, He will shake the nations for your sake and abundant gold and silver shall be unleashed upon you.

"Therefore I say unto you, What things soever ye desire, when ye pray, believe that ye receive them, and ye shall have them."
Mark 11:28 KJV

The silver is Mine, and the gold is Mine, says Jehovah of Hosts.
Haggai 2:8 MKJV

"Turn to the stronghold, prisoners of hope; even today I declare that I will return to you double."
Zechariah 9:12 MKJV

Legally Protected While He Resides In The Host Country

Even though an ambassador may live in the host country for so many years, the fact remains that he is a stranger in it. He is never a citizen of the nation. However, during the term of his assignment, he enjoys the benefit of being a legal resident of the host nation; his residency is protected by the law of the two countries.

If he continues to operate within the agreed memorandum of his assignment, he cannot be removed by the host country. He can only be recalled home on the discretion of the leader of his home country. It could be after he completes his office tenure or if he voluntarily retires. Also, his legal residency could also seize if he dies on duty.

Likewise, you, Christian ambassador. You are de jure resident on earth, adequately protected by divine laws. They are set in motion by God to give you adequate security. Moreover, angels are on assignment for you, watching over you. Therefore, no power of hell can touch or remove you from the place of your divine assignment on earth. After completion of the term of your assignment, your Leader, Jesus Christ would call you home.

"For we know that if our earthly house of this tabernacle were

dissolved, we have a building from God, a house not made with hands, eternal in the heavens. For indeed in this we groan, earnestly desiring to be clothed with our dwelling-place out of Heaven; if indeed in being clothed, we shall not be found naked."

2Corinthians 5:1-3 MKJV

"...In My Father's house are many mansions; if it were not so, I would have told you. I go to prepare a place for you. And if I go and prepare a place for you, I will come again and receive you to Myself, so that where I am, you may be also."

John 14:1-3 MKJV

Hence, while you are still on earth, focus on your divine assignments where you are today, for a day will come when the Lord Jesus Christ, your Commander-In-Chief will call you home that you may give a full account of your stewardship. It could be sooner or later, nevertheless, now, you have the time and opportunity to serve Him acceptably; never be a moment slothful on your assignment. Spread the gospel of God's kingdom all over your community, village, town and nation and conquer them for Jesus Christ.

"For though I preach the gospel, I have nothing to glory of: for necessity is laid upon me; yea, woe is unto me, if I preach not the gospel!"

1 Corinthians 9:16 KJV

Principal Link Between His Country And The Host Nation

Besides, an ambassador is the principal link between his home country and the host nation. So, he does not live incommunicado or at independence of his home nation's government. He ceaselessly relates with his leader and nation to know and receive policies; he is privileged to be the custodian of his home country's policies in the place of his assignment. He likewise maintains a cordial relationship between his nation and the host country.

Sometimes, there may be communication breakdown between the two nations; however, because he is the link between the two countries, he must ensure that the leader of his home nation is sufficiently briefed, and necessary consequential actions are taken in line with to his home country's policies.

Christian, as God's ambassador, akin, this is part of your privileges on earth; you are the bodily link between heaven and earth. Jesus Christ is in you; you are in Him, just as the Father is in Him, and He is in the Father.

"At that day you shall know that I am in My Father, and you in Me, and I in you."

John 14:20 MKJV

"I in them, and You in Me, that they may be made perfect in one; and that the world may know that You have sent Me..."

John 17:23 MKJV

Now, Christian, you are the custodian of God's kingdom's policies on earth. It is a privilege that you are a bodily link between heaven and earth, because you a part of the Church. And whatever God wants to do on earth, He first communicates it to His Church on earth, to disseminate and uphold.

For so long, satanic hosts have infiltrated the world with contrary ideologies, and by deception, they have conquered many territories in the life of people. Today, people of the world have misgivings regarding God's agendas on earth. But as an ambassador of the heavenly kingdom, you must uphold heaven's policies. Never compromise God's intentions.

You must stand your ground on God's standards and in reverence of Him to defend the policies of His kingdom, no matter the opposition, and ensure you claim back the territories that satanic hosts have annexed from people.

Prerogative Powers To Act On Behalf Of His Country

Among the citizens of any nation, there is no one that has the prerogative powers to act on behalf of their country in a foreign nation like an ambassador. He is arrogated this privilege in the nation of his assignment.

The fellow citizens of an ambassador's home country may visit the nation of his assignment, notwithstanding, they are not given powers to represent their home country in the nation. An ambassador is exclusively assigned this prerogative, and he acts at different levels of diplomacy for his country. Also, he helps the fellow citizens of his home country whenever the need arises.

Christian, as God's ambassador, the authority and power to act on behalf of the kingdom of heaven has been invested in you. God has given you supernatural powers to act on His behalf and do greater works than Jesus Christ did.

"Verily, verily, I say unto you, He that believeth on me, the works that I do shall he do also; and greater works than these shall he do; because I go unto my Father."

John 14:12 KJV

What works did Jesus Christ do? He manifested the will of the Father by His good works. He delivered those that were oppressed of the devil, opened the blind eyes and set the captive free. He went to the cross and tackled all satanic hosts and triumphed over them.

"How God anointed Jesus of Nazareth with the Holy Ghost and with power: who went about doing good, and healing all that were oppressed of the devil; for God was with him."

Acts 10:38 KJV

You may ask yourself "what shall I do that I may work the works of God in my current place"? You are not the first person to ask this question. So many people during the days of Jesus Christ on earth asked the same question in John 6:28.

Nevertheless, it is very simple. The first step to engaging in the works of God is receiving and believing that Jesus Christ is the Son of God, sent by the Father into the world of man. It is your believing in Jesus Christ that will give you the opportunity to become His ambassador and be granted the necessary privileges to work His works.

"But as many as received Him, He gave to them authority to become the children of God, to those who believe on His name,"
John 1:12 MKJV

Now that you are Christ's ambassador you have been ordained to go about your territory and do the good works that Jesus Christ did. Heal the sick, raise the dead, set the captive free, and deliver them that are oppressed of the devil.

Proclaim that salvation and redemption have come to man. Declare the second return of Jesus Christ and give hope to the hopeless. You have been given the prerogative authority and power to act freely on Christ's behalf, as Holy Spirit leads.

"Behold, I give unto you power to tread on serpents and scorpions, and over all the power of the enemy: and nothing shall by any means hurt you."
Luke 10:19 KJV

One of the words translated *'power'* (underlined) in Luke 10:19 is the Greek word *'Exousia.'* It was also interpreted as, ability, privilege, force capacity, competency, freedom, mastery, delegated influence, authority, etc.

These interpretations indicate that you have been given the ability, privilege, liberty, mastery, authority and power of influence to do things as it pleases you in righteousness on behalf of Christ.

Likewise, it is the measure of power of rule that you possess that makes you a ruler indeed over your territory. The reality is that the power is universal and immeasurable. It is not limited to any region or nation of the world like the powers of nations; there is no end it cannot reach.

For example, it will be wrong for the president of America, even though he is the most power person in the world to exercise his power of governance over a nation in Europe. If he does, he will incur the wrath of other nations of the world.

However, God's kingdom's power is not like the power of man. It is the only type of power that can be used wherever in the world, either by you or any believer. It is an ever-present power and its strength never diminishes, nor know any limits.

Now, the power is on you. What are you waiting for? Dear ambassador of Christ, the highest representative of the kingdom of God on earth, arise in the strength of your power. Take charge and rule over your territory.

Did you ever notice that everywhere Jesus Christ went He established His domain over the territory? His presence was felt all over the area and ripples of His good news were spread abroad. Demons screamed out and fled and the oppressed was delivered. People gathered and praise God for His wonderful works.

Now is your turn to reign. What are you waiting for? Establish your domain over your territory now. Kick the devils out and destroy their works. **'NEVER LET SATAN ANNEX YOUR DIVINE GOODLY HERITAGE!'** It is time you dominate your world.

Dominion Over A Specific Territory Within Another Nation

The place where the office of an ambassador is situated is called an *'embassy.'* In some cases, it is usually an ambassador's residence.

Moreover, if the leader of his country visits his nation of assignment, and he does not have any suitable place to stay, he may decide to reside at the embassy for the period of his visit. This is where the government of his home country is based in the country in any foreign nation. It is the heritage of his home country.

The *'embassy,'* no matter how big or small, is a territory that is supposed to be free from the control of the host nation. It is completely under the ambassador and his home country's government control. It is the property of his home government.

Whatever is done within the embassy territory is an internal affair of the ambassador's home country, and it is protected under the 'international non-interference principle.' In other words, the host nation cannot interfere except on invitation by the ambassador or approval of his home government. As a result, the embassy is always given maximum protection from external incursions.

An embassy is supposed to be a place of first contact of the host country with the ambassador's home country. It is the place of the highest authority of the ambassador's home country in the host nation. Besides, it is the place from which businesses of interests of the ambassador's home government is transacted with the host country.

From the embassy, necessary diplomatic, political and commercial businesses are done and maintained with the host country by the ambassador on behalf of his leader and country. Whenever his leader and country want to have any dealing with his country of assignment, it passes through the consulate.

In a real sense, the embassy must be in place before an ambassador is appointed and sent forth to the host country.

Christian, the embassy is a mystery in relation to your salvation and call. You are first God's spiritual embassy before you are made His ambassador. The real you (the inner man) is the ambassador, living inside your physical body (embassy) in a foreign place—the world, wherever you are.

Remember, God is the Leader of your home country. He is on a visit to the earth now, by the Holy Spirit; and just as the leader of a nation may visit and live in his nation's embassy for the period of his visit to a foreign nation, God is residing with you (the ambassador) inside your body (the spiritual embassy), by the Holy Spirit.

God first started His work of edification in you (spiritual embassy), and afterwards, He sends you out as His highest representative to the territory you are now. He will continue to furnish his divine business in and through you, (the spiritual embassy) until the day of Jesus Christ.

It does not matter if you were born and reared up in the same area you are at present, you are both God's spiritual embassy and an ambassador there; you are God's heritage. He is at work in and through you. Hence, as you go here and there to attend to His intentions within your territory, you are still His spiritual embassy and ambassador, carrying God about.

Now, you are God's spiritual building that is supposed to be absolutely controlled by God, the Holy Spirit.

Christian, take note of the mystery of spirits. Whether it is Holy Spirit or demonic spirits, it is the fact that, wherever they reside, they like to have absolute control. Thus, your life is supposed to be a territory, controlled by God through the Holy Spirit thoroughly.

As God's spiritual embassy on earth, He has set you up as His spiritual heritage base on earth, where His business interest and dealings can pass through to the nations of the world. Due to this, anyone that wants to have any information about God would first come to you, just the way people may go to an embassy and to the ambassador to inquire about his home nation.

Holy Spirit inspired Peter as he wrote in *1Peter 2:5*, and said:

"You also as living stones are built up a spiritual house..."
1 Peter 2:5 MKJV

Therefore, God said:

"... I will dwell in them, and walk in them; and I will be their God, and they shall be my people."
2 Corinthians 6:16 KJV

Many people, including Christians have wrong impressions and believe that the building where Christians gather for fellowship and worship God is the Church. No, it is not. The Christian believers are the Church of the Lord Jesus Christ. He is not coming back for houses built by man's hand, but by God; you are the house, the temple of the Holy Spirit, built by God.

After you were saved, God fills you with the Holy Spirit to perfect what He has begun in you. One day, in a moment, Jesus Christ will return for His Church and Christian people that are filled with the Holy Spirit will be raptured.

While the Church (the spiritual embassies and ambassadors) is taken away, the physical buildings built by men will remain on earth. No matter how magnificent they are, they will not be raptured. So, concentrate more on building people as God's holy edifice and prepare them for rapture instead of man-made material buildings, although it may be beneficial for the Church while on earth.

When a nation removes its ambassador and closes its embassy in the host nation, it shows, in most cases that the relationship has gone sour and horrific things could happen. Comparably, when God removes Christians, (His spiritual embassies and ambassadors) from the earth, it is the sign that the dispensation of grace for the generality of man has ended; His wrath will be unleashed, and the people of the world will not escape it.

Dear Christian, the rapture of the Church will soon take place. Are you ready? Jesus is coming soon; we will soon be going home. How prepared are you?

As an embassy is a territorial heritage of the government of the home country of an ambassador, so, your entire life should be to God. You should see and declare all areas of your life a territory separated to and for God, one hundred percent. No interference from the demonic spirits, no entanglements with the world.

If any demons dare attempt to invade your life's territory, it is a violation of the laws of your heavenly home country that are at variance with their assignments. Demons are strangers to you and heaven your home country, never accommodate them for a moment. Instantly unleash God's judgment on them; rebuke, bind and cast them out. Be at peace with God and let Holy Spirit take over all positions in your life.

"And what agreement does a temple of God have with idols? For you are the temple of the living God..."

2 Corinthians 6:16 MKJV

Apart from the mystery that God has made you to be His spiritual embassy and an ambassador, He has equally given you some places as your territories. They include your place of work, socialization places and other places you may find yourself at any point in time.

While you are in these places, God's presence is with you. As God's ambassador, you must mark out these places as your physical embassy, where no demonic force should operate either directly or indirectly. If they do, it is a violation of the laws of heaven, your home country, and divine laws override any other laws on earth. Reject and root out those demonic forces and take control in Jesus' Name.

Let me tell you this story. It is a true story. There was a time, then I was living in Nigeria. During this period Nigeria used to be a place where there were security lapses here and there. No adequate security was provided by the government agencies. As necessary, residents everywhere had to arrange some sorts of private securities, chiefly against armed robbers and other criminals.

Often, despite the privately arranged securities, armed robbers could still invade wherever and whenever. At times, they could notify the residents of their intentions in writing by giving time of their operations.

On an occasion, a notice was given to the residents of the area where I was living that armed robbers were coming for operations. Everyone was in panic, except me.

As soon as I got the news that they were coming to sack my area, I saw it as an assault and insult on my person as an ambassador of the Most High God. My life and house are God's embassy, a heritage where God's Presence is. It is the first physical place where I transact His kingdom business. This is my territorial heritage, the territory of the Living God. It is not for the devils.

I went to God, the Leader of my heavenly home country in prayer and briefed Him on the matter. He instructed me to release decrees on His behalf and His heavenly government; whatever I decree is in this situation is the final.

In earnest, I issued decrees all over the area, proclaiming it as God's and my territorial heritage. Any invasion of demons of robbery in the area is a violation of the laws of heaven, my spiritual home country. Therefore, any armed robbers that dare step into my territory would be arrested and be brought to justice. I gave thanks to God and be at peace.

On their appointed night of invasion, the armed robbers came, and while my neighbours were fully awakened because of the invasion, by the grace of God, I slept like a baby, no worries. In fact, it was a sweet, sound sleep; the Lord's beloved, He gave me a sound sleep.

In the morning, some neighbours came knocking on my door and narrated what had happened overnight to me. They asked if I heard gun shots, shouts and screams. Indeed, the armed robbers came, and before they could attack any home, there was a divine intervention, and they were all miraculously caught and arrested by the security agents and the community had peace afterwards. Let God take all the glory. Amen.

Another incident occurred in my neighbourhood in London, England a few years ago. There was a notorious gang leader who had just moved into the area to live with his grandmother. Soon after he moved in, all hell was let lose.

An area within the neighbourhood that was very peaceful round the clock suddenly became a den of criminals. Day and night there were all sorts of disturbances. It was nightmare period for the residents. The irony of things was that this gang leader was living in front of my house.

Members of this gang did not always meet during the day. They usually held their meetings in the dead of the night, when people in the neighbourhood were very deep at sleep.

As part of their activities, they engaged in motorbike racing competitions. They used the type of bikes with big exhausts that emit loud irritating sounds to pollute the air with noise, and they shout and scream without any consideration for the residents. The situation was a nightmare, and no one could sleep at night anymore. The neighbourhood suddenly became an ambiance of terrors.

One day, the gang leader met me in front of my house as I was trying to park my car. He told me to give him my car key because he wanted to drive it for some time. I objected his request immediately. Soon after this, day after day, my car was vandalized.

I reported the matter to the police authority, and they said there was nothing they could do. They claimed there was no evidence to prove the gangs had committed the offense. So, I sold the car and bought a much more expensive one; I thought they would not vandalize it. Within two weeks, the new car was vandalized, and I had to spend some money to fix it.

A few days after, I had an idea of what to do, possibly it would work, however, it did not work. I thought of closer familiarization with the gang leader to witness Jesus Christ to him.

Immediately I told the guy about Jesus Christ, he was so furious. He told me to keep my Jesus Christ to myself. He started showing off that the area was his territory, whereby he could do whatever he wanted. All my neighbours dreaded him and his gang members.

As soon as he claimed my neighbourhood as his territory, I knew that a battle line has been drawn. The battle line was not between him and me, but between the demons that were ruling his heart and my spiritual home country's government. I am God's ambassador, and if I live within the neighbourhood, it is my territorial heritage for the period. I would never allow any satanic hosts to annex it.

Hence, I decided to exercise my ambassadorial authority and powers over the territory. My community is my territory; God's embassy is established within. It belongs singularly to God and me as our heritage. No violence or any form of demonic invasions are allowed. It does not belong to Satan and his hosts, it is mine, it is God's. In earnest, I issued decrees that the man and his gang members be rooted out totally from the territory, and never return.

About two weeks after, on a Sunday as I was returning from the Church service and I saw scores of police officers all over the neighbourhood and police helicopter was hovering all over the area. I spotted the gang leader running for his life, trying to find a place to hide.

I asked my neighbours what had happened, and I was told the police have come to arrest the notorious gang leader and his members. He had just committed a crime somewhere and was chased down to my neighbourhood.

At last, he was fished out, arrested and whisked away. Finally, he and his grandmother were evicted from the neighbourhood and never to return to the area again.

Since then, peace that had eluded the area for months returned and the people rejoiced. Let God be glorified in Jesus' Name. Amen.

Listen carefully, your body and life are God's embassy; they are His property. Preserve and fortify them as territorial heritages for God only. Your geographical area should be a consulate in God. Delineate and claim it as your territorial heritage, never let Satan annex any of them.

Heritages are always protected all over the world, because they confirm and preserve history of cultures and traditions for posterity. Thus, dominate and rule over everything that is working contrary to the knowledge of God within your territory; overcome every demonic principality and power that may want to annex them. Establish God's will and counsel and glorify His holy Name. Satan must not have them, they are your possessions. Amen!

As said before now, your life should be a territorial heritage that solely belongs to God. Let Him own and indwell it.

Additionally, members of your family: your spouse, children and household members are also your divine goodly heritage, because they are part of your life. Establish and set them apart as a territorial heritage for God.

From your family members and households, spread your territory to cover every other thing that belongs to you financially and materially; including your workplace and community. Encompass them for God and declared them as a no-go area to the devils. Let them be held as God's heritage.

Until you realise that your family and households, finances, material possessions, neighbourhood, city, nation are your territorial heritages, you cannot claim them for God. What you do not claim cannot be in your possession, even though they belong to you.

Give Satan and his demons quit notice and evict them. They are not the rightful owners; they are intruders. You have rightful ownership to the territories, satanic hosts do not. You are God's embassy; you are God's ambassador; you are God's heritage. You are an overcomer, go forth now and win.

Chapter 15

Overcomer Wins All Whenever

So far, the message of this book has been how you can reign as *'lord and king'* over the territories God has given you, and correspondingly preserve them for posterity as godly goodly heritage. You cannot have dominion over those territories until you overcome the enemies that are striving to annex them.

The summary of what Jesus Christ came to do for all humanity is this, He overcame satanic hosts and redeemed all mankind from sins and offers eternal life and gives total restoration of life of glory. The redemption of man did not just materialize from the blues, Jesus Christ fought decisively and won the battle over Satan and sin once and for all, while He gave His life on the cross. On the third day, He resurrected.

Therefore, after His resurrection day, Jesus Christ declares:

"...All power is given unto me in heaven and in earth."
                                        Matthew 28:18 KJV

Dear Christian, Satan can no longer say *'all this power'* as he declared in *Luke, 4:6,* except if you are ignorant of what Jesus

Christ has accomplished.

When Satan tempted Jesus Christ in the wilderness, what did he say to Him? He said to Jesus Christ,

"...All this power will I give thee, and the glory of them: for that is delivered unto me; and to whomsoever I will I give it."

Luke 4:6 KJV

The only final answer Jesus Christ could give was,

"...Get thee hence, Satan: for it is written, Thou shalt worship the Lord thy God, and him only shalt thou serve."

Matthew 4:10 KJV

Why did Jesus Christ only reply, *"Get thee hence, Satan"* as stated in the above scripture? The reason for the response was that Jesus Christ had not yet paid the price for the redemption of man and retrieved the stolen dominion from Satan. Legally Satan had the ownership of the dominion because of what Adam did in the Garden of Eden. However, after His resurrection from the dead, Jesus Christ declared that the power to reign in life is no longer in the hands of Satan. He, Jesus Christ has overcome all satanic hosts triumphantly and reclaimed all power. All power now belongs to Him.

"And having spoiled principalities and powers, he made a show of them openly, triumphing over them in it."

Colossians 2:15 KJV

"(Now that he ascended, what is it but that he also descended first into the lower parts of the earth? He that descended is the same also that ascended up far above all heavens, that he might fill all things.)"

Ephesians 4:9-10 KJV

From Colossians 2:15, the Greek word translated *'spoiled'* was *'Apekduomai.'* It also reded 'to divest wholly oneself.'

In other words, by His death on the cross, Jesus Christ stripped

Satan and his hosts at all levels of their ranks and hierarchies of all power stolen from the first Adam. After Satan stole the power from Adam, he delegated the power to various hierarchies in his kingdom to rule over the earth through man.

Indeed, Jesus Christ died on the cross, and he was brought down from the cross and was buried. Within three days of His death, He went to lower parts of the earth where the departed souls of the Old Testament saints were confined. There He divested Satan of all dominion in his possession, absolutely. He left nothing in his hands.

Afterwards, He came out of the grave on the resurrection morning and afterwards heralded that *"All Power Has Been Given To Him in Heaven And On Earth."* Subsequently, He gives every Christian believer authority to use the dominion power in His Name.

You Can Only Rule By Dominion Power

Dominion power is the power that overcomes whatever Satan, and his hosts may stand for. It is the power that gives you 'Rulership' over all satanic hosts, no devil can overcome. It cannot be taken from you again by any satanic hosts.

Christian, carefully note this, your dominion power is useless to Satan because it can only be used by the Name of Jesus Christ, the Son of God. And before anyone can possess the dominion power unlimitedly, Jesus Christ must be alive and active in him.

Jesus is not alive in Satan; therefore, it is impossible for him to have the same dominion power you have in Jesus Christ. Your possession and use of the dominion power already put you in your position as an overcomer.

You may have this question, 'if Jesus Christ dispossessed Satan of all powers, why is Satan still active in the world?' This is the answer; Satan and his fallen angels still possess their corrupted angelic prowess. It was the dominion power that he subtly took away from the first Adam that was retrieved from him. The dominion power that he stole from Adam put him in the position as the *'crowned prince and god'* of this world; the right to rule on earth instead of man — *2Corinthians 4:4; John 12:31; John 16:11.*

Additionally, satanic hosts are also cursed with darkness. If you can recollect, the word *'darkness'* was elaborately explained in chapter two as God's judgment upon them. From the time he was judged, he ceases to be an angel of light. So, the reference to *'darkness'* in *Genesis 1:2* was satanic presence.

'Darkness' in *Genesis 1:2* means destruction, sorrow, wickedness, death, ignorance and death. Due to the above reasons, Satan is presently active and could be discerned by all the above traits. With his angelic powers, he dispels destruction, sorrow, wickedness, death, ignorance, and miseries directly or indirectly.

Angels have powers to do certain things just as human beings have natural abilities to do certain things too on earth. In Luke chapter one, angel Gabriel, by his angelic power, decreed in righteousness that Zechariah, the father John the Baptist, would be dumb for a while; it came to pass. Note, angel Gabriel is a holy angel; he did not steal any dominion from Adam. Also, in *Genesis 19:1-11*, angels of God decreed that the people of Sodom be struck with blindness, and it was so.

The above incidents give us some clues about the angelic powers and what they can do. Angels of God do not use their powers in evilness like Satan and his hosts, but they operate in righteousness to serve divine judgment.

Regardless, as a child of the Most High God, you are maximally protected from whatever any evil angel or satanic hosts may be up to concerning God's purposes for your life. No weapon formed against you, by them shall prosper.

The power that Jesus Christ gives to every believer is the power that is far greater than what any angel possesses. It is the presence of the Holy Spirit, the Lord God Almighty Himself in us. It is, far above all principality, authority, power and dominion, and names that are named in this world and in the world to come. This power is in your possession now.

A greater demonstration of this power raised Jesus Christ from the dead on the resurrection morning, and Paul describes it as,

"...the surpassing greatness of His power toward us, the ones believing according to the working of His mighty strength which He worked in Christ in raising Him from the dead, and He seated Him at His right hand in the heavenlies, far above all principality and authority and power and dominion, and every name being named, not only in this world, but also in the coming age."
Ephesians 1:19-21 MKJV

You Are Admonished To Overcome

Severally, in the book of Revelation, Jesus Christ stresses the need for the Church to overcome. Overcome signifies 'prevalence over an opponent or enemy in a challenge or battle to successfully get things under control.' Anyone that does not overcome the enemy cannot control what belongs to him. God gave a similar command to Adam after his creation. He must *'subdue'* all things on earth to have control over his heritage sphere.

"And God blessed them, and God said unto them, Be fruitful, and multiply, and replenish the earth, and subdue it..."
Genesis 1:28 KJV

As stated earlier, the word translated *'subdue'* is 'to subject, force, keep under, bring into bondage'. The deduction from these meanings is that something must be overcome.

The entire planet earth was Adam's to keep as his heritage territory. In the broad sense of divine blessedness, it has been given to all mankind to rule and reign over; it is not given to any other being. Due to this, God told Adam that things must be under his control to be what He had intended for him. Hence, Satan, his demons and any contrary views must be conquered.

Every Christian is supposed to be an overcomer, and that includes you. It is the core message of Jesus Christ to the early Church, and He has the same message for today's Church, including you.

To *the Church in Ephesus*, Jesus Christ said,

"He who has an ear, let him hear what the Spirit says to the churches. To him who overcomes I will give to eat of the Tree of Life, which is in the midst of the paradise of God."

Revelation 2:7 MKJV

To *the Church in Smyrna*, Jesus Christ said,

"He who has an ear, let him hear what the Spirit says to the churches. He who overcomes will not be hurt by the second death."

Revelation 2:11 MKJV

Again, Jesus Christ said to *the Church in Pergamos*,

"He who has an ear, let him hear what the Spirit says to the churches. To him who overcomes I will give to eat of the hidden manna, and will give to him a white stone, and in the stone a new name written, which no man knows except he who receives it."

Revelation 2:17 MKJV

Jesus Christ said to *the Church in Thyatira*,

"And he who overcomes and keeps My works to the end, to him I will give power over the nations."

Revelation 2:26 MKJV

To *the Church in Sardis*, Jesus Christ said,

"The one who overcomes, this one will be clothed in white clothing. And I will not blot out his name out of the Book of Life, but I will confess his name before My Father and before His angels."

Revelation 3:5 MKJV

Also, to *the Church in Philadelphia*, Jesus Christ said,

"Him who overcomes I will make him a pillar in the temple of My God, and he will go out no more. And I will write upon him the name of My God, and the name of the city of My God, the New Jerusalem, which comes down out of Heaven from My God, and My new name."

Revelation 3:12 MKJV

And finally, to **the Church in Laodicea**, Jesus Christ said,

"To him who overcomes I will grant to sit with Me in My throne, even as I also overcame and have sat down with My Father in His throne."

Revelation 3:21 MKJV

To you today, Jesus Christ says, **'You Must Overcome.'**

What Must You Overcome?

Satan and his demons know categorically that they cannot overcome a Christian who understands what Jesus Christ meant by the word *'overcome.'* Various Christians take the victory of Jesus Christ passively. They think they must overcome satanic hosts all over again as if Jesus Christ did not entirely defeat them before now.

Please recognize that all satanic hosts have been defeated entirely. There is no God's goodness that belongs to you that Jesus Christ left at the mercy of any satanic hosts. He has retrieved everything for you; He has recovered everything for me; He got back everything for us. He has triumphed over all enemies for His Church.

Christian, what must you overcome? Holy Spirit reveals one of them by Paul, the Apostle. It is how Satan and his demons work against believers today by wiles.

"...that ye may be able to stand against the wiles of the devil."

Ephesians 6:11 KJV

324

From the scripture in *Ephesians 6:11* above, the word translated *'wiles'* was a Greek word *'Methodeia.'* Its other translations are cunning arts, deceit, craft, and trickery.

'Wile' is the use of tricks to deceive someone. It also means to lure or entice. In other words, satanic hosts largely use tricks to entice and attack a Christian believer.

Where does the attack take place? It always begins on the mind.

Satan's main target on the mind is to create confusion. Once there is confusion, if care is not taken, doubt will set. Hence, faith in Jesus Christ will gradually diminish and the promises of God would be of no effect.

It could be on your health, marriage, finances, job, business, etc. Whatever they may be, all satanic attacks always manifest through scheming, by suggestions, ideas, thoughts, ungodly advice, etc. They always happen in the field of mind.

For example, he may attack your mind with a thought to attack God's integrity, and you may say, "If God wants you well, why did He allow your body to be afflicted with diseases that are incurable?" You may also imagine, "If God loves you, why does it take Him time to turn your situations around?"

Except you are fully persuaded that, no matter the situation, God is love and does not tempt with evil. Thus, in no time, your mind could be streaming the doubtful thought, and finally admit that God's promises are not sure. Do not ever settle for such suggestions; it is Satan's device. He is the originator of evil. No matter what, God is faithful and always good; His promises are sure and will never fail.

A True Story

One evening a parent and I discussed God's love and Jesus Christ's sacrifice. I always see him at my child's nursery school whenever he comes around to drop his children and perceived he was not a

Christian. On this evening, in other to witness and invite him to our Church fellowship, I decided to tell him about Jesus Christ.

He waited for me finish my message. After I had finished, he responded, and his response revealed that he was once a Christian who had allowed demons to sell their lies about God to him; he bought the satanic lies at the cost price of his redemption and made a shipwreck of his faith. Now, instead of being a defender of the cross of Jesus Christ, he was completely against it, making fun of Jesus Christ's accomplishments for humanity.

One of his comments on God was on the condition of things in the world. With rage, he asked, "if God was in charge, why didn't He stop wars and all kinds of evil that are in the world? Why didn't God do this, why didn't He do that, he continued. Hence, he rubbished everything about Christianity and made fun of me. I made all efforts to convince him, however, he hardened his heart.

During our conversation, I realized that he had fallen for the satanic wiles, while he accused God of being weak and incapable of subduing the evils in the world. He could not identify the origin of sin. He did not know that satanic hosts are contending for mastery in the world to control mankind, especially his own soul, and he must overcome them. He refused to recognise that if he keeps the faith, he will possess dominion to subdue and overpower all satanic hosts and their weapons, whoever or whatever they are. Regardless, whatever the situation may be, God is mighty, and He loves, everlastingly.

Unfortunately, today, there are many people, particularly people that were once Christians that are like the man in the above incident. Because of trials of life, they have abandoned God and rejected Jesus Christ. Satanic hosts have attacked their minds and bewitched them, and they have failed to overcome their wiles.

What they do not understand is that, as Christians, their minds and hearts are parts of their life that must be jealously protected as territories for God. The Word of God must replace the stronghold of deceit that demonic hosts have built up in their minds and hearts.

If they refuse to fill their hearts and minds with the words of God and His promises, when the hosts of darkness come with their weapon of deceit, they will not be able to overcome them. Accordingly, they will not keep the divine goodly heritage territories they are supposed to reign over.

There is no Christian on earth that satanic hosts do not attempt to attack, directly or indirectly. They attack directly or indirectly by demons and their human agents. Whoever you are in the Church, a minister, or lay member, satanic hosts will always attempt to attack you. The attacks are always unleashed at different levels. They could be by temptations and other difficulties of life.

Nonetheless, only a few Christians always prepare to overcome the demonic onslaughts by equipping themselves with the truth of God's Word; and many are not discerning to see the attacks as Satan's ploy against their salvation.

Attacks on your mind are parts of Satan's cunning devices to make you believe his lies and then doubt your capabilities in Jesus Christ. He profitably attacked Adam and Eve in the Garden of Eden, and they lost control of their divine goodly heritage dominion to him. Similarly, he tempted Jesus Christ in the wilderness to steal His dominion, and he lost woefully. Hallelujah!

Satan's objective is to make you lose faith in God and Jesus Christ in order to overcome you. Once he succeeds, you may not be able to please God and claim and reign over the territories God has given you.

Remember that your territories include your life, spouse, children, finances, jobs, property, community, city, nation, and the ends of the earth. You are a child of God. And in all the above-mentioned facets of your territories, you must overcome all satanic hosts, and keep your territories intact for God.

"For everything that has been born of God OVERCOMES the world. And this is the victory that OVERCOMES the world, OUR FAITH. Who is he who OVERCOMES the world, but he who

believes that Jesus is the Son of God?"

1 John 5:4-5 MKJV

Your active faith is very crucial to your overcoming Satan's lies and consequently, dominates your territory. When your faith is active, you can possess all things that Jesus Christ has won for you.

By faith resist Satan! By faith claim back those things he has stolen from you! By faith chuck him out of your life! By faith spread God's protection over your life and territories! By faith know that all is well, and all shall be well! It is only by faith through grace, and by faith and grace alone!

Through faith, you can be ahead of all satanic hosts by infinite steps. By faith everything Jesus Christ has accomplished for you would manifest. Equally, by faith you can enter and remain in the rest that God has for you, not only in this life but throughout eternity. Your faith is the victory that overcomes the world and Satan. As a result, God is glorified, and you are glorified.

Chapter 16

Keeping Your Pace Ahead Of The Hosts Of Darkness

Surely, you can be ahead of all satanic hosts by infinite steps, and they will never be able to catch up with your pace. But how? It is by knowing how they play their games in their attempts to beat you indiscernibly.

Satan and his demons always capitalize on certain elements that are indiscernible by Christians to take advantage of them. They use such elements to make an average Christian vulnerable and simply forget and forego their dominion, as they advance in their Christian faith in life.

Except you recognize and make every diligent effort to overcome the elements, you might not be able to be ahead of the hosts of darkness, and reign over your territories.

Some elements are listed below for considerations.

- ➢ Ignorant Of Your Authority
- ➢ Unbelief, Fear And Unwillingness Elements
- ➢ Non-Strategic Methodical Preparations

➤ Non-Spiritual Vigilance Posture
➤ Conformance To A Complacent Posture
➤ Inability To Possess And Manifest Gifts Of The Holy Spirit
➤ Covetousness For The Glory Of This World
➤ Other Unrecognized Little Foxes

Ignorant Of Your Authority

Ignorance is not of God; it is from the devil. As it has been unequivocally stated many times in this book, ignorance is one of God's judgments on Satan after his insurrection.

Before his fall, Satan knew what to do and how to do them right before God. After Satan's falls from glory, he is cast out of God's presence and invested with ignorance. The plans of God in all ramifications are always hidden from him moment by moment. In consequence, he is always caught unawares.

"Which none of the rulers of this world knew (for if they had known, they would not have crucified the Lord of glory)."
1 Corinthians 2:8 MKJV

Ignorance is a disease contracted by mankind from Satan after the fall and all must be delivered from it. By ignorance, mankind is unable to know God's plans for them. By ignorance, people reject God's plan and embrace unprofitable mundane projects.

By ignorance, some Christians feel that God has abandoned them to whatever challenges they may be facing, not knowing that He has promised not to leave nor forsake them. By ignorance, they think that God does not want them well, forgetting He cares for them.

If you are ignorant of your blessings in Christ Jesus, it could probably be by a demonic attack. And if you are ignorant of the benefits already available to you, how would you be able to possess them. However, if you are aware of what belongs to you, then make necessary efforts to take possession of them. God declares:

"My people are destroyed for lack of knowledge: because thou hast rejected knowledge..."

Hosea 4:6 KJV

From the above scripture, you can recognise the impact of ignorance on a life; it is a power that slowly destroys. Before now, it has destroyed many lives as they grope in darkness, battling hardship.

It is of satanic hosts' agenda, by attack of ignorance for you not to dominate your God gifted heritage territories. Therefore, to overcome ignorance, you must 'know' your privileges in Christ.

These privileges are spelled out in the scriptures, to reveal God's will and what He can do. So, immerse your mind and heart in the Word of God and saturate your life with the Truth. Study and meditate on the Word to acquire and appropriate God's promise given in it for you; let the Word become part of your life.

You have an enormous authority in Christ Jesus. Your authority will manifest the anointing upon your life to make demonic hosts flee. Your authority in Jesus Christ is so great that no devil can withstand it.

Hence, as God's child, if you understand your authority and use it, you will prevent Satan from coming into your territory. All satanic hosts will be subdued in all facets of your life, and they will have no reign over your heritage. Praise God!

Unbelief, Fear And Unwillingness Elements

Today, a larger percentage of Christians take their spiritual authority passive because they do not really understand its significance. Taking your authority passive is like a freedom pass you give to satanic hosts to intrude and take advantage of and prevent you from reigning over your divine goodly heritage territory. If they intrude, they may steal, kill, and destroy your goodly heritage.

The situation could be likened to a policeman on duty, extensively dressed up in the uniform of his delegated authority and armed. He is sent to arrest a thief, yet he is unwilling to arrest him due to unbelief in the authority of his position and weapons. While he is face to face with an active thief, despite enormous weapons and authority he has, he starts crying like a little child and pleading, because he is afraid to use his weapons and authority.

Many Christians are like the 'policeman' in the above narrative. When they notice Satan and his forces have trespassed into their territories, to steal, kill and destroy, they develop cold feet.

It is not that they do not know that Satan and his demons are around to steal, kill and destroy. It is not that they do not know that, as Christians, they have enormous power and authority in the Name of Jesus Christ to subdue all satanic hosts, bind and cast them out. It is just that they are unwilling to exert their authority in the Name of Jesus Christ, because of fear and doubts.

While you fail to exert your spiritual authority over the hosts of darkness as God intends, you may give them absolute liberty to do whatever they desire; therefore, they can steal, kill, and destroy, and you might not be blessed as you are supposed. Because of your posture, people around you would not witness the great impact of your authority and be blessed too and glorify God.

An incident occurred in *Matthew 17:15-20* and Jesus Christ rebuked His disciples for their inability to use their authority over a lunacy demon.

"Lord, have mercy on my son: for he is lunatic, and sore vexed: for oft times he falleth into the fire, and oft into the water. And I brought him to thy disciples, and they could not cure him. Then Jesus answered and said, O faithless and perverse generation, how long shall I be with you? how long shall I suffer you? bring him hither to me. And Jesus rebuked the devil; and he departed out of him: and the child was cured from that very hour. Then came the disciples to Jesus apart, and said, Why could not we cast him out? And Jesus said unto them, Because of your unbelief: for verily I

say unto you, If ye have faith as a grain of mustard seed, ye shall say unto this mountain, Remove hence to yonder place; and it shall remove; and nothing shall be impossible unto you."

Matthew 17:15-20 KJV

In the above scriptures, why did Jesus Christ rebuke His disciples? Jesus rebuked His disciples because, while they possessed authority, they entertained unwillingness, fear, and unbelief. The captive that could have been set free and be blessed if they had used their spiritual authority was not blessed, and God was not glorified through them.

Look at the situation in the above scriptures this way. The devil of lunacy came into their territory, while he masked himself with his victim's body. The disciples knew that the demon of lunacy has taken over the territory of his victim's body, as he manifests before them. Yet, due to fear and unbelief, they could not cast him out and set the captive free.

I hope you do not have the same posture as the disciples in *Matthew 17:15-20*. If you do, you must overcome your unwillingness, fear, and unbelief. You cannot get your desired results with a power you believe you do not have, or afraid of using, even though you possess it.

Until you are convinced that you possess the power, either by ownership or on borrowed terms, and willing to employ it, you cannot maximize its use. The spiritual power and authority you possess are outrightly yours in Jesus Christ; they are not borrowed. Use them and chuck out the satanic hosts. Your divine goodly heritage must be protected.

Non-Strategic Methodical Preparations

Preparation against an insidious enemy that does not give warnings before his invasion and assaults is essential. To oppose such enemy, moment by moment well-structured preparations should be employed. On the other hand, if you have not been preparing yourself against an enemy like that, you may be in for a rude surprise of attacks.

In *Matthew 17:20*, Jesus Christ opens our eyes to see a certain factor that must be present to exert our spiritual authority decisively. It is faith. However, faith must be complemented with prayer, and prayer with fasting as a facilitator in an organized preparation to overcome.

Jesus Christ teaches in *Matthew 17:21* and says:

"Howbeit this kind goeth not out but by prayer and fasting."
Matthew 17:21 KJV

Without doubt, a Christian life must comprise adequate consistent spiritual warfare. Notwithstanding, the spiritual warfare must be complemented with fasting to be effectual, in order to prevail. The fasting period is not a hunger strike time, but to support an all-round prayer life.

For such a prayer time, the help of the Holy Spirit as the Strengthener must not be secondary, but the principal force. Holy Spirit knows the battles ahead; He knows your spiritual strength and the enemy's capacity. He must be the strength you substantially covet.

As Holy Spirit leads you into a fasting period while you pray, He will infuse new spiritual strength into you, and the impact of your authority will be decisive over the enemy. Your victory will be sweet, and your heritage will be bulwarked, while you reign over your heritage territory.

There was a time I was chosen to lead my fellow ministers to an all-night outreach at a Church. During the time, I was yet an associate minister with Faith Clinic Ministries, Lagos branch, Nigeria. For a reason that I could not at once understand, Holy Spirit led me into a seven-day intensive prayer with fasting, as I stayed in His presence for those days.

While I commune with Him in prayer and fasting, I did not go for any of the ministers' meetings at Faith Clinic ministries or attend to any secular business endeavours. I was indoor alone, communing with God.

At the end of the seven-day prayer and fasting period, I thought of joining other ministers at the fellowship Centre for the mid-week fellowship. Suddenly, in the morning of the eight day as I woke up, the Lord instructed me to observe another three days of prayer and fasting, which would end on a Friday, and then join the fellow ministers on the day.

On Friday, the third day of my second round of prayer and fasting, I joined the ministers at Faith Clinic ministries, Lagos for prayers. To my ultimate surprise, the leader of the ministry in Lagos disclosed to me that he had been praying that I should come for the ministers' meeting. He said we were going out that Friday night for an outreach, and he would not be able to attend. He said that the Holy Ghost told him that I should lead other ministers to the event.

At this time, I told him my experience on prayer and fasting that I had observed, as I waited in the presence of the Lord. Even though I did not know why the Lord instructed me to observe an intensive prayer time with fasting, but Holy Spirit knew what was ahead.

At the outreach event, the impact of our corporate anointing and authority was highly evident and significantly decisive over the demonic forces that had held people in bondage. Many people were healed and delivered; Jesus Christ was glorified, and satanic hosts were put to shame. Amen.

Christian, momentary preparation creates a great opportunity to be ready against the satanic hosts to protect the goodly heritage within your territory. You cannot pray enough, and you cannot fast too much.

If you are well-prepared and equipped, the impact of onslaught, by your spiritual power and authority will be seriously detrimental to the satanic hosts; they will be chucked out of your territory instantaneously than you can imagine.

Non-Spiritual Vigilance Posture

Vigilance is one of the virtues that you need to prevail over the enemy of your soul. If you are not vigilant enough, the cunning enemy might take advantage of you, to steal, kill and destroy your goodly heritage.

As previously stated, satanic hosts often use temptations to subdue Christians, but God tests His people, to strengthen their relationship with Him. Nevertheless, Satan's temptations are frequently subtle, and a Christian may fall for them because of their non-vigilant posture. Thus, Jesus Christ says,

"Watch and pray that you enter not into temptation..."
Matthew 26:41 KJV

The Greek word translated *'watch'* is *'Gregoreou.'* Other words derived from it are, 'to keep awake, watch, be vigilant and wake'.

Also, the word translated *'temptation'* was interpreted from the Greek word, *'Peirasmos.'* It has other translations like, experience of evil, solicitation, trial, enticement to sins, etc.

The message of Jesus Christ in *Matthew 26:41* is that you should be observant and fully awake spiritually while you watch out for Satan's enticements, as he subtly attempts to encroach into the territories of your life.

Satan's best method of invasion is by enticement to sin by lust of the flesh, lust of the eye, pride of life and other elements of world's glory. Hence, Peter, in *1Peter 5:8* amplifies as he warns,

"Be sober, be vigilant; because your adversary the devil, as a roaring lion, walketh about, seeking whom he may devour:"
1 Peter 5:8 KJV

Furthermore, let us examine the word *'devour'* in *1Peter 5:8*. It was translated from the Greek word, *'Katapino.'* Its other interpretations are, drink down, swallowed up, drown and destroy.'

The deduction from these translations is that Satan's main objective as he entices a non-vigilant Christian is to swallow up and destroy them. So, you must be alert step by step. While he tries to swallow up and destroy, he could do it by associations, thoughts, communications, and other means.

One day, I watched the testimony of a Christian lady on the television. During a Church service, she spoke of how a friend influenced her into a sexual relationship with an unbeliever. In due course, she lost her virginity before marriage, which she regretted her action greatly.

She claimed she was brutally abused again and again through the unholy relationship. Suddenly, she realized that Satan was all the way out to kill and destroy her. Glory to God, she cried out for help, and she was delivered and restored.

Due to nonspiritual vigilance, the church has allowed abominable lifestyles to creep in. Therefore, homosexuality, witchcraft, heresies, occultism, greed, polygamy and many other works of the flesh and darkness are becoming the acceptable norms within the territories of the Church.

Today, the Church has embraced worldliness and the Faithfuls within her territories are becoming helpless, more and more. Mockers of God and impostor 'Christians' are gradually occupying spiritual positions, while they exhibit sinfulness without genuine remorse. They claim God loves.

Indeed, God is love, but He will never condone sins. If a jeerer minister in the Church is banking on God's love to prevent the consequences of his abominable lifestyle without a sincere repentance, then, he should be making a grave mistake.

If his view on God's love is right, then, God would not have called mankind to repent of their sins. He would not have sent His only Son, the Lord Jesus Christ to die on the cross to atone for the sins of humanity. Equitably, God would not have been justified while He punished Sodom and Gomorrah for their sins.

Christian, it is part of Satan's ploy to deceive anyone with such absurd mindset on God's love. Should abominable lifestyles become norms in the Church in the name of 'God is love? God forbid.

Hence, Paul emphatically states in *Romans 1:26-32*,

"For this cause, God gave them up to dishonorable affections. For even their women changed the natural use into that which is against nature. And likewise also the men, leaving the natural use of the woman, burned in their lust toward one another; males with males working out shamefulness, and receiving in themselves the recompense which was fitting for their error. And even as they did not think fit to have God in their knowledge, God gave them over to a reprobate mind, to do the things not right, being filled with all unrighteousness, fornication, wickedness, covetousness, maliciousness; being full of envy, murder, quarrels, deceit, evil habits, becoming whisperers, backbiters, haters of God, insolent, proud, braggarts, inventors of evil things, disobedient to parents, undiscerning, perfidious, without natural affection, unforgiving, unmerciful; who, knowing the righteous order of God, that those practicing such things are worthy of death, not only do them, but have pleasure in those practicing them."

Romans 1:26-32 MKJV

Church, it is time to wake up from slumber. Satan, like a roaring lion is all out on rampage; he wants to swallow up and destroy many souls. God has not changed His mind; without holiness, no one can truly relate with him and be empowered to resist Satan. If you are not empowered from on high, how can you prevail over satanic hosts?

Christian, make up your mind to live holy; be wholly separated to God and be empowered, and then, arise and resist satanic hosts. While you take those steps, they will flee, and you will overcome.

Take note, as Christian Faithfuls gather for fellowship, they become one territory that must be guarded for God. Devils must not dwell in the congregation of the saints of God nor stand behind the pulpit to mock God's grace. Demons must not take over their bodies as territories. In any way they may manifest, they must be instantly chucked out, to protect the collective divine goodly heritage of the Church and preserve them for posterity.

God's Everlasting Love And Its Terms

According to the Bible and as amplified in the Church everywhere, God's love is everlasting, however, not all receives it. Thus, God's love is everlasting to only those that have humbly accepted it on His terms and abide in it to the end in this world. And for those that have rejected His love on His terms, it is not everlasting.

What is God's everlasting love? God's everlasting love is a sacrificial and unconditional infinite love that He manifested through the Person of the Lord Jesus Christ on the cross.

"As the Father has loved Me, so I have loved you; continue in My love."

John 15:9 MKJV

"...Yea, I have loved you with an everlasting love; therefore with loving-kindness I have drawn you."

Jeremiah 31:3 MKJV

"...having loved his own which were in the world, <u>he loved them unto the end</u>."

John 13:1 KJV

One of the words that came from the Greek word translated *'end'* in *John 13:1* is *'eternal.'* This means Jesus Christ loves His own endlessly; now and forever.

What is God's everlasting love's term? The term is very simple; you must repent of your sins and receive Jesus Christ as your Lord and Saviour and live for Him by grace, to abide in God's love forever.

Love naturally manifests best in its genuine reciprocity and continuous maintenance. God's love will be everlasting to you if you receive and continue to abide in it while you are alive on earth. If you reject God's love, on the day you die in your sins, it will expire. God's love does not continue in second death; after the first death, you enter His judgment, to go into the second death.

"...If a man loves Me, he will keep My Word. And My Father will love him, and We will come to him and make Our abode with him."
John 14:23 KJV

For instance, God said to the people in the days of Noah,

"...My spirit shall not always strive with man, in his erring; he is flesh...And Jehovah said, I will destroy man whom I have created, from the face of the earth. But Noah found grace in the eyes of Jehovah."
Genesis 6:3-8 MKJV

"And as it is appointed unto men once to die, but after this the judgment."
Hebrews 9:27 KJV

According to the above scriptures, God's everlasting love was extended to the people in the generation of Noah by the Holy Spirit, but they rejected it. However, Noah embraced it. As a result, he entered God's everlasting love for all eternity after his physical death.

Because of God's unending love for Noah and all the Old Testament saints, Jesus Christ went to the lowest part of the earth after He died on the cross. On the resurrection day He led captivities captive, and Satan, principalities, powers, sin, death, grave and all spiritual enemies lost them forever. And Noah and other Old Testament saints were rescued, and they resurrected with Jesus Christ.

To abide in God's love, you must maintain a holy life. If you have not been living a holy life, check yourself. Maybe, you have resisted the Holy Ghost and chucked the Spirit of grace out of your life. If Holy Spirit is indeed in you, He will not strengthen you to continue in your sin, but by grace, He will help you live above sin and preserve you blameless for heaven.

So, if indulgence in sinful lifestyle has dominated your life, it is not too late to cry out to God. Repent and ask for His mercy. God will deliver you because of His love and restore you into fellowship with the Holy Spirit, and you will reign over your world.

"He who covers his sins shall not be blessed; but whoever confesses and leaves them shall have mercy."
Proverbs 28:13 MKJV

And John, the beloved said,

"...If we say that we have no sin, we deceive ourselves, and the truth is not in us. If we confess our sins, He is faithful and just to forgive us our sins, and to cleanse us from all unrighteousness. If we say that we have not sinned, we make Him a liar, and His Word is not in us."
1 John 1:5-10 MKJV

Conformance To A Complacent Posture

If a Christian feels he has attained the highest level of satisfaction in his relationship with God, then you have seen a Christian that is already on a complacent and sleep modes. He is a Christian that is no longer on the move with the Holy Spirit to advance the course of God. He has been left behind on the adventures of faith.

Due to his complacent posture, he does not see any reason to press on with God for more spiritual adventures to attain greater spiritual heights; he is pleased with his current plane in God. While his relationship with God dwindles away, he does not any longer have desires to acquire more spiritual strength. A Christian at this level is often the target of satanic hosts. Ultimately, he may become a casualty of faith. May God forbid.

A Christian life should be constantly be refreshed by the presence of the Lord through communion, as he presses toward the mark for the prize of high calling of God in Christ. The Place of Communion with the Lord is the point where, Holy Spirit gives more benefits, to be well-equipped, to prevail over the enemies. It is place of spiritual replenishment.

A self-satisfied soul cannot be refilled; every effort engaged to replenish him will be a futile exercise. If you are not replenished with spiritual vigour, how would you be invigorated to face the battles ahead.

A Christian that is not well rejuvenated and best equipped with God's arsenals will be an easy target for the satanic hosts. In the end, he may become a prey and be overcome. May God forbid.

Hence, complacency is the pathway to lukewarmness, a state of neither hot nor cold. And Jesus Christ warns in Revelation,

"I know your works, that you are neither cold nor hot. I would that you were cold or hot. So because you are lukewarm, and neither cold nor hot, I will vomit you out of My mouth."
Revelation 3:15-16 MKJV

Let us further consider the words *'lukewarm'* and *'vomit'* from the above scriptures. The word *'lukewarm'* was translated from the Greek word *'Chliaros.'* Other translations from it are 'tepid' and 'fluctuation between a torpor and a fervor of love.' Tepidity is a state of having a feeling or showing little interest or enthusiasm.

The word translated *'vomit'* was interpreted from the Greek word *'Emeo.'* It has other interpretations like 'spew' and 'throw up.' The words *'vomit'*, *'spew'* and *'throw up'* have similar meanings. They mean to eject the contents of the stomach through the mouth.

The implication of Jesus' warnings in *Revelation 3:15-16* is that, if you are feeling or showing little interest or enthusiasm for the things of God, it is a sign that you are on spiritual decline, and you could be on the way to spiritual rejection by the Lord. It is a sort of unnoticed backsliding mode, a situation where you could lose your place in Him.

Ejection is a label of rejection. It is like food in the stomach. When in the stomach, it is in a secret place, going through the process of digestion for the benefit of the whole body, and it is hidden from garbage. If vomited, it is purged into a garbage and exposed to destruction; it gives no benefit to the body.

Jesus Christ is the secret place that gives you a maximum protection from any destruction in life. While you remain in Him, you are supposed to be a blessing to His Body, the Church. If you are ejected from Him, you will be vulnerable to the enemy's attacks, and the Church will not benefit from you as she is supposed to.

Furthermore, your relationship with God starts from your heart; it is the place where He fellowships with you. It is the place where you have a firsthand witness that Jesus Christ is in you and you are in Him. In your heart, the presence of the Holy Spirit should be burning like fiery coals, to attest His presence in you.

A Christian that is complacent is not always spiritually flammable to deter satanic hosts from his territory. So, do not let your heart be lukewarm; let it be an altar with fervid coals that burn for the Lord Jesus Christ. It will be the proof of your holy zeal.

And to overcome and have control over your territory, you must always exhibit your zeal against the enemy, by your spiritual flame. By the flame of your zeal, be quick in response, moving with greater speed to beat the enemy in all his wiles.

So, change your complacent and sleepy postures to prevail over the enemies that want to steal, kill, and destroy from your territory. It is time to dominate your world, never let Satan and his hosts annex your goodly heritage.

Inability To Possess And Manifest The Gifts Of The Holy Spirit

Another reason there is not much difference between the Church and the world today is the inability of many Christians to manifest the gifts of the Holy Spirit as they should. These gifts are divided into two categories as:

➢ The Fruit Gift(s) Of The Holy Spirit

➢ The Charismatic Gifts Of The Holy Spirit

Their origin and components are of the Holy Spirit. They are gifts that no natural mankind can generate independently on their own. They are infused and endowed by the Holy Spirit.

The Fruit(s) Gift(s) Of The Holy Spirit

Just like an average unsaved person in the world, at the point of spiritual birth, an average Christian had one weakness or the other that manifested the works of the flesh in them. Those works of the flesh are emblems of an unregenerated soul; never accepted by God and must never be retained in any way.

Hence, as a Christian receives Jesus Christ as his Lord and Saviour, He abides in him/her by the Holy Spirit. And while Holy Spirit indwells them, they are infused with His 'fruit(s)' as a gift(s). The fruit(s) are the first virtues that reveal the genuineness of their spiritual regeneration and rebirth. By the fruit(s), people around could remark the difference as they see a new person and then believe that, indeed he/she is now a true Christian.

Works of the flesh are some demonic spirits that Satan uses to gain control over a life's territory. They are forces that find their ways into many lives to ruin divine goodly heritages of marriage, financial prosperity, good social relationships, godly endeavours, relationship with God and many other beneficial things to life.

Therefore, Paul the apostle lists these works of the flesh as,

"...adultery, fornication, uncleanness, lasciviousness, Idolatry, witchcraft, hatred, variance, emulations, wrath, strife, seditions, heresies, Envyings, murders, drunkenness, reveling, and such like: of the which I tell you before, as I have also told you in time past,

that they which do such things shall not inherit the kingdom of God."

Galatians 5:19-21 KJV

Entrance Doors For The Works Of The Flesh

Christian, the entrance door for the works of the flesh into your life must be identified, and every effort should be made to dislodge the enemy out of your life's territory; shut the door against him and lock him out completely. While you take these steps, it will be very difficult for the satanic hosts to gain access again.

Moreover, lust of the flesh, lust of the eye and pride of life are primary entrance doors for the works of the flesh into any life. They are the ungodly desires and unhealthy spiritual factors that magnetise the eye, to create appetites, emotions, and senses for the flesh to crave after unrighteous gratifications; by them, many lives have been destroyed.

When ungodly desires are not tackled, they grow to become the keys that open the door for demonic spirits to seize control of the body, to exhibit the works of the flesh and manifest evilness in a life's territory. Therefore, their access door must be blocked totally.

How To Lock Out Satanic Hosts From Your Territory

How can you thoroughly lock out the demonic enemy from the territory of your life? Ungodly desires are like a doorstopper sitting in the way of a door; it prevents the door from shutting. It keeps a door opened perpetually until it is removed. If a doorstopper remains in its position, by its weight, it can obstruct the door and stop it from shutting entirely, to lock out intruders.

A life that is absolutely controlled by the Holy Spirit always manifests godly desires. By godly desires, remove those evil desires (the doorstoppers) from obstructing the door of your life, to shut out the enemy. Submit your thoughts and imaginations to God, and He will control your desires to align with His will. Do not allow ungodly desires to control your life; let Holy Spirit does absolutely.

Inclusively, shut your eyes, ears, and mind from receiving any unrighteous messages. The messages could come to you inform of music, movies, scripts and directly from worldly people. These are some of the ways satanic hosts gain their access into a soul. They use them to entice a soul and utilize them as doorstoppers.

Furthermore, use prayer and fasting, scriptural meditation to renew your mind, anointing and authority in the Name of Jesus Christ as overpowering forces to remove those ungodly desires (the doorstoppers) and dislodge the works of the flesh from your life. Afterwards, covet and use the Fruit(s) of the Holy Spirit as keys to lock out those satanic hosts from your territory.

Now, what is Fruit(s) of the Holy Spirit? Fruit of the Holy Spirit is a cluster of divine virtues that are supernaturally infused by the Holy Spirit into a Christian to manifest godly attributes as part of divine nature.

Although each virtue in the cluster can manifest individually, equally, they can be evidenced corporately. Regardless, Holy Spirit is the Holder and love is the principal virtue that controls the rest.

Apostle Paul listed them as follows,

"But the fruit of the Spirit is love, joy, peace, longsuffering, gentleness, goodness, faith, Meekness, temperance..."
Galatians 5:22-23 KJV

If you are a Christian, Holy Spirit should be actively at work within you. If Holy Spirit is not allowed to have His way in your life, it will be difficult for you to manifest His fruit.

Sanctification is part of Holy Spirit's works in a Christian life, and it is continuous. He sanctifies every Christian life moment by moment when there is humbleness and total surrender. By sanctification, He purges all works of the flesh and makes a soul pure, and then infuse the vessel's heart with His fruit(s).

The righteous fruits that you bear are the manifestations of the works of Holy Spirit in you. So, your sensitivity and total submission to Him is very crucial for more manifestations of His Fruit(s).

It does not matter if you think you have the anointing and bears the power of the Holy Spirit. Without the virtues of His Fruit(s) evidencing in and through you, you would not be able to put works of the flesh out of your life's territory.

Many anointed Christians have not been able to go far in their exploits for God because of the works of the flesh that create ungodly lifestyles in them. As a result, they have not been able to dominate their territories and protect their divine goodly heritages. You cannot manifest the works of the flesh and virtues of the Fruit(s) of the Holy Spirit simultaneously. They do not mix up. One must give way for the other.

The first of these virtues is love as stated above. It is like the main rachis of a cluster of fruits that holds the peduncles of the other fruits in place. If love is not evidencing, it will be difficult for the rest to genuinely unveil; their unwrapping will be by hypocrisy.

Hence, let joy, peace, longsuffering, gentleness, goodness, faith, meekness, and temperance bubble out of you by love, to bless the people within your territory. In this, God is glorified as you bear more acceptable fruits.

Essentialities Of Bearing And Overcoming By Your Fruit(s)

Fruit bearing is very essential in overcoming the enemy of your soul. The expectation of God concerning you is that your life bears many fruits.

"Herein is my Father glorified, that ye bear much fruit; so shall ye be my disciples."

John 15:8 KJV

Evidencing the fruit of the Holy Spirit is one of the marks of

Christian maturity. Apart from anointing, it is fruit bearing that will distinguish you from the rest of the world, as they notice your Christlikeness. The people of Antioch concluded that the disciples were Christlike when they observed their fruits and benefited from their anointing. So, they called them Christians.

"And when he had found him, he brought him unto Antioch. And it came to pass, that a whole year they assembled themselves with the church, and taught much people. And the disciples were called Christians first in Antioch."

Acts 11:26 KJV

The disciples did not just earn the honor of being Christlike just like that. They earned it because of Christ's attributes that were seen in them. Holy Spirit produced and manifested God's love through them, by joy, peace, longsuffering, kindness, goodness, faith, meekness, and self-control.

The Fruit(s) of the Holy Spirit became the virtues of the relationship between the disciples and the people they wanted to reconcile to God. As a result, they won the hearts of the people for God, kicked the devil out, and dominate their territories.

Where there was hatred, they evidenced love. Where there was anger, they attested self-control. Where there was sadness, they manifested joy. Where there was supposed to be vengeance, they evinced compassion and mercy. Where people were neglected and cast out, they embrace and received them into the family of God.

Thus, while Satan wanted to take advantage of them through weapons of cynicism and antagonism, they overcame him by the Fruit(s) Gift(s) of the Spirit. They dominated their world and preserved their goodly heritage.

Christian, note, Satan does not want anyone within your territory to believe in Jesus Christ. He would attempt to frustrate you from evidencing the Fruit(s) Gift(s) of the Holy Spirit because he knows they are the virtues that reveal Christlikeness.

How can Satan prevent you from evidencing your godly fruit(s)?

He does it indirectly by people, through demonic control, incitement, and attacks. He does it in his attempt to rubbish the attributes of Christ in you.

Supposing there is an outburst of anger against you, if you cannot demonstrate self-control in the face of it, then you have lost a portion of goodly heritage, and you may lose a space within your territory.

If you are surrounded with hatred, and you cannot manifest love, then you have lost another part of your heritage and you may forfeit a part of your territory.

Assuming people are emotionally down within your reach and you cannot show compassion and lift them up, then you have missed an opportunity to retrieve a territory from Satan.

And once there is a reason to retaliate evil with evil and you give goodness, you have just acquired a ground from the devils.

When your goodly Christian character is under attack, you should perceive Satan is on the loose to annex your goodly heritage and territory. How you react in the face of negativity will reveal if you have a firm control of your territory or not. You must overcome by the fruit of the Holy Spirit.

People do not physically see, or touch or feel the Lord Jesus Christ, but you are His bodily revelation to them. They want to see, feel, and touch His person through you. Let Jesus Christ manifest through your affairs, and they will believe you are Christlike.

A True Story Of Physical Altercation Between Allegedly Christian Parents

There was an incident at my children's primary school one day, a few years ago. About four major parent actors were involved. The school is a Christian school, and its community assumes that every parent is supposedly a Christian, exhibiting goodly virtues, at least to some extent.

The school has a parking area within its premises at the frontage and parents could drop off and pick up their children within the area during opening hours. However, the available spaces in the car park were limited; not enough to meet the parking needs.

Parents rapidly drop off their children at school in the morning and afterwards proceed with their day's endeavours. So, if any parent does not park in the right place or refuses to leave on time after dropping off their child, they may incur the wrath of other parents that need the parking spaces or parents that may be in a hurry to leave the premises. If a parent is unable to get a space, they may have to use a public 'park and pay' car park facility opposite the school.

As usual, it was a morning rush-hour period of the day, and it was raining. Whenever it rains, the school rules allow the pupils to go straight into their classes without filling up at the front of the school building.

On this day, a parent came late to drop her child and instead of parking her car behind the last car or use the public 'park and pay' car park facility, she parked at the front of other vehicles and blocked the exit way and prevented other parents from leaving the school premises on time. Three other parents that parked at the forefront had already dropped their children, waiting in their cars for her to move her car out of the way.

Still, having dropped her child, the parent that blocked the exit way deliberately stayed behind, while she had discussions with some other parents. She was so inconsiderate to other parents that wanted to leave immediately.

By this time, emotions were already running higher than normal as parents were complaining about her inconsideration. I overheard the three parents that parked at the forefront discussed that they would approach her and complain. I walked over to them and advised them otherwise, because I perceived it could degenerate into a quarrel. However, respectfully, they could let her know how they feel later.

After the 'inconsiderate parent' returned to her car, the other three parents approached her and politely complained about her insensitivity to their conditions. They complained of how they wanted to leave immediately for their places of work, but they could not, because of where she parked her car.

As the conversation was on going, to the surprise of other parents, the 'inconsiderate parent' grabbed one of the three parents by the collar of her blouse and slapped her on the face. The impact was so great to the extent that the parent's mobile phone and handbag dropped, and her stuffs were scattered all over the ground.

The altercation could have become a physical fight if the other three parents did not show restraint, as they exhibited the fruit of the Holy Spirit. Everyone that witnessed the scenario was shocked and castigated the 'inconsiderate parent.' They praised the other three parents for their display of self-control Christian attitude in the face of an assault.

"See that none render evil for evil unto any man; but ever follow that which is good, both among yourselves, and to all men."
1Thessalonians 5:15 KJV

Satan, by human agent wanted to annex their territories and steal and destroy their goodly heritage of self-control and godly attitude, however, they refused to hand it over to him.

Dear reader, get rid of the works of the flesh and allow the Holy Spirit to manifest His Fruit(s) in and through you, and you will bear more fruits acceptable to God. Let your light shine forth through the fruit of godly attitude.

By your fruit, anyone around you will either want to emulate or repudiate you. By your godly fruit, display goodly heritage and win people for Jesus. Through your fruit, you can overcome devils and reign over your territory. Now, you can dominate your world.

Charismatic Gifts Of The Holy Spirit

As stated in Chapter Four, the Charismatic Gifts of the Holy Spirit are weapons of warfare that must be employed in spiritual warfare. They are the game changers in spiritual battles, and if engaged befittingly, they could be used to draw a wall between the Church and the world.

For example, Elisha, in *2Kings 6:8-12* used the Charismatic gift of the Word of Knowledge severally against the plots of the king of Syria to deliver the king of Israel from abduction. The king of Syria was perplexed until he was told that it was Elisha that has been revealing his secret plots. Consequently, the king of Israel escaped abduction many times.

"And the king of Syria warred against Israel, and took counsel with his servants, saying, In such and such a place shall be my camp. And the man of God sent to the king of Israel, saying, Beware that you do not pass such a place, for the Syrians have come down there. And the king of Israel sent to the place of which the man of God told him and warned him, and saved himself there, not once nor twice. And the heart of the king of Syria was enraged for this thing. And he called his servants and said to them, Will you not show me which of us is for the king of Israel? And one of his servants said, None, my lord, O king, but Elisha the prophet, who is in Israel, tells the king of Israel the words that you speak in your bedroom."

2Kings 6:8-12 MKJV

Covet all the Charismatic gifts of the Holy Spirit for your profitability. Engage them against the hosts of darkness that have or may want to encroach into your territory and chuck them out, to preserve your divine goodly heritage.

When Charismatic Gifts are backed up by the Fruit(s) Gift(s) of the Holy Spirit, they become your stabilizers, and there is no way you will be less effective in any battle against the satanic hosts. While you use the Charismatic Gifts of the Holy Spirit as offensive weapons, the Fruit(s) Gift(s) can become a wall of defense around you against the enemies that want to fault and ridicule your Christlikeness before the people of the world.

Thence, be infused with the Fruit(s) Gift(s) and crave for the endowment with the Charismatic Gifts of the Holy Spirit. With both categories of these divine gifts at work in you, the enemies will be shut out altogether and a wall of defense will be built around your goodly heritage and territory; no enemy can surmount you or annex your territory to steal or destroy.

Covetousness For The Glory Of This World

The world is a place of diminishing glory; the elements of its glory are temporal and often radiate many shades of depravity, and they evanescence with time. However, the quality of God's kingdom's glory surmounts them, in all ramifications.

Unlike the elements of the glory of this world that can be measured by human senses, God's kingdom's glory and its properties cannot be quantified by natural mind. Its sublimity is mind-boggling, beyond what all-natural mankind can comprehend. God's kingdom's glory is exceptionally resplendent; it is the best that awaits the Church.

All elements of the glory of this world are part of what make life comfortable and pleasurable, and they are part of the daily benefits that a Christian should enjoy without abandonment of their divine assignments, and without compromising their relationship with God. These elements include, money, riches, honour, etc. They are all parts of divine providence.

Nevertheless, oftentimes, Satan and his hosts use these elements to lure many Christians into covetousness until they eventually abandon God's call and their relationship with God. Subsequently, they might become just mere people, and be deprived of exercising their dominion over satanic subtle incursions into their territories to steal, kill and destroy their goodly heritage.

Satan, being who he is, tried playing the same game with the Lord Jesus Christ in the wilderness in Matthew 4:8-11. He exhibited the elements of the glory of this world before the Lord Jesus Christ, to lure Him into covetousness, submission and abandonment of His purpose and relationship with God. Notwithstanding, Satan failed deplorably in all his attempts, as Jesus Christ vehemently rebuked him.

"Again, the devil taketh him up into an exceeding high mountain, and sheweth him all the kingdoms of the world, and the glory of them; And saith unto him, All these things will I give thee, if thou wilt fall down and worship me. Then saith Jesus unto him, Get thee hence, Satan: for it is written, Thou shalt worship the Lord thy God, and him only shalt thou serve. Then the devil leaveth him, and, behold, angels came and ministered unto him."

Matthew 4:8-11 KJV

Covetousness is a force that weakens a soul to a detrimental submission to insatiable desires. Whatever you covet at all cost could become a force that controls and dictates your actions momentarily. If you are captivated by it, you may abandon the real purpose of your existence and pursue its shadow. Nonetheless, if you obey God and utilize your dominion to protect your territory and preserve your divine goodly heritage for posterity, you will not become complacent and forfeit them.

Therefore, Jesus Christ says something about covetousness for the elements of the glory of this world in *Luke 12:15*.

"And He said to them, Watch and keep yourselves from covetousness. For a man's life is not in the abundance of the things which he possesses."

Luke 12:15 MKJV

Hence, be careful of covetousness for world's glory and never let it dominate your soul; it could be detrimental. At all times, you will deliver your soul from satanic bewitchment and control and dominate your territory appropriately and preserve your divine goodly heritage for posterity.

Other Unrecognized Little Foxes

Additionally, there are some other unnoticed openings that Satan could use to gain access into the territory of a Christian's life. They are things done in error, and unperceived.

They could also be ungodly matters done on behalf of a Christian without their knowledge or approval, and they are harmful to their spiritual well-being. The initiators of such things could include parents, ancestors, leaders of their country and other people. The initiators might not be aware of the negative impacts of their actions on the Christian.

Often, they are always shrouded in mysteries. And until they are resolved, Satan and his hosts could use them as entries into the territory of a Christian's life, to prevent them from dominating their world effectively.

They are the spiritual forces that create mysterious circles of defeat in the life of a Christian. Anytime the Christian is about to advance, they suddenly show up to prevent them from moving forward to dominate their territory. David says:

"Who can understand his errors? cleanse thou me from secret faults. Keep back thy servant also from presumptuous sins; let them not have dominion over me: then shall I be upright, and I shall be innocent from the great transgression."

Psalms. 19:12-13 KJV

They are the little foxes that spoil the vine of a Christian's life. Potentially, they have been showing up within the territory of your life; they must be dislodged. If they continue unchecked, they might stop you from having controls over the territories of your life.

Even though they may be mysterious, and you may not know how to unravel them. Holy Spirit knows all things, no matter how hidden they may be; you can ask Him to reveal them to you.

Testimony Of Breakthrough And Progressive Success

A while ago, a young Christian man came to see me, and narrated a chapter in his life. It had been like the case of Jabez. Any of his endeavours did not end in success. If they did, they always came by struggle; nothing happened with ease. He had tried all he could, but nothing changed. The whole thing had remained a mystery. As a result, he was concerned.

After telling me his situation, I told him there could be an opening in his life that the enemy has been using to stop him from moving forward. What he needed was spiritual eyesight to perceive how the enemy has managed to intrude into the territory of his life. So, we prayed that Holy Spirit would open his eyes to see the little foxes that have been ruining the harvest of his labour.

A few days after, he returned with a testimony. The Lord has revealed certain things to him by dream. He saw certain rituals and covenants that were made on his behalf by a certain member of his family. As part of the rituals, a covenant was initiated on his behalf unaware when he was an unbeliever.

Even though he was now a believer who loved the Lord dearly, anytime he wanted to advance, he was always intercepted by the spirit of failure and stagnancy. So, the rituals were neutralized, and the covenants were broken and destroyed. Afterwards, he had breakthroughs and started having progressive successes. Let Jesus Christ be glorified.

Testimony Of Restoration Of Peace In A Marriage

One day a lady came to me for counseling on her marriage. The issue was that her marriage has broken down and about to breakup; she was at the brink of divorce.

She and her husband always had quarrels over anything; just over anything; including minor things that should be no issues. During each quarrel, the atmosphere was always filled with rage, bitterness and unforgiveness. While they yelled at each other, they always use the phrase, "Get out of my life"; "You are a cancer to me." She got fed up with the marriage and about to initiate divorce as her final option. However, she quested for a godly counsel, possibly it could save the situation.

While she finished narrating the issues in her marriage, I perceived it was a generational issue and asked for a little information on her family background. By what she told me, she exposed a pattern that has become a force of a circle of defeat for generations. It was the force of anger.

She claimed she was the fourth generation that their marriages would break down and totally collapse because of uncontrollable anger. She confirmed that no marriage among the previous four generations had lasted a lifetime. Her siblings were not spared; the goodly vines of their marriages had ended in divorce, because of the attacks of the fox, called 'anger.'

As far as she could recollect, it all began with her great grandmother. It was a curse that had been raging through generations, manifesting uncontrollable temperaments. Regardless, as a Christian she knew God's counsel, and wanted to chuck Satan out and keep her goodly marital heritage intact.

In earnest, prayer of deliverance was ministered to her and generation curse of anger was broken. Satan and demon of anger were chucked out of her territory, while peace, understanding, harmony and love were restored to her home. She began to reign over her territory as God ordains and her divine goodly marital heritage was protected from the satanic hosts. Let Jesus Christ take the glory.

"Catch the foxes for us, the little foxes that spoil the vineyards, for our vineyards are in blossom."
Song of Solomon 2:15 ESV

If demonic foxes are not cast out of your goodly vinery heritage, they will prevent your life from blossoming. Continuous spiritual blooming is a sign that your territory is free of satanic interference, and you are in control of it. Therefore, tackle every weight and sins that undeniably beset you; remove and destroy them one hundred percent.

"...let us lay aside every weight, and the sin which doth so easily beset us, and let us run with patience the race that is set before

us,"

Hebrew 12:2 KJV

Spiritual weights and sins must be laid aside so that they do not render you ineffectual in your Christian race. Supposing they are not laid aside, they could slow down your spiritual pace and drag you backward, until your final withdrawal from your Christian race. Once you are at this moment, satanic hosts can attack and seize the territory and goodly heritage you have in your life. May God forbid.

In earnest, catch those little foxes and get rid of them quickly. Do not let Satan annex your divine goodly heritage. It is time you dominate your world; and be continuously victorious, to always give glory to God.

Chapter 17

Glorify God All The Time

Whatever you do or say, God wants the glory; it is His due right. The testimonies of your faith are some of the things that unleash glory to Him. Your continuous testimonies are beyond the testimonies of your conversion, they evidence your uninterrupted walking in victory despite satanic hosts' attempts to destroy your faith.

It is one thing to be a Christian, it is another thing, more importantly that, in your daily walk with God, despite enemies' onslaught against your faith, you have overwhelming victories. Reigning over your world is only possible in a sustained victory over the forces of darkness that want to steal, kill, and destroy your territory. By your reigning over your world, you can show forth that, hitherto, all satanic hosts are subdued; and in this God is glorified.

Many Christians limit the testimonies of their faith to the time they received Jesus Christ as their Lord and Saviour. They never realized that the testimonies of their rebirth are just the beginning of their victories of faith against the satanic hosts. Each day, as they progress in life, there are more battles of faith that must be won, for God to be glorified through them, again and again.

While Satan unleashes his temptations to try your faith, it is your righteous resistance that will m̲   st your victory. As he attempts to use human masks to annex your territory and steal your divine goodly heritage, it is the caliber of substantive Christian attributes that you display that will demean his ensnarement. By your attributes you will safeguard your territory and preserve your heritage.

However, you must recognize that you are not a lone warrior. The Lord is constantly with you, fighting on your side; you are a co-warrior with God; your victory is sure. God is the source of your spiritual might to overcome any enemy. Hence, while each day's victory is attained, always retire into His presence to say, 'THANK YOU, LORD.' It is His right; He deserves all praises.

"But thanks be to God who gives us the victory through our Lord Jesus Christ."
1 Corinthians 15:57 MKJV

"Now thanks be to God, who always causes us to triumph in Christ..."
2 Corinthians 2:14 MKJV

Perhaps you perceive that the battles are still on and hitherto, the enemy is on the prowl despite your confidence in God. Yet, God deserves a thanksgiving for how far He has helped you in the race of life, amid the battles of life. Many have falling, but thus far you are standing. For the fact that the battles are still raging is a sign that God is still at work on your behalf, fighting for you.

Therefore, what looks like a day's loss to you will not end in defeat for God. The fact of the matter is that, when you feel you have lost a ground on your territory, it shows that the victory you want to attain is still ahead. Once again, note, the battles of life are in phases and victories are stages. God will not give up until He manifests your victory; and those victories will be sweet. Likewise, you must persevere and never give up until the battle is over. Satan cannot annex your territory while you willingly engage him and stand your ground, as God fights for you.

No Christian Should Be Defeated Again

There is no child of God that is still in the faith that can be defeated by Satan again. Not now, and never again! The battle has heretofore ended in our victory through Jesus Christ, our Lord.

You might have felt overwhelmed and had a temporary intermission as Satan attempted to annex your territory, and you thought you could lose, or have lost a ground to him. Potentially, it could be in your relationship with God, marriage, finances, social relationship, health, or any other areas of your life; never look at things from the point of defeat again. Relate with your circumstances from the point of victory of Jesus Christ. Offer thanksgiving to God while you recoup and again launch an onslaught against the hosts of darkness.

Note, Satan and his hosts have been defeated, and the victory cannot be reversed, because it is a triumph. So, they are not in control, since God is still busy on your territory, working things out in your favour. Hence, it is not over until God says it is over, and it will not be over in your defeat if you are willing and obedient; it will always end in your victory. Thus, retreat into God's presence and recharge; forge ahead with greater might to dominate your world.

Look at the story of ten lepers in *Luke 17:11-19.*

"And it came to pass, as he went to Jerusalem, that he passed through the midst of Samaria and Galilee. And as he entered into a certain village, there met him ten men that were lepers, which stood afar off: And they lifted up their voices, and said, Jesus, Master, have mercy on us. And when he saw them, he said unto them, Go shew yourselves unto the priests. And it came to pass, that, as they went, they were cleansed. And one of them, when he saw that he was healed, turned back, and with a loud voice glorified God, And fell down on his face at his feet, giving him

thanks: and he was a Samaritan. And Jesus answering said, Were
there not ten cleansed? but where are the nine? There are not
found that returned to give glory to God, save this stranger. And he
said unto him, Arise, go thy way: thy faith hath made thee whole."
Luke 17:12-16 MKJV

Despite their desires to have excellent health as their heritage, for
some time, Satan had dominated their territories and stole their
health heritage through the demon called, leprosy. Possibly, they
were at loss each time they rose to chuck out the enemy by other
means, as Satan devoured their resources financially, materially,
socially, emotionally and some other divine goodly heritages. It
had become a battle they could not win alone without God's
intervention, and it was like God and victory seemed so far away.

One day Jesus Christ appeared on their territories. He threw out the
demon of leprosy and gave each of them a clean bill of health to
keep as their divine goodly heritage. The health territories Satan
had claimed from their lives and replaced with leprosy were
recovered and given back to them.

Nevertheless, instead of all of them returning to give thanks to
Jesus Christ, only one of them returned to showed gratitude. He
went back to Jesus Christ, fell at His feet and glorified God.
Consequently, by showing gratitude to God, he was made whole,
and he regained all the remaining divine goodly heritages from
Satan.

Christian how often do you offer thanksgiving to God for what He
has done for you, no matter how insignificant they are? If you have
not been giving God the glory, you can start now.

Fall before Him and declare and appreciate His worth in your life.
Let Him know that you are an example of those that value Him
more than anything. And by your gratitude to Him, you will be
strengthened more and more to safeguard your divine goodly
heritage and dominate your territory. Sweet victories will be
attained today, tomorrow, and forever.

Never let Satan annex your territory by your ingratitude to God; it is time you dominate your world. Do not surrender your divine goodly heritage to demonic hosts; *SATAN DOESN'T OWN IT, YOU GOT IT!* Henceforth, keep it intact and preserve it for posterity.

About The Author

Joseph 'Sola Adedoyin has been in the service of the Lord Jesus Christ for more than 30 years, preaching the gospel and touching souls, one at a time in the nations of the world.

Before now, He was the Chartered Prayer Secretary at the Maryland Chapter of the Full Gospel Businessmen's Fellowship in Lagos, Nigeria and Bible College Principal and National Executive Council Member at Faith Clinic Ministries, Nigeria. He was a pastor at the Redeemed Christian Church Of God and a lecturer at the Redeemed Bible College, Lagos, Nigeria.

Joseph is currently the President of Rhema Aflame Ministries and Senior Pastor at Life Expressions Tabernacle, UK. He is positively impacting lives for Jesus Christ by the power of the Holy Spirit, and testimonies are abounding for God's glory.

He is married to Seyi, and they are blessed with Children.

Other Titles
By Joseph 'Sola Adedoyin

Created To Be A Warrior Like God

In this powerful book, Joseph 'Sola Adedoyin reveals the methodology of spiritual warfare in relation to a Christian's daily challenges, especially in these Last Days, in order to live in the overwhelming victory that Jesus Christ has won for you. You will never be the same again.

ISBN 9781628715200

The Great And Final Conquest
(Victory Is Surely Guaranteed)

This powerful book is an expository on how to overcome all oppressive demonic spirits in all facets of life; and then set yourself, family, and nation apart for God's purpose. It also discusses how you can triumph over death and its oppressive fear in this life and live forever more. Full of breakthrough prayer targets for decisive spiritual warfares, to obtain lasting victories.

ISBN 9798645025755

Quest For Divine Purposes To Fulfill Your Destiny

Every soul is created by God to fulfill some divine purposes, to have a destiny in Him; and purposes of life are not supposed to be gambles. However, since the fall of man, life purposes have become mysterious, and must be searched for. This great 700-page book unlocks the methodical guides on how you can quest and discover your divine purposes in life, reach the divine demarcated Places Over-There, possess the earmarked divine provisions to fulfill them, and have the destiny God has ordained for you, now and for all eternity.

ISBN 9798715362360

Printed in Great Britain
by Amazon